Pragmatism's Advantage

Pragmatism's Advantage

*American and European Philosophy
at the End of the Twentieth Century*

Joseph Margolis

Stanford University Press
Stanford, California

Stanford University Press
Stanford, California

© 2010 by the Board of Trustees of the Leland Stanford Junior University. All rights reserved.

No part of this book may be reproduced or transmitted in any form or by any means, electronic or mechanical, including photocopying and recording, or in any information storage or retrieval system without the prior written permission of Stanford University Press.

Printed in the United States of America on acid-free, archival-quality paper

Library of Congress Cataloging-in-Publication Data
Margolis, Joseph, 1924–
  Pragmatism's advantage : American and European philosophy at the end of the twentieth century / Joseph Margolis.
      p. cm.
  Includes bibliographical references and index.
  ISBN 978-0-8047-6268-7 (cloth : alk. paper) — ISBN 978-0-8047-7046-0 (pbk. : alk. paper)
    1. Pragmatism—History—20th century. 2. Philosophy, American—20th century. 3. Philosophy, European—20th century. 4. Analysis (Philosophy) 5. Continental philosophy. I. Title.
  B944.P72.M268 2010
  144'.3—dc22
                                              2009035622

Typeset by Bruce Lundquist in 11/15.5 Adobe Garamond

for camaraderie among contested views

Contents

Preface — ix

1 Pragmatism's Advantage — 1

2 Reclaiming Naturalism — 49

3 Vicissitudes of Transcendental Reason — 93

Epilogue: Pragmatism and the Prospect of a Rapprochement within Eurocentric Philosophy — 131

Notes — 145

Index — 167

Preface

IN THE SECOND HALF OF THE LAST CENTURY, American philosophy yielded three unusually influential, heterodox, more or less lopsidedly doctrinaire texts that caught up the subterranean intuitions of an otherwise undistinguished academy and now count as the vanguard of its greatest surge of influence to date within the whole of Eurocentric philosophy. Their convergence is also clear, though it seemed like scatter when each book appeared in turn, and their shared instruction and promise came into focus only by reviewing the drift of Western philosophy against the piecemeal manifestos each favored in its time. All three authors are now gone, though they were marvelously alive when I began to put the present story together. I've benefited from knowing them somewhat, possibly because I came to see that each was much more intuitive than deliberate, in spite of seeming evidence to the contrary, and that none of them was entirely clear about the fuller meaning of the exclusionary direction each chose to champion. Moreover, their optimisms were eccentrically off the mark, yet they were always close to the center of the energy that, at the end of the century, began to take explicit form—or so it seems to me.

They were on their way, it's now clear, to offering pragmatism new options of an unexpected kind, though they had cast themselves initially as opponents of successful orthodoxies. Looking back, most discussants would now accept their being characterized as pragmatists of a new kind, or conceptual cousins at least. In fact, Richard Rorty explicitly claimed that when, early in the second half of the twentieth century, American philosophy took "the linguistic turn," pragmatism's career seemed no longer relevant. A few decades later, pragmatism began to coopt the linguistic turn itself and thereupon began to reclaim and penetrate the work of the best-known analytic champions—on meaning and truth and reference and allied topics—who were often determined opponents of pragmatism's supposed laxity. There is now a sizeable company of admired analysts who are clearly pragmatists of the newer breed (sometimes self-identified as such), and as a result, the work of the original pragmatists now seems made of sterner stuff than the analysts' appraisals in the early decades of the century originally supposed.

I've come to see the future of Western philosophy in terms of the many strands of what is now identified—loosely, it must be said—as pragmatism, analytic philosophy, and continental philosophy. The serendipity of their convergence has led me to imagine an entirely fabulous creature, the pragmatist of the future! Such a creature could easily be the agent of a genuine rapprochement among the different movements of Eurocentric philosophy. He may not come our way. But I draw together in his name the largest promise of our philosophical age captured, obliquely, by three emblematic American texts of the second half of the twentieth century: W. V. Quine's *Word and Object* (1960), T. S. Kuhn's *Structure of Scientific Revolutions* (1962, 1970), and Richard Rorty's *Philosophy and the Mirror of Nature* (1979).

All three authors, I would say, were pragmatists of a dawning sort: none of them could have been easily reconciled with the main thrust of pragmatism's classic period. But then, when "official" pragmatism seriously declined in the 1940s, there was no reason to believe the movement would ever revive again. Nor was there reason to believe the vigorous analytic philosophies of the 1930s and 1940s would ever revive (those associated with the scientism of the positivists and the unity of science movement) or, more baffling still, the triumphal, altogether different inquiries associated with the spectacular influence of Martin Heidegger and Edmund Husserl on the Continent.

The whole of Western philosophy was, I think, becalmed, traumatically affected by the Second World War and the cold war; and by and large, almost nothing got through the conceptual haze that was not a recycling of the seemingly successful inquiries of the first half of the century. What *would have been* novel for the future of the second half of the last century *was*, however, already inchoate in the three texts mentioned. In making this explicit, I admit I am recommending the reinvention (more than the extension) of pragmatism along the lines of what is still inadequately perceived in the new beginnings tendered by the three texts noted. Because, of course, although they may all be judged to have taken the linguistic turn, the "turn" itself proved to require a richer enculturing and historicized setting than the analysts were prepared to admit: to have taken the "turn" in Rorty's sense seemed to threaten (for instance, among the champions of the unity of science program) to reintroduce without a struggle the dubious logic and semantics the analysts had fought so hard to disallow. But if that is indeed the mark of analytic purity, then almost no important figure among the American analysts could possibly ensure his bona fides.

Quine's and Rorty's new starts are, finally, failures, I would say, but they unmistakably confirm the need to think in new directions that they themselves obliquely introduce. Kuhn's new start I deem the best of the three, a genuinely fresh beginning; but it was also the most savagely rejected of the lot—only grudgingly reclaimed at the end of the century, in a way unperceived even by Kuhn, who found it difficult to accept his own findings and even to explain them in terms of the philosophical canon centered in Immanuel Kant and G. W. F. Hegel. I've published my reading of all of this in two previous books: *Reinventing Pragmatism* (2002), centered on the abortive revival of pragmatism due to what really proved to be a minor skirmish between Rorty and Hilary Putnam; and *The Unraveling of Scientism* (2003), regarding the wider failing of analytic philosophy's best-known inquiries.

The volume now before you ventures, well beyond the Anglo-American limits of both pragmatism and analytic philosophy, to explain the three-legged promise of the Eurocentric world in terms of the new alignment glimpsed in the "pragmatisms" of my specimen texts but read through confrontations between American pragmatism and the leading currents of continental philosophy, as well as with the more familiar themes of analytic philosophy. Predictably, the upshot is that the "pragmatism" that now makes itself felt is no longer merely or even distinctly American. It requires the reclamation of the once-radical themes of historicity and enculturation, inexplicably neglected or diminished by the classic pragmatists themselves but already brought to center stage in the interval that belongs to Kant, the German idealists, and Hegel especially, whom the British analysts (Bertrand Russell and G. E. Moore) hoped, at the very start of the last century, to erase completely (or at least to supersede) and whom the American pragmatists largely failed to champion adequately.

What follows, then, is a lean but hopeful narrative of philosophically linked arguments that threads its way through false starts, deflections, retrograde currents, excessive zeal, and blindness on all sides and that emerges, wiser and chastened, with a thoroughly justified sense of having recovered the principal strengths of what it should never have lost—what I call "pragmatism's advantage"—which now lies as much outside pragmatism in the narrow sense as it does outside analytic and continental philosophy.

I don't mind spelling out the saving themes I've collected. I'm convinced that the pragmatists were right to reinterpret Hegel's critique of Kant along naturalistic and (largely) Darwinian lines and to attenuate as far as possible the idealist extravagances with which a constructivist realism might be defended. I also endorse their good sense in favoring the flux of history over fixity, invariance, substantive necessities, universalisms of every sort, cognitive privilege, abstract truths drawn from facultative powers: that is, favoring what, effectively, is the culturally artifactual, second-natured "nature" of a society of human selves—impossible to account for in terms of biological sources alone.

The age of "Kantian" conceptual closure is over, and its replacement by a "Hegelian" policy that holds fast to the view that there can be no disjunction between our would-be conceptual truths and our empirical truths now seems assured. Pragmatism has begun again with renewed conviction—and decidedly less baggage than before. Furthermore, to come to findings such as these is, perhaps, no more than a preliminary effort at rationalizing our entire history on the edge of an even larger encounter of a global sort. There you have the motivation of my tale, if not the argument. But the argument *is* the principal thing, as I very much hope you will confirm by reading on.

I can put my intuition a little more provocatively. If you read the master theme of Hegel's *Lectures on Fine Art*, the claim that "art is higher than nature," as signifying that *Geist*'s role in the arts and in the forms of human intelligence that make art (and language and encultured action and history) possible is "higher" than the linkage that holds between physical and biological nature and *Geist*, you touch (no more than touch) on the intriguing possibility that Hegel has glimpsed the thread of an argument that would in time enable us to construe the evolution of language and culture as a sui generis process that depends on biological evolution (in the Darwinian sense) but that cannot be explained solely or primarily or in its most important innovations in Darwinian or neo-Darwinian terms. Add to this the evidence that Charles Peirce, who held conflicting opinions regarding Hegel's achievement but who also acknowledged the undeniable fact that his own evolutionary conception of reality came to respect the import of a growing convergence between his own version of "post-Kantian idealism" and Hegel's synoptic vision, was very strongly attracted (for instance, in his reviews in the American journal the *Nation*) to the double theme of "Darwinizing Hegel" and "Hegelianizing Darwin," it dawns on you that the classic phase of American pragmatism was ineluctably drawn to a theme (one among a good many) that never really flowered in the strong form that now beckons. I reclaim these themes in the name of "pragmatism's advantage," and I take note of the fact that not altogether dissimilar temptations have begun to be applied to the reading of Husserl and Heidegger. I concede at once that these temptations are distinctly heterodox. But then I myself am in the business of changing philosophy (if I can), not in any merely textual explication, although I'm also unwilling to deny that the new themes I have in mind were already budding in their original sources.

 A final caveat, then. I have no interest in a mere rereading of the overall history of "modern" modern philosophy from, say, Kant and the idealists to the beginning of our new century. I have no reason to think that that would not be a worthwhile labor, but it's not mine! Some readers (of early drafts of the book now before you) find it much too easy a slide to go from the inquiry I intend to the one just mentioned—apparently a better choice (in their view) than the one I favor. But I see no point to any such undertaking if it's not motivated by arguments of the sort I mean to provide. Furthermore, *if* my own argument is at all convincing, then the economies I intend will lead us to see that a very large part of Kantian, post-Kantian idealist, and, more pointedly, Hegelian work will have been exposed as rhetorically and philosophically extravagant (excessively so), too purple for words (though perfectly unavoidable), open to radical interpretation (if worth preserving at all), important more in persuading us to abandon (at long last) some of philosophy's most egregious mistakes than in collecting once again those encyclopedic histories that avoid harsh economies.

 That's a heterodox notion, I don't deny. But on my own account, it cannot be separated from the true import of classic pragmatism stretched a little beyond its accustomed practice—that catches up as well the main threads of existentialism, Marxism, hermeneutics, late phenomenology,

Lebensphilosophie, *Weltanschuuungsphilosophie*, poststructuralism, postmodernism, and similarly motivated innovations. If that's conceded, then from my own point of view, to favor history over philosophy is to put the cart before the horse. Also, it's perfectly clear that the way in which competing arguments would have to be weighted would be very different if we gave priority to the historical narrative over the philosophical argument—though I would never deny that "doing" the history of philosophy *is* a way of "doing" philosophy and that philosophy makes no sense unless it incorporates the evolving history of philosophy as the narrative form of its own evolving lessons.

Thus, for example, the great theme of Reason (*Vernunft*: finally inseparable from *Verstand*, but not a form of higher knowledge) is absolutely central to the history of philosophy spanning Kant and Hegel (the beginnings of "modern" modern philosophy); but it is also the principal source of conceptual disorder when viewed from the vantage of the story I'm about to tell. In short, the history of philosophy without philosophy is pointless, and philosophy without the history of philosophy is impoverished and arbitrary.

Furthermore, if you allow a conceptual leap in advance of my story, I confess I also hold that Hegel without Darwin is conceptually wild, and Darwin without Hegel is very nearly philosophically irrelevant. The double lesson that I draw (which the account that follows is meant to support) maintains, first, that the human being we call a "self" or "person" is an artifact of cultural history made possible by late biological evolution but not explained primarily by biological means; and second, that the Darwinian discovery (not any theoretical doctrine we might call "Darwinism") makes it clear that *both* the reductionisms of analytic scientism and the extravagant efforts of continental philosophy to elude the constraints of naturalism (as the continentals see the world) are stalemated at a stroke by the first part of the lesson I tender. That needs to be spelled out, of course; but it *is* the essential clue to what I am calling "pragmatism's advantage."

The trouble is that the original pragmatists somehow sold us short with regard to both historicity and enculturation *and* with regard to the artifactuality of the self favored by a naturalistic reading of Hegel along lines made possible by Darwin's innovation but not confined to any sort of biologism. The philosophical simplifications achieved by construing the self as the formation of a new kind of being, "a natural artifact," so to say, are quite extraordinary. They show all three movements to be vulnerable in a way they'd never seriously considered before—but show them now to be open to a genuine rapprochement and a stronger future. There's the tale that remains to be told.

The account that follows traces a philosophical history meant to make the intended "advantage" palpably familiar, agreeably accessible, and plainly worth conjuring with. I mean the idea that the human self (or person, subject, agent, ego, *ich, yo,* I) is not a natural-kind kind at all but a "natural artifact" engendered as a regularly emergent transform of the primate offspring of *Homo sapiens* through its ability to internalize the mastery of a natural language (and its enabled and enabling culture), a self thereby *gebildet* (instructed, reared) among the apt members of its own encompassing society. I track the nerve of the argument in favor of this "advantaged" doctrine largely by tracing the false turns and developing rapprochement of the pertinent history of Eurocentric philosophy: I sketch the philosophical argument in favor of the artifactual self only in terms of its general orientation and likeliest resources. It will need a sustained account of its own, a fresh beginning, bits of which I admit I've already broached in earlier inquiries.

The present narrative (the third of three linked studies) serves to bring to a close a larger history of the philosophy of the second half of the twentieth century viewed from the vantage of American pragmatism within the ambit of the whole of Eurocentric philosophy and focused jointly on the stalemate of the principal currents of the period and the glimpsed promise of a strong breakthrough that lies—has lain for a long time—essentially unclaimed, ignored, somewhat dismembered, not entirely inchoate, but definitely in need of a recovery capable of rejoining the best forces of the now-dysfunctional divisions of pragmatism, analytic philosophy, and continental philosophy so that the envisioned achievement might actually bring the larger history of modern philosophy, possibly even the history of the whole of Western philosophy, to at least one convincing resolution of a conserving and firmly simplified sort.

It would have to give up the parochial divisions that still plague Western philosophy but now show signs of being judged tiresome and perceptibly unnecessary. The sense of the doctrine's "advantage" is the main issue, however. I find its potential gains decidedly grand. For instance, I take it to afford a plausible replacement for the various reductionisms of the unity of science program that have remained in play since the dissolution of positivism. That is, the new conception might adopt as its principle of scientific unity the premise that all the sciences are human sciences (that all depend on the same resources of human inquiry) and that the natural sciences are, therefore, deliberately shaped as an efficient abstraction within the enabling resources of the cultural world—say, along the lines of predictability and technological control more than mere loyalty to the ideologies of reductionism and extensionalism.

The thesis of the artifactual self would greatly facilitate the Darwinizing of both Kant and Hegel, the abandonment of biologism and teleologism in nature at large, the very prospect of interpreting the main lines of Western philosophy naturalistically and without disallowing the unique powers of the human mode of being. As already remarked, it would also facilitate strong gains in the direction of a rapprochement of the whole of Western philosophy, without insisting on any uniquely valid doctrine: it would, for instance, reopen the possibility of drawing on conceptual strategies developed from largely disallowed sources (analytic from continental, continental from analytic) that might then overcome the self-impoverishing tendencies of so much of recent philosophy. (This is no longer a remote concern.)

It would fit very well with the scruple of a constructivist form of realism, without yielding to any of the extravagances of idealism that are all too easily favored in attempts to incorporate the seminal lessons drawn from Kant and Hegel. Constructivism in epistemology, which the post-Kantian tradition has made all but unavoidable, need not yield to idealism in the metaphysical sense; but it cannot fail to ensure the profound contingency of the norms of truth and knowledge and moral and other forms of worth. These are simply some of the anticipated benefits of supporting the artifactuality of the self and the corollary economies of the leanest possible rapprochement among the best resources of pragmatism and analytic and continental philosophy.

The story that follows lays a proper ground for a genuinely recuperative philosophy but sketches its main lines no more than glancingly. I have my own inkling of how the argument should go, but I see no point in keeping it hostage to my personal convictions. I read the recovery as a sort of larger pragmatism fulfilling the promise of its classic beginnings. But even here it has eclipsed its beginnings by turning to a deeper analysis of the meaning of the transcendental and posttranscendental turn in philosophy during the fifty-plus years from about the last quarter of the eighteenth century to a little more than the end of the first quarter of the nineteenth.

I take that interval to mark the true beginnings of "modern" modern philosophy: the joint rise of constructivism and historicism and the developing need to reinterpret its inflated claims in finite, a posteriori, naturalistic, epistemically unprivileged, existentially adequate but transient terms that were variously first provided by Marxist, existentialist, Darwinist, and pragmatist conjectures.

Now, near the end of the first decade of the twenty-first century, the picture has become reasonably clear. My own suggestion rests entirely with the guess that the Darwinizing of Hegel and Kant and the Kantian/Hegelian absorption of Darwin—which I find most clearly manifested (though hardly deliberately) in the somewhat convergent philosophies of Charles Peirce and Ernst Cassirer—provides the best clue regarding the importance of the doctrine of the artifactual self. In any case, it's the best clue to what my own philosophical labors are committed to.

I must add a word of thanks to Ruth Brooks, who manages my scatter better than I can; and to two young friends, Robert Main and Aili Bresnahan, who have helped with various chores the manuscript's preparation required. (Main, I should add, introduced me to Peirce's reviews in the *Nation*.)

J. M.
February 2009

Pragmatism's Advantage

1

Pragmatism's Advantage

WHAT I MEAN BY "PRAGMATISM'S ADVANTAGE" I shall draw out slowly from the enormous scatter of contemporary Eurocentric philosophy. (These first words will hardly be enough.) What I have in mind is as much an invention as a discovery. I'm speaking of the need to find a unity of purpose where the academy doubts one can be found but would like to believe it can be eked out nevertheless. Thus, in this first pass, perhaps something of the stakes involved, something of an underlying problematic, the principal players, economies tested and intended will make their presence and history known legibly enough. I've fitted a simple armature to the details of what follows—for the sake of sheer manageability. I identify the principal philosophical movements of our day—that is, a three-legged contest between pragmatists, analysts, and continentals, and I expect that pragmatism's advantage will become increasingly explicit within the terms of that familiar simplification.

Some will regard this as a terrible distortion pure and simple. I view it, rather, as an innocent economy the benefits of which may be rightly judged at the end of the account—though it will surely gain plausibility and force as the analysis unfolds. The separate movements are genuine enough in terms of the perceived loyalties of their current champions; but their true natures, given in terms of implied convictions and related uniformities of thought, remain too simple to be trusted at face value. I don't believe, however, that the actual arguments I advance need distort our final reckoning. On the contrary, their validity should confirm the good sense of yielding to what may prove to be more than a passing convenience.

In fact, the simplification is already pretty well adopted by the philosophical community and is easily rectified wherever needed. In the process, I hope it will become clear that the agon favored is itself a lightly displaced proxy for a deeper reflection on philosophy's future. You will have to be the judge of it.

PRAGMATISM'S REVIVAL, even its persistence, continues to baffle explanation, as in a way its history always has. It was deemed exhausted by the end of the 1940s and 1950s but was unexpectedly revived in the 1970s, though its principal champions, Richard Rorty and Hilary Putnam, prominent members of the American philosophical community, faded rather quickly by the end of the century.[1] Yet now, still close to the beginning of the new century, its prospects seem startlingly improved, as if something of special promise had been discovered or rediscovered apart from the energies of its classic figures and its "second-wave" enthusiasts (that is, its accidental vivifiers).

It was originally a parochial success, though it did gain adherents abroad; and it began to attract a wider Eurocentric interest in its short second life, despite a distinctly poor showing at home. We may even speculate about a third career. For pragmatism has begun, possibly for the first time in its history, to be seriously treated as a distinct alternative to—more than an alternative, perhaps a connective tissue spanning the great divide between—analytic and continental philosophy. At any rate, it now counts as a distinctly strong constellation of doctrines and strategies potentially capable of contesting the hegemonies of the day—within both the English-language analytic movement of the last half of the twentieth century and the trailing forces of the Cartesian, Kantian, Husserlian, and Heideggerian movements of late continental Europe. It would not be unreasonable to say that pragmatism's promise at the present time is a function, in part, of the fatigue of its principal competitors and of the economy and fluency with which, without betraying its own conviction, it coopts the principal strengths that remain attractive among the many movements of Eurocentric philosophy. (I use the term "Eurocentric" to range over all the currents of mainstream European philosophy and, in particular, worldwide, all those currents—notably, the Anglo-American—that derive in important ways from the transformative work spanning Kant and Hegel, which, in my opinion, marks the period of "modern" modern philosophy.)

Rightly perceived, pragmatism's best feature lies with its post-Kantian ancestry coupled with its opposition to the extreme forms of analytic scientism with which it has shared a gathering sense of conceptual rigor. It forms, for that reason, a natural bridge between analytic and continental philosophy, for rigor is not inherently scientific—not bound, say, to reductive materialism or the extensionalist regimentation of the language of science. None of the three movements mentioned (hardly unified within themselves) is separately likely to overtake its own limitations or incorporate the best work of the others in a compelling way. Still, within its own conceptual space, pragmatism favors a constructive (or constructivist) realism drawn from post-Kantian resources in as spare a way as possible, freed from every form of cognitive, rational, and practical privilege, opposed to imagined necessities of thought and reality, committed to the continuities of animal nature and human culture, confined to the existential and historical contingencies of the human condition, and open in principle to plural, partial, perspectived, provisional, even nonconverging ways of understanding what may be judged valid in any and every sort of factual and normative regard. (I shall come back to the meaning of "constructivism.")

There may be a touch of reportorial distortion in going beyond these clichés; but, in risking that much, it would not be unreasonable to say that pragmatists believe that analysts are likely to favor scientism and that continentals are likely to exceed the bounds of naturalism, and both tendencies are more extreme or extravagant than their policies require. In this fairly obvious sense, pragmatism's strength rests with the possibility of a rapprochement by way of the corrections mentioned. It could never have claimed such an advantage earlier had not the main efforts of analytic and continental philosophy persisted too long, in turn, in their own most vulnerable commitments. Pragmatism has delayed as well, of course, but it seems poised now for a larger venture.

Improbable though it may seem, the most confident analysts have lost touch with an essential thread of the transformative history of late eighteenth- and nineteenth-century Critical and post-Critical philosophy. It was still easily discerned in the late-Kantian reflections of the earliest phase of logical positivism and allied currents, but it dwindled and all but disappeared by the time it went transatlantic. By the end of the last century, for instance, in the work of John McDowell and Hilary Putnam, analytic philosophy pointedly discovered the need to recover what it had so cavalierly ignored, but it now lacked a sure-footed command of the deep import of any such effort. The pragmatists and continentals never lost sight of the original critique: without venturing any appraisals for the moment, you will find its continuing influence easily enough in Peirce, John Dewey, C. I. Lewis, Husserl, Heidegger, and Cassirer, among others. The narrative wanted requires its effective recovery (and adjustment) well beyond Rorty and Wilfrid Sellars, for instance.[2] It is in fact essential in regaining any effective rapprochement within the Eurocentric world. It depends quite precisely on coming to terms, one way or another, with the essential lesson that *joins* the transformative and matched contributions of Kant and Hegel: that is, it depends on tethering the distinct inquiries of any contemporary Eurocentric movements to just this uniquely orienting source. McDowell and Putnam, for instance, reclaim Kant, but Hegel almost not at all; pragmatism, however, makes no sense under any such restriction.

At the beginning of the new century, Eurocentric philosophy (both analytic and continental) maintains its technical competence in every sector of inquiry in which it invests its energies—but it is plainly played out by now. It is philosophically becalmed, no doubt afloat, but bound for no particular port of importance beyond what its best progenitors had originally identified. Very nearly all of these large programs are known to be seriously defective, though their inertia remains impressive. Contemporary "pre-Kantians" or "Cartesians," for instance (if you allow these terms), continue more or less to ignore the import of the original seventeenth- and eighteenth-century aporiai (effectively exposed in the interval spanning Kant and Hegel) within their own most up-to-date efforts; nearly the whole of late analytic philosophy may be counted among their self-appointed victims: notably, W. V. Quine and Donald Davidson and such familiar representatives of recent analytic scientism as Daniel Dennett and Paul Churchland. I give the whole of contemporary Eurocentric philosophy scope enough, therefore, in a somewhat unfettered way, in order to get clear, initially, about its largest pretensions; once it is formulated, however, I impose more sober constraints on its prospects and ambitions.

Kant and the post-Kantians posit a more than merely human cognizing competence, examining which they and their advocates discover (to no one's surprise) transcendental powers that they cannot confirm within the limits of actual human reflection: Jürgen Habermas and Karl-Otto Apel afford more than enough evidence (regarding reason in practical affairs) to show that the dream of such a mythical resource has easily survived two hundred years of disbelief.[3]

Habermas, for instance, unlike Apel, has never been able to decide whether "reason" is a determinate natural faculty or a transcendental faculty; whereas the better claim denies that it is a determinate faculty of any kind: its mention (that is, the point of mentioning reason) merely collects a would-be formal feature of what we call thinking viewed as the muster of argumentative rules beyond (but including) deduction, regardless of whether it addresses theoretical or practical questions. Habermas has always been uneasy about admitting any allegiance to the a priori powers of Reason; but increasingly, in more recent years, he shows (in admitting the vagaries of natural reason) an uncertainty as well about the possibility of securing the reliable universality he needs. He is caught, therefore, in a dilemma of his own devising; for the prospects of an objective universalism, whether in practical or theoretical matters, whether normative or factual, cannot be freed from consensual contingencies: in effect, cannot be secured by any ready means confined empirically or by reference to historical experience.

Kant effectively demonstrates in the first *Critique* that the very idea of a "natural faculty of reason" cannot rightly claim the cognitively privileged or universalist powers Kant's rationalist predecessors regard as a confirmed entitlement; and of course, Hegel's insistence on the historied nature of reason (*Vernunft*), which, in finite time, cannot assign more than a provisional and inherently horizoned interpretation of any sensorily grounded understanding of our apparent experience of the world (*Verstand*), completely undermines any assurances, empirical or transcendental, that exceed the provisionality of what we may consensually construct (in our own time) as a workable conjecture about the way the world is.

Add to this the Darwinian evidence (as well as can be surmised) that *Homo sapiens*, as an animal species, seems to have been uniquely endowed biologically among the primates but never exceeded the primate forms of intelligence until the species (very possibly, earlier species of *Homo* as well) began to build on the incipience of true language, somewhere on the human side of the primate divide, which shows no promising beginning anywhere else in the primate world (and indeed, no biological gifts to begin to account for it) like that of the unique, species-specific interest on the part of human infants in entering into and sustaining complex forms of play and prelinguistic communication with the adults of the species, whom, in contrast to the higher apes, they seem to recognize for the purpose.[4]

Habermas's problem is precisely the same one that confronted John Rawls, when Rawls found himself obliged to rechristen his own theory of justice as a form of liberal ideology. Pragmatism in the American vein eschews any and every strict or assured form of necessity, of which the so-called Kantian pragmatisms of Apel, Habermas, and Rawls cannot afford to be deprived. There is no way to draw universally necessary conditions from contingent or historical experience except by pretensions of cognitive privilege: after Kant, quite often, this is managed by aprioristic pretensions (that is, by versions of transcendentalism). Habermas fails because his venture is plainly self-defeating—broken backed, I would say. Apel does not fail for Habermas's reasons because, of course, he embraces transcendentalism quite willingly. The Anglo-American analysts largely fail because, in the latter half of the twentieth century, they were never seriously tempted by Kantian apriorism (favoring Hume instead) and because, not being thus tempted, they denied themselves the resources of the contingent and historicized successors of transcendentalism as well. That suggests, also, why the pragmatists "escaped" and what the contemporary Eurocentric contest signifies.

It's worth mentioning that both Hume and Kant, the eighteenth-century champions of empiricism and transcendentalism, are remarkably weak in their treatment of the human self. Hume, famously, cannot find any simple idea of the self in the entire empiricist repertory, and Kant seems to have thought of the *ich* that is the presumed custodian and source of the apriorist system of categories as a sort of default concession. But disputes about the right analysis of the self are precisely what distinguish in the most pointed way what separates the pragmatists, the analysts, and the continentals in our own time.

Moreover, though I can only hint at the argument here, to admit the Darwinian discovery to the effect that the evolution of *Homo sapiens* was a very long process that brought the species to the point of exploiting an entirely different form of evolution—the evolution of language and culture, which, on the best evidence, cannot itself be explained in terms suited to the mature forms of neo-Darwinism (that is, of natural selection united with the forms of genetic explanation)[5]—threatens the validity of analytic scientism (reductionism, particularly) and continental extranaturalism at the same time and for the same reasons. What is most extraordinary here is that, in principle, Kant's transcendental Reason, Hegel's Absolute *Geist*, Heidegger's *Dasein*, and Husserl's Transcendental Ego are open to potentially fatal challenge for very nearly the same reasons. It's true that neither Kant nor Hegel could have considered the import of Darwinian evolution, but that cuts no ice now.

Hegel, incomparably the best of the post-Kantians, who sought to bring Kant's abstract cognizing Subject back to the unavoidable contingencies of the quotidian world, could not quite keep his own effective Subject from swelling beyond any merely mortal *ich*—in a way that threatened to encompass the whole of humanity, the whole of history, *Geist*, Reason, even (through a sort of Spinozistic exuberance) the Trinity, within the compass of his singular Subject. The telltale clue that challenges the entire Hegelian tradition rests with the assured sense of a kind of subjective continuity of thought and experience that no merely human agent could possibly confirm—the so-called identity of the finite and the infinite, the transient and the absolute, the contingent and the necessary, the subjective and the objective: that is precisely what figures like Friedrich Nietzsche and Michel Foucault effectively challenged, and figures like Karl Marx and Jean-Paul Sartre manfully tried to render in naturalistic terms.

At his best, Hegel (unlike Kant) introduces a mythic or heuristic Subject to facilitate his deliberate constructions, but two hundred years have failed to yield much in the way of leaner assumptions. Indeed, Hegel may not have been well served by his own progeny. For a great many admiring commentators find it unlikely that Hegel did not subscribe to a collective Subject—a *Geist*—somehow more real than any human subject could be, though *Phenomenology*, the linchpin of Hegel's extraordinary effort, as well as other texts, gives us more than ample reason to view *Geist* as a convenient nominalization of its own, a device for managing predicative complexities abstracted and idealized from the thought and life of aggregates of humans who share a common history.[6] If Hegel opposed the reading just sketched, then so much the worse for him. (In any event, this suggests the kind of inventive liberty pragmatism would require if it were ever to recover the deeper promise of its second wave.)

Very early on, the young Karl Marx precociously isolated the nerve of Hegel's excesses in an introductory essay for a proposed critique of Hegel's *Philosophy of Right* (never completed), which, in the Feuerbachian spirit in which it begins, tellingly affirms: "[M]an is not an abstract being, squatting outside the world. Man is *the human world*, the state, society," which, read in Ludwig Feuerbach's way, succinctly signified (however inexplicitly) the simple fact that Hegel had somehow reversed the denotative and predicative foci of the analysis of the human.[7]

Of course, Marx was at least partly—certainly not entirely—right, though the mature Marx was open to a similar charge. The best that can be said for the post-Kantian idealists is that they collected, pell-mell, every intuition about the human (the encultured and enlanguaged) world but had no analytic patience for isolating what exactly was the human condition itself as distinct from the whole of societal life. Two hundred years later, within the boundaries of English-language analysis, we have hardly put our minds to the matter with more conviction or success; we have all but lost any reliable sense of the cultural and historical questions the idealists pondered so flamboyantly. (Consider Daniel Dennett's charmingly mad neurophysiological replacements for a culturally artifactual self: Dennett throws all caution to the winds when he construes the executive unity of the "self's" interventions as somehow due to the near chaos of the brain's random neuronal firings.[8] I take all that to be an admission of defeat.)

In any event, Marx's phrase confirms (however unintentionally) that Hegel opposed "Cartesianism" in all its forms (including the Kantian version) and grasped the sense in which there cannot be a disjunction between the human subject and its world—including its evolving cultural history.[9] Marx may not have been quite clear about the extent to which he was himself a Hegelian in his best work: for instance, in the seminal (but entirely heuristic) sense in which *Geist* requires the unity and difference of cognizing subjects and cognized world.

Edmund Husserl stubbornly championed what has proved to be the self-deception of the Transcendental Ego fortified, conceptually, in a palpably impossible form: where, that is, he explicitly disjoins phenomenology from "natural" reason and experience (from which it had to be functionally separated in order to ensure, somehow, an otherwise inexplicable competence free of all natural encumbrances). Here is what Husserl says in *Ideas*—it needs little in the way of explication—when he introduces the essential project of what he terms the phenomenological *epoché*:

We put out of action the general thesis which belongs to the essence of the natural standpoint, we place in brackets whatever it includes respecting the nature of Being: *this entire natural world therefore* which is continually "there for us," "present to our hand," and will ever remain there, is a "fact-world" of which we continue to be conscious, even though it pleases us to put it in brackets. . . . Thus *all sciences which relate to this natural world*, though they stand never so firm to me, though they fill me with wondering admiration, though I am far from any thought of objecting to them in the least degree, *I disconnect them all, I make absolutely no use of their standards, I do not appropriate a single one of the propositions that enter into their systems, even though their evidential value is perfect. I take none of them, no one of them serves me for a foundation*—so long, that is, as it is understood, in the way these sciences themselves understand it, as a truth *concerning the realities* of this world. *I may accept it only after I have placed it in the bracket.*[10]

Husserl, however, nowhere demonstrates that "bracketing . . . any judgment that concerns spatio-temporal existence" *ever* frees any of our predicative distinctions from being indissolubly influenced by the "natural standpoint." His argument may expose the naiveté of Descartes's version of the cogito, of Kant's naturalistic constraints on the sheer pertinence of transcendental assurances of the very "possibility" of natural cognition; but surely his own replacement is at least as arbitrary and naive. The entire fortune of phenomenology depends on it! (I shall come back to a closer reading of Husserl's best-known proposals.)

Furthermore, just this unaccountable privilege may be judged, fairly enough, to have been the partial inspiration for Martin Heidegger's abandonment of Husserl's *epoché* in favor (as it turns out) of a potentially even deeper, more problematic penetration of the would-be self-disclosive power (*aletheia*) lying in wait at the very source of the mystery of Being—which (to be sure) no merely human *Dasein* could possibly affect or control or fathom.[11] The result has been an unmatched privilege in matters of philosophical and political prophecy: whatever had been assigned to determinate transcendental sources earlier—beyond the merely human, as, preeminently, in Kant—now needed only to be assigned to the mystery of Being itself (that is, *Sein*), incomprehensibly close, yet utterly inaccessible, to *Dasein*'s initiatives. Proceeding thus, Heidegger betrays, in much the same way the transcendentalists do, the privileged certainty thereby gained, though now seemingly without the scruple of confining speculation within the play of the "natural world." Heidegger freed himself from the disadvantageous transparency of actually positing a transcendental structure in Kant's or Husserl's sense, though (against his intent) he has been read (wrongly, of course) as an unwilling, possibly a failed late Kantian. In any case, his withdrawal from Husserl, which Husserl himself took to be a retreat to naturalism (a kind of anthropologism) has surely revealed itself to be something altogether different, something that, through the entire interval spanning the *Kehre* and the end of his life, has become increasingly difficult to identify—let alone explicate.

THIS PUTS THE LESSON IN TENDENTIOUS TERMS. But it matches in a perfectly fair-minded way the ambiguous, if not equivocal, claims of the actual texts of Hegel, Husserl, and Heidegger: Hegel does indeed abandon strict necessity and any commitment to the literal existence of a collective *Geist* or Subject or any strictly privileged cognitive source of any kind; Husserl does seem wedded to a transcendentally pure *epoché* and the ultimate disjunction (at the level of "science") between natural and phenomenological reason; and Heidegger (after the *Kehre*) does seem stubbornly committed to the revelatory powers of *Sein*, or Being, possibly of an even deeper power. Together, all three figures begin to isolate the agon of our age, because they signal some of the most stubborn lines of thought by which the continental tradition challenges the adequacy of the conceptual resources of pragmatism and analytic philosophy functioning under their own self-imposed naturalistic constraints. This way of putting matters ensures a more manageable contest, because the continentals must then explain why their own extravagances should not be forced to identify and defend the constraints they are themselves prepared to abide by, which they suppose the others demonstrably fail to meet; and then, at the very least, the relevance of the empirical puzzle, cast in Darwinian terms, regarding the difference between primate biology and culturally artifactual selves, cannot be ignored.

I foresee the deep vulnerability of all three movements: the reductionism of the analysts seems likely to fail to accommodate the unique emergence of our historicized, enlanguaged, and encultured world; the extranaturalism of the continentals may be ruled out by the actual facts of the evolution of a particular species (*Homo sapiens*) that has invented its own mode of being (qua self, person, subject, or agent) by the gradual artifactual transformation of primate communication into true speech and languaged thought in ways that cannot be accounted for in Darwinian or genetic terms; and the pragmatists, though they plainly rely on Darwin's discovery, have hardly begun to articulate the conceptual linkages and differences between the metaphysics of physical nature and the metaphysics of human culture in any fine-grained way.

Let me put the point another way (which I shall examine more closely later). The entire history of Western philosophy that spans the biologism of the Greek conception of *paideia* (education, child rearing) informing Aristotle's *Nicomachean Ethics*, the *geistlich* conception of *Bildung* that, in remarkably varied ways, unites figures like Johann Herder, Hegel, and Hans-Georg Gadamer in their adherence to enculturing processes that are already clearly contrasted with the natural processes of primate forms of rearing; and the hapless efforts of genuinely perceptive contemporary philosophers like John McDowell and Charles Taylor, who, though they rightly grasp the impoverishment of analytic philosophies deprived of the resources of *Bildung*, still cleave unaccountably to the essential adequacy of Aristotle's paideutic model or (in McDowell's case) to the supposed conceptual congruity between Aristotle's ahistorical biologism, Kant's transcendentalism, Hume's empiricism, and Hegel's historicism![12]

The entire tradition from the beginning to its provisional end (thus far) is committed to what we may call "internal *Bildung*"—the effective process of instructing the young of a human society in some preferred way of living (as in Aristotle's *Ethics*) drawn from that society's more inclusive cultural resources. My point is that all the important philosophical questions regarding the analysis of culture are ignored by beginning any account of the human condition in such a way. Apart from the profound incommensurability of the biological and the cultural, which McDowell does not actually consider (which Taylor is clearer about), the entire trajectory of Western philosophy has barely explored the import of what I shall call "external *Bildung*," the long evolutionary process that accounts for the emergence of the unique primate gifts (of *Homo sapiens*) that bridge for the first time the advanced forms of primate communication and their transformation into true speech: a process that entails the original formation and continually evolving transformation of the artifactually "second-natured" site of linguistic and cultural competence—the being that we call a self or person.

I suggest that external *Bildung* is the metaphysically decisive novelty that Darwinian evolution makes possible but cannot rightly explain, which, in turn, accounts for that kind of cultural "ontogeny" (mixing terms for convenience) that answers to internal *Bildung*. It's quite plain that both Peirce and Dewey rely on some version of external *Bildung*: Peirce, speculating on the continuity between protoplasm and the inventions of advanced scientists; Dewey, speaking (in *Logic*) of the transformation of an "indeterminate situation" into a "problematic situation."[13] But these are no more than the slimmest of beginnings. The prevailing intuition has it that the innovations of true language, however continuous with primate communication, cannot be explained essentially in terms restricted to any familiar biological or physical processes, that the evolution of language and culture is effectively sui generis, though the cultural must be suitably incarnate in the physical.

I concede that if pragmatism may be read as "implicitly" hospitable to the artifactual emergence of the "self" or "person" (or "ego"), then so may Husserl and Heidegger, though I think the pragmatists were drawn to Darwinian (and post-Darwinian) themes in a way Husserl and Heidegger were surely not. Nevertheless, both Husserl and Heidegger have their recent interpreters who view them as overcoming their well-marked animus against the distorting continuities that might join the "natural" and the existentially "transcendental." I say only that to read Husserl in this way would require the abandonment of apriorism altogether, and to read Heidegger conformably would make most of "late" Heidegger impossible. (Nevertheless, I welcome the revisionist reading!)

One can easily imagine trying to free Kant from his transcendental idealism (whether it would succeed or not); but it is not easy (in a similar way) to imagine Husserl "freed" from pure phenomenology, though Maurice Merleau-Ponty makes a splendid effort at doing just that. Heidegger frees himself by a deeper form of gnomic wisdom, but the result is barely legible on any known reading, which is to say, Heidegger's insights regarding intersubjectivity might never be paraphrased well enough to test any naturalistic reading. Kant may be weaned from transcendentalism, because his own arguments claim to discern no more than familiar necessities explained by reference to extraordinary circumstances; whereas Husserl introduces a novel methodology that must be mastered if we are to discern its characteristic necessities at all, and Heidegger simply announces what the mystery of Being reveals.[14] There's room for invention here, so far as Kant and Husserl are concerned, whereas either the invention made possible by Heidegger's *Being and Time* is displaced after the *Kehre*,[15] or the claim of the *Kehre* can be found to have been lurking in *Being and Time*, though largely undetected. You see how the bare admission of the Darwinian theme affects our assessment of the largest currents of contemporary philosophy.

No one would believe we would be willing to bear so much conceptual baggage without complaint, were it not for the easy conviction that its arguments were actually true, or trust the stubborn confidence with which analytic philosophy continues to ply a calling that belongs somewhere, in time, so we may claim, between the mid-seventeenth century and the beginning of the nineteenth! This is not, however, to allow the pragmatists to go scot-free. They are themselves obviously slack in their own reading of naturalism: they have hardly distinguished their own account from that of the "naturalizing" extremes championed, for instance, by Quine and Davidson, and they have never returned in any significant depth (pace G. H. Mead) to the analysis of what a person is, or indeed what social history is. These themes belong to their post-Kantian origins, but they need to be rescued from analytic and continental excesses *and* from pragmatist inertia. The classic pragmatists are genuinely interesting and ingenious figures; but as a single movement pragmatism is a disappointing hodgepodge that must be redirected. And even at the present time, when the opportunity has made itself felt, continuing inertia has, with rather little resistance, pretty well remained the rule.

Still, pragmatism's best intuitions have been applied to eliminating the extravagances of its Kantian sources (by Charles Peirce) and of its Hegelian sources (by John Dewey) in such a way as to lead us back to the ordinary aptitudes of *human beings* (ourselves) viewed within a generously Darwinized ecology, without transcendental, revelatory, or privileged presumptions of any kind. Frankly, Dewey, despite his technical limitations (in logic and the methodology of science), does manage to penetrate the corrective themes—in a commanding way—in *Experience and Nature*.[16] No other American philosopher, it seems, has succeeded nearly as well, though his detailed treatment needs a stronger hand.

Broadly speaking, the pragmatists are not usually wrong in their principal views, though Dewey is often banal—less so than usual, I hazard to say, in *Experience and Nature*. Peirce simply veers off more and more insistently from what he originally took to be pragmatism's theme. William James supplies a necessary ingredient in the pragmatist arsenal—the theory of truth—but he does so lamely, so utterly without skill and for such an unlikely reason that he accomplishes little more than the betrayal of his own minor standing—that is, in his compulsion to reconcile the "truths" of religion and the truths of science—which of course puts the movement's reputation at great risk.[17] Peirce was infuriated with James's "misreading"—piracy was what he saw—but he condemned James (indirectly) for the wrong reasons, for he himself became more of a German idealist (of a homegrown American sort) than a pragmatist in the terms *we* now acknowledge: that is, in terms of a pragmatism more Dewey's than Peirce's. (Philosophy's infelicities begin to mount.)

Peirce simply lost interest in the narrow primacy of the "here and now" with which he began.[18] Even so, he never returned to the transcendentalist's excesses: he betters Kant by collecting Kant's kinds of certitudes as no more than pragmatic conjectures or projections of rational Hope. Though why such articles of faith continued to be needed remains inadequately explained: they ultimately belong to Peirce's quite original, decidedly ingenious reinterpretation of transcendentalism. The fact is that they are inseparably linked to Peirce's version of fallibilism and the "long run," that is, to Peirce's account of truth, which is utterly contrary to James's remarkably canny intuitions *and* the best-known strains of Peirce's earliest papers. The account goes far toward explaining the stalemate between Peirce and James. But it also anticipates in the profoundest way the Hegelianized Kantianism of Ernst Cassirer's *Philosophy of Symbolic Forms*, perhaps the most important neo-Kantian contribution of the last century (which, on my reading, converges in a striking way with Peirce's fallibilism and even explains the pragmatist import of Peirce's own doctrine).

The mature Dewey makes almost no mistakes of this sort, but no one can be genuinely satisfied with Dewey's resolutions: adopting them so often strikes the mind as platitudinous, hardly worth the labor. Yet, when one keeps in mind the outrageous alternatives promoted by the grand thinkers already mentioned, one realizes how much better Dewey is than he sounds. In the same sense, the analytic philosophers are generally not merely wrong but wrongheaded in the very thrust of their most distinctive programs, that is, wrong in their various scientisms.

They could never, in fact, confirm the validity of their best-known, most unyielding forms of reductionism; though it must be conceded that their mistake is rather a noble and ambitious one, not lightly set aside. Quine, however, believes that haecceity can be replaced by quiddity; David Armstrong believes that real possibility can be explained in terms of actuality if modeled on the *Tractatus*; Nelson Goodman believes that predicative similarity can be explained in nominalist terms. These are troublingly elementary mistakes that accumulate (among justifiably admired philosophers) with alarming ease,[19] though they happen to be advanced in the service of a contest favoring a thoroughgoing extensionalism whose latest inning we must stay to witness.

Analysts often view the principal strands of continental thought—those linked to Kant, Hegel, Husserl, and Heidegger—as concoctions pure and simple, concoctions of great skill no doubt, by which opposed philosophies of high presumption are defeated rather handily or said to lead to conclusions no one would willingly support. They are, in turn, themselves often thought to be impossible to defend: each toys with holding fast to the life and capacity of ordinary human beings. But each seems to "relent," so to say, in order to save the genuine grandeur of its own invention. The truth about these charges will have to be sorted, but they point to the difficulty of the present undertaking: there is no neutral idiom or agreed-upon set of essential problems. There is nothing in the viable philosophies of our day to compare with the marvelous extravagances of Kant, Hegel, Husserl, and Heidegger, unless it is the way in which our lesser figures catch fire from the fire that belongs to these. We shall have to see.

What is most interesting about the pragmatists is this: first, they begin, as Husserl and Heidegger do, with the problems posed by Kant and Hegel (which neither pragmatism nor phenomenology ever abandons); and second, they are never tempted by the self-deceptions of analytic scientism or the analysts' refusal to admit the sense in which they themselves have never rightly overcome the pre-Kantian or Kant's own pre-Kantian paradoxes. Pragmatism is one of a very small number of Western philosophical movements—certainly it is the only sustained American movement—that, within the terms just mentioned, never exceed the natural competence and limitations of mere human being. That at least is the brief I favor. The necessary arguments are close at hand. Kant's transcendentalism, after all, was a noble effort to outflank the otherwise insuperable paradoxes of pre-Kantian cognitive privilege, which have persisted, effectively, through the whole of the twentieth century and beyond. But Kant failed for reasons Hegel masterfully exposes; and pragmatism is very nearly the only Anglo-American movement to have remained true to that exposé. There's the clue to the right concerns of the new century.

Every well-ordered inquiry, alert to the prospects of the rapprochement I've bruited, must see that what's still needed is a reasonable replacement of the strict transcendentalism Kant introduces (or of surrogates like those of the idealists or Husserl or Heidegger) that would be able to recover the simple continuity of ordinary human experience and the distinctive questions of an a priori legitimation of objective knowledge. There is, as it turns out, only one way to proceed: the a priori must itself be conceived as being an a posteriori posit! There's the minimal lesson that follows from reading Kant and Hegel as concerned, at different phases of the argument, with the same problems of elucidation. This is as close to the nerve of the account that follows as we are likely to come. I shall need your patience here.

Against the analysts, the pragmatists' motto might be "natural but not naturalizable"—that is, to favor the reasoned rejection of every form of scientistic reductionism spawned in the spirit of Quine's "Epistemology Naturalized" or Davidson's "Coherence Theory of Truth and Knowledge."[20] Against the continentals, it might be "realism on no more than human terms"—that is, the unavoidability of a constructivism or constructive realism as a result of conceding the generic argument Kant and Hegel share through first invention and revision, trimmed down from the "extranatural," transcendental, "supersensuous," or idealist extravagances of Kant's and the post-Kantian world—always, of course, with an eye to their identifying the single would-be constant Subject of every form of knowledge, understanding, and agency. Put in the flattest way: we humans are the only *agents* and *subjects*, formed as selves or persons, that we find in the natural world. There's an enormous innovation tethered there that, in my opinion, depends on Darwinizing historicity and historicizing the meaning of Darwin's discoveries, has remained largely inert or inchoate, and could easily provide the inspiration of a new surge of Western philosophy that would focus its entire career in a suitably redemptive way. It's an essential part of the convergent impulses of late twentieth-century philosophy that I espy, though the full brief has still to be provided.

We might recast the second motto this way: "naturalism but not extranaturalism" (to exclude obvious supernaturalisms as well as doctrines of cognitive privilege and the like that have no prospect of ever being convincingly construed in terms of the more modest naturalisms that now prevail). By "constructivism," I mean nothing more than the conceptual indissolubility of the subjective and the objective (the true theme of the rhetorical extravagance of the "identity of difference," which Hegel collects as *Geist*). Faute de mieux, it signifies obliquely an epistemological constraint on whatever in evidentiary terms we elect to count as objective knowledge; it has nothing to do with positing substances of any novel kind. (I'm hinting here at "pragmatist" economies applied to Hegel that will draw on figures as different as Peirce, Dewey, and Cassirer.) We cannot go beyond the indissoluble union of subjects and objects—epistemically.

(That should have been Kant's thesis.) In this obvious sense, constructivism equals constructive realism (if we wish); effectively, the thesis eclipses both idealism and representationalism. The real world (at least physical nature) is not a "construction" of mind or Mind in any sense at all; but the paradigm of knowledge or science is certainly confined to the discursive powers of the human.[21]

I find it perfectly fair to say that many of the extreme formulations of continental philosophy that seem to oppose the human and the natural (or the "naturalistic") may mean no more than to insist on the sui generis distinctions of the human when contrasted with the rest of "nature": where they mean more (you will have to judge Heidegger's and Husserl's intent yourselves), we may with a clear conscience simply reject their philosophical exertions. There's the advantage of the Darwinian economy: the natural artifactuality of the "self" concedes nothing firmer than a "constructivist" legitimation of our theories of the self's cognizing powers. Faute de mieux, there is no apodictic knowledge, no privileged faculties, no preestablished harmony, no exceptionless universals, no assured natural necessities, no access to the noumenal, no timeless "conceptual truths," no human grasp of the totality of all "there is," no escape from the contingencies of whatever we report as "given" within human experience. The Darwinian limitation is a variant of the flux of life itself, deprived of any and all resources of reflexive validation that are not themselves infected with the same limitation. In short, knowledge, finally, is an extraordinary form of bootstrapping.

The theme may be focused a bit more forcefully. After the work of Kant and Hegel, the admission that the analysis of knowledge cannot be made to rest on any disjunctive account of the contributions of "subject" and "object" signifies that (1) transcendentalism is as indefensible as pre-Kantian cognitive privilege; (2) realism cannot fail to be constructivist, though reality is not itself (for that reason) constructed; (3) what we count as objective reality, as independent of our thinking of what is real, must be an epistemic (not an ontic) construction if it is to be distinguished from noumenalism; and, therefore, (4) it is no longer possible to disjoin the realist and idealist aspects of objective knowledge—the canonical contrast between realism and idealism no longer makes sense. Minimally, "idealism" (in the sense favored by the post-Kantian Idealists: Peirce as well as Friedrich Schelling and Hegel—and Johann Fichte before them) signifies the indissoluble unity (in cognitive contexts) of the subjective and objective sides of phenomenological experience. It's in this sense that Peirce speaks of "mind" in nature independently of human thought: it's a formulaic admission of the metaphysical congruity between human knowledge and what is known objectively, not anything that could possibly stand in either Kantian or Hegelian terms as autonomous Reason, *Geist*, or a supersensuous cognizing source of any kind. But to correct the rhetorical extravagance, which admittedly often appears as metaphysical discovery, *is* plainly an important part of the essential charm of classic pragmatism. Post-Kant and post-Hegel, metaphysics and epistemology are inseparable but not identical. Idealism in the post-Kantian sense signifies (or should signify) no more than that inseparability. Idealism in the metaphysical sense champions the preposterous doctrine that the natural world is itself constituted or constructed by the cognizing mind. Furthermore, the (Kantian) argument that what human cognizers can possibly know is only what is transcendentally constructed supposes wrongly that this is the only way to escape noumenalism; in fact, it rightly addresses only the epistemological question: it is entirely straightforward to argue that, though knowledge is dependent on the indissolubility of the subjective and objective, *what* we know (if we know the world at all) may, without paradox, be known of the "independent" world.

Pragmatism is poised between the extremes of analytic and continental philosophy of the sorts now mentioned. It isolates as distinct the question of the right analysis of the human being as such, in the very context in which we arrive at a realist picture of the world ample enough for all intelligent life. Analytic scientism precludes constructivism: hence, precludes the Kantian and post-Kantian resolution of the "Cartesian" paradox. Yet Kant's own and the usual post-Kantian efforts to capture the "subjective" condition on which a constructive realism is said to depend tend to go extravagantly haywire, to exceed anything that might be said to be at all "natural" or familiar to our ordinary sense of ourselves.

The fact remains (as the idealists never tire of reminding us) that Kant failed to provide a transcendental argument to legitimate the necessity of his own transcendentalism. No one has succeeded in this regard. At least in part, this helps to define what idealism signifies (whether German or British) insofar as we exceed the sense of the two mottoes just given and secure thereby some questionable kind of necessity—telic, historical, rational, or totalized. Pragmatism is committed to bringing the account of the human down to scale, without yielding to any premature form of "naturalizing" (reductionism) or to any form of extranatural privilege, ontic necessity, unexaminable faculty, or, worse still, the revelations of Being itself, which (as Heidegger candidly admits) is utterly alien and unbidden!

Put metonymically: pragmatism's form of naturalism precludes any indefeasible necessities affecting knowledge or reality. That is the basis of its opposition to the extreme proposals of analytic scientism and Husserlian and post-Husserlian phenomenology: the one, in the direction of naturalizing; the other, in the direction of extranaturalism. But once one grants the pragmatist postulate, one will find it impossible to hold the line against admitting some form or other of constructivism, historicism, relativism, incommensurabilism, and similar proposals (to whatever extent they prove independently coherent). You see here how our dwelling on the fortunes of pragmatism begins to organize a unified conception of the whole of Eurocentric philosophy. I propose as yet no more than the promise of an argument.

IT CANNOT BE DENIED that, within the continental fold, there are comparable efforts to save these themes (or something like the themes already flagged) as defining, in the Kantian and post-Kantian way, the constructivist cast of any realism likely to be viable. The epistemological competence those efforts display must themselves be construed in constructivist terms. For if *they* were cognitively privileged in a facultative way, we would have exceeded once again the reasonable limits of naturalistic tolerance and nullified the advantages of a constructive realism. Pragmatism is of course just such a naturalism or realism; it is already, therefore, cousin to any corresponding movement from the continental side that recoils from whatever remains of privilege in the work of figures like Kant, Hegel, Husserl, and Heidegger: for example, in Kant's speaking of the determinative role of noumena that we cannot possibly know, or of the "deduction" (from the contingent data of sensory perception) of the pure concepts of the understanding, or of the assured representational nature of perception itself, or of the supposed a priori arguments confirming the conceptual indefeasibility of Euclidean geometry and Newtonian physics; or of Husserl's claim that the transcendental *epoché* can be effected even within the confines of natural experience, or that noematic invariances can be reliably freed from the contingent constraints of language, perception, or any other expression of naturalistic experience (now dubbed the "natural attitude").[22]

Once the temptations of new forms of privilege are set aside, one begins to glimpse the prospect of an abundance of continental theories that may claim a history pertinently similar to pragmatism's history and something of a cognate idiom. There's the clue to pragmatism's "advantage": a prospect more than merely prefigured in Merleau-Ponty's phenomenology and, say, the Frankfurt Critical program, both of which have been judged hospitable to themes very close to those favored by pragmatism.[23] But the evidence (often tantalizing and inconclusive) may be drawn as well from figures like Jacques Derrida, Michel Foucault, Jean-François Lyotard, and others loosely collected as poststructuralists. And once we go this far, we may also welcome the inclusion of that isolated figure—the Ludwig Wittgenstein of *Philosophical Investigations*[24]—who bridges in an incompletely developed way (through *Sprachspiel* and *Lebensform*) a sort of proto-pragmatism and a Kantian-like inspiration.

Other names may now be added, the names, for instance, of some considerably less well-known figures who write in the spirit of the so-called American continental movement, such as Frederick Olafson and Joseph Rouse.[25] Both feature a Heideggerian reading of what it is for a human being "to *have* a world" or to investigate physical nature scientifically within the terms of a human world. "Having a world," Olafson maintains, cannot be captured by, or reduced to, the conceptual idiom usually thought adequate, in Anglo-American analytic philosophy, for the descriptive and explanatory work of the natural sciences.[26] We find ourselves here in the neighborhood of a fresh beginning bridging the shared strengths of pragmatism and continental philosophy and directed (at least in part) against the egregious scientisms of analytic philosophy. "Having a world" (in Olafson's sense) is, I would say, meant to stake out common ground between Husserl, Heidegger, and Dewey—and, for that matter, Hegel and Cassirer. Is that reasonable?

You realize that the convergent instruction here, for example, the sense of Dewey's "problematic situation" (in the *Logic*) and Heidegger's *In-der-Welt-sein* (in *Being and Time*), signifies an ineliminable constraint on would-be objective inquiries regarding whatever may be claimed (propositionally) to be found in the encountered world. So truth itself (in the sense in which, according to Heidegger, we presume our cognitively enabling aptitudes may be counted on to yield determinate statements about the way the world finally is) is problematically subject to the "existential" vagaries of the very condition of "being" that the dependent inquiries cannot fathom (unless in a question-begging way) by their own dependent assertions. Here, indeed, is the point of convergence between Deweyan naturalism ("Darwinian," let us agree) and Heideggerian extranaturalism (possibly an existential, holist, atheoretical analogue of transcendental speculation that affirms no constative truths of its own, except that what it concedes to be thus disclosed is itself insuperably aletheic—disclosed—in its own right). This, I surmise, is the point of fundamental divergence between Heidegger's existential phenomenology and Dewey's pragmatism, which is standardly misread by commentators hospitable to both philosophers and to the idea that Heidegger is or may be a pragmatist.[27]

Merleau-Ponty characterizes science (in *Phenomenology of Perception*) as "second-order," which means to privilege whatever may be phenomenologically recovered from some deepest bodily contact with the world, ourselves, and others, where the latter is said to harbor "primordial," "prethetic" elements of experience beyond whatever is thought to be contingently and familiarly empirical, as among the experienced data of the natural sciences.[28] (Here Merleau-Ponty is still very close to his Husserlian beginnings.) But Merleau-Ponty may also have come to mean, particularly toward the end of his career, that science is second-order in the ineluctable sense that, however confined or revisable our primordial resources may be, science cannot escape its dependence on the endlessly recovered, conjectured, forever incompletely retrieved (or interpreted), already chiasmically undecomposable data (the "given") from which its own disciplines arise.

It is there that pragmatists and Husserlian phenomenologists diverge—as do Husserlian and Heideggerian phenomenologists. The crucial question is this: how can it be shown that what is extracted from the "given" (read without privilege, say, in the spirit of Hegel's *Erscheinungen*: "presuppositionlessly") could possibly yield a principled disjunction between the naturalistic and the transcendental or between the Husserlian transcendental and the Heideggerian existential? The Husserlian sense of natural science's "second-order" standing is, in its own terms, an assurance that Husserl's apriorism is also, finally, a "presuppositionless" method of recovery! But no Husserlian (not even Husserl) ever demonstrated (or could) that this was true or open to actual confirmation.

Perhaps most notably in his "Course Notes" on Husserl's "Origin of Geometry," Merleau-Ponty sketches the sense in which he finds his own conception of phenomenology amply anticipated in Husserl's first and last work and in what he finds to be the final convergence between Husserl and Heidegger. He may have been too sanguine about the privileged resources Husserl and Heidegger reserve for themselves (in their very different ways). But he points the way to what, from a pragmatist perspective, might arguably be viewed as a naturalistic turn within phenomenology itself—a turn, however, whose coherence is finally unclear.

Following are some lines from Merleau-Ponty's "Course Notes," cited entirely out of context, which give a clear sense of his own struggle with what he regards as a false disjunction between phenomenological objectivism and phenomenological subjectivism—in favor of a potentially infinite chiasm, the interweaving or entanglement of language and lived experience ("idea" and "flesh": *Verflechtung* is Husserl's term, which Merleau-Ponty coopts as *entrelacement*), a would-be "third" way of phenomenology:

[A] thought is not *some ideas*. It is the *circumscription of an unthought*. . . . Cf. the lived or perceived universe: not only made out of things but also out of reflections, shadows, levels, horizons, which are not nothing, which are *between* the things and delimit their variations in one sole world. . . . The method that we are extolling is already one of Husserl's final thoughts. Circle: we presuppose his final thoughts and they presuppose this method. . . . Exactly this leads description to the place where consciousness is *apperceived* as connected to body-world-truth-language-history, man. Can one *constitute* that, envelop it, in the system of apperception? How can one found on acts that which is *"vor aller Theorie,"* the "pretheoretical," the *Vorgegeben*? Does reflection rediscover the source from which it descends? Being eidetical, isn't reflection always different from production. . . . How would it unveil the *Ursprung* of passivity?[29]

These extraordinarily perceptive remarks may be read as temptations to incorporate the "natural" in a *deeper* phenomenology that risks being finally inchoate while remaining very different from the explicitly reportable *Erscheinungen* of Hegel's *Phenomenology* and (too baldly put) the discernible sense of Dewey's notion of "an indeterminate [or problematic] situation"—or I now add without instant explication the discernibly simpler warning of Wittgenstein's famous question (at § 621 of the *Investigations*) of explaining the difference between "raising my arm" and "my arm's rising," which begins to suggest the relevance of such tangential figures as Wilhelm Dilthey and Henri Bergson in recovering the common ground that is all but shared by, say, Dewey and Heidegger (without, of course, making Heidegger out to be a pragmatist or Dewey a lesser Heideggerian).

It's here, precisely, that some are persuaded that Heidegger thought he discerned a deeper source for centering the account of *Dasein*'s existence in the variant forms of Chinese and Japanese approaches to the Void.[30] But whatever the attraction of such a turn, we are painfully aware that it cannot yield a formulable linkage to the determinate questions of natural inquiry. (The appeal to the inexpressible will always appear as privileged if it helps us surmount an expressible difficulty!)

The point at which divergent phenomenologies begin to matter is plain enough: *vor aller Theorie* might signify *either* what is "given" within natural experience (without theoretical commitment, even where what is given may yet be shown to be theory laden) or what is unconditionally prior or primordial, putatively shorn of all theory, in terms of transcendental "recovery"; the first accords with the spirit of Dewey's intuition; the second, with Husserl's. The first is naturalistic; the second, extranaturalist. The first is given in the sense of being presuppositionless in intent, hence not privileged in any epistemic way though finally accessible to human inquiry; whereas the second is posited *as* theory free by way of a problematic theory and determinate method of cognition: by being the very source of the given!

Merleau-Ponty's "Course Notes" challenge in a perfectly reasonable way the final closure and apodictic confidence of Husserl's transcendental reduction *and*, by that reflection, the assurance of any principled disjunction between the naturalistic and the transcendentally phenomenological. But in that daring union (the achievement of what he calls *la chair*, beyond what he had called *le corps vécu*), Merleau-Ponty completely disorganizes the ordinary possibilities of manageable reportage. The Husserlian insists on the recovery of what is constitutively originary in experience; the Hegelian and pragmatist are content with what may be fairly constructed from what is as close as possible to being given in experience without privileged sources or privileged reliability. In effect, in pursuing his "third" way, Merleau-Ponty exposes (though that is hardly his intention) the seemingly inescapable arbitrariness of Husserl's painstakingly defined facultative claims and a priori method. He therefore leaves the field to a recuperable naturalism, if only naturalism could escape scientism and if indeed a full recovery of what is primordially given can never be more than an infinitely postponed objective.

But to speak of science as second-order is either a misdescription of the inherent limitations of phenomenological experience that we already know from naturalistic sources or else an exaggerated acknowledgment of the thoroughly constructivist nature of human knowledge and understanding. All we need insist on here (on pragmatist grounds) is that invariances cast in naturalistic terms can never be assured in any modal sense and that phenomenology is never more than a search for the largest and most nearly invariant—constructed—constancies that may be deemed to organize our experienced world conceptually, that can be tested *within that same world*. Read that way, phenomenology cannot be counted a separate—foundational—science: it must be an idealized abstraction drawn from the naturalistic sciences themselves or from their informal sources.

Olafson is completely straightforward when, following Husserl (but not Husserl's argument) and following Heidegger (whom he finds more congenial), he attempts to recover what Husserl calls "the natural attitude," the competitive strength of which he then proceeds to test. Here is Olafson's clear-sighted proposal, therefore, which may help to secure an important conceptual economy:

> I propose to reverse the traditional procedure and to accept the claim of the natural attitude unless and until it can be shown to be false by proofs that are more persuasive than those that have been offered so far. This means that the natural attitude will not serve simply as a datum for the kind of philosophical interpretation that is quite free to replace it with theses of its own devising. Instead, it will represent in some sense the primordial achievement implicit in having a world at all—an achievement that all philosophical and scientific accounts of our nature as perceiving and thinking beings have somehow to acknowledge and find a place for in the theories they construct.[31]

Olafson's very neat challenge suggests a way of recovering the nerve of the continental tradition while avoiding the excesses of the Kantian/post-Kantian period *and* the excesses of his own champions. What he offers converges very nicely with the main thrust of the pragmatists' own way of resisting scientism, reductionism, dualism, transcendentalism, and other conceptual megalomanias of the Kantian/post-Kantian world. Olafson manages to isolate what he and I both take to be the pivot of the entire future prospect of Western philosophy: locally, what amounts to pragmatism's potential third life; Eurocentrically, what anticipates the rapprochement bruited between pragmatism and continental philosophy. I would say Olafson favors the full play of what I am calling "constructivism" or "constructive realism" (even within the space of Husserlian "constitution").

Read that way, the best of the "continental" themes drawn from phenomenology (generously construed) insists on the primordial or, perhaps better, the empirically indefeasible standing of whatever is uniquely and irreducibly human. In this sense, Olafson sees a way of recovering the naturalistic theme in both Husserl and Heidegger. By "rapprochement," beyond the merely apparent "convergence" of disparate philosophies, I mean only the promise of my intended argument: that is, the quarrels that appear to mark the three-cornered opposition of pragmatism, analytic philosophy, and continental philosophy can be made to yield to a reformulated problematic capable of incorporating coherently and without unacceptable distortion the best energies of the most important movements of Western philosophy that remain salient at the close of the last century.

The nearly invisible point of convergence surfaces compellingly in Merleau-Ponty's seemingly opaque formulation that "a thought . . . is the *circumscription of an unthought.*" Extraordinary conceptual risk. Merleau-Ponty marks here the inexhaustible, continual presence of contingently sampled, horizonally prejudiced intrusions of an undefined *Umwelt* of potential significations that bear on whatever we are able to affirm but cannot, in doing that, capture in the same way.

I take that to stalemate the closure of Kant's transcendentalism, the apodictic reliability of Husserl's *epoché*, any literal-minded success in bridging the finite and the infinite in Hegel's Absolute *Geist*, the inchoate possibilities of Heidegger's *In-der-Welt-sein*, the insuperable indeterminacies of Dewey's "indeterminate situation." Merleau-Ponty's confession is not a retreat to ineffability at all but an admission of the unspecifiable inexhaustibility of whatever may play the part of what is "given" or "apparent" or "reportable" within the human ken; so, for instance, survival is itself a marvel—though also given. Merleau-Ponty has found a way of admitting the pregiven given that impenetrably yields what we affirm to be given at any point in our conjectured history; in effect, he's stalemated every form of apriorism—every constituting "I" *vor* (prior to) every constituted "given"—without disallowing the inchoate standing of any determinately a priori posit that we happen to elect. There's the gist of his implied reconciliation between pragmatist naturalism and what is salvageable from Husserl's and Heidegger's alternative forms of phenomenology. Behind the scenes, it begins to dawn that, for all his extravagance, Hegel had already grasped the point of the extraordinary joke of cognitive confidence.

THERE'S A FURTHER STRATEGIC GAIN that Olafson may have had in mind in weighing the compatibility of Dewey and Heidegger. For if we view *Dasein* under the functional role of agency, then what a self does or thinks is "too close" to its own nature to support, *there*, the "externalist" model of causality that the analysts (going beyond David Hume) favor; although, by alternative causal formulations, we can always recover the canonical model without disadvantage. Otherwise, Heidegger's *In-der-Welt-sein* and Dewey's "indeterminate situation" overlap inexplicitly (in ontic terms), though they are articulated in very different ways.

The contrast between analytic scientism and what is convergent between pragmatism and phenomenology may be put this way. First, scientism treats the world as independently *determinate* and knowable as such; whereas pragmatism and continental philosophy view the determinacy of the natural world as a construction (of potentially endlessly different sorts) within the terms of its *determinability*: that is, its apparent determinacy's being "given" within the epistemic space of its larger untapped determinability. Second, analytic scientism supposes that the foundational determinacy of the entire world can be adequately expressed in terms confined to the description and explanation of inanimate physical things so that the fully human world can be described, bottom up, *from* that same foundation; whereas pragmatism and continental philosophy are not persuaded that the mental, behavioral, cultural, linguistic, and historical aspects of the human world *can be reduced* to the terms favored by the other, even where they remain naturalistic. They insist instead on a fundamental asymmetry between top-down, part-whole, functional and subfunctional accounts and bottom-up accounts that are thoroughly atomic, compositional, adequately rendered in extensionalist terms.[32]

Third, as a consequence of the two sorts of opposition just mentioned, scientism sees no reason, *in principle*, to think of human beings as radically different, conceptually, from inanimate things, even with regard to consciousness, intentionality, reflexive thought, language, freedom, care, and responsibility; whereas the pragmatists and continental theorists, believing otherwise, construe whatever is judged to be a part of reality or true about the world, or valuable in any sense whatsoever, as practically and epistemologically (though not, for that reason alone, ontologically) dependent on the initiatives of human inquirers. (Here, I am obliged to bracket the extreme Buddhist and Daoist themes Heidegger apparently found congenial. I confess I've never seen a sufficiently articulated analysis of what "relationship" might hold between, say *śūnyatā* and the determinate/determinable world; on the contrary, to admit a relationship is already to deny the deeper pretensions of the Asian themes—which cannot be "doctrines" of any familiar sort.)

The difference between the pragmatists and the continentals—if there is any difference finally—seems to be confined to formulating the difference between persons and "things" and what, in this regard, we should understand by the adequacy or inadequacy of naturalism itself. Beyond that, the pragmatists and continentals view the dual role of the human (1) as discernible, within nature, as a distinct kind of being and (2) as the "subjective" (a priori) pole of any objective science of the real—hence, as constituting the supreme test of the adequacy or inadequacy of naturalism or extranaturalism. The analysts regularly minimize the strategic importance of the question or answer it in reductive terms. For the moment, convergence provides the most interesting lesson.

At the risk of adding further, as yet unredeemed allusions to instructive philosophical confrontations (which I shall redeem in due course), let me suggest that the demonstrable inadequacies of recent forms of reductionism and of the classic forms of the unity of science program (as in Jaegwon Kim's supervenientism) and the equally demonstrable inadequacies of recent versions of hermeneutics (as in Charles Taylor's review of the differences between the natural and the human sciences) lead inexorably in the direction of the rapprochement I've been hinting at. The analysts are simply unable to explain the reliability of their cognitive grounds and drive for contextless certainty. It's in this same sense that McDowell's wish to reclaim Hegel's *Bildung* engenders the pathos that it does: it explains, for instance, why, finally, the classic pragmatists were so much more convincing than the analytic masters of "truth," "meaning," "reference," "predicative" generality, and the like: they had a sense of Merleau-Ponty's "circumscription of an unthought" without the least instruction.[33]

To grasp the full import of the agon before us, we must be clear about Olafson's intent in speaking of "the primordial achievement implicit in *having* a world." This is, of course, a theme central but obscurely linked to the ontological in Heidegger's account in *Being and Time*, problematic but equally central in Husserl's reckoning of a shared "world." Olafson is well worth pondering here. Commenting on what was cited earlier from his account, he continues:

> This may seem an excessively weighty entitlement to confer on what some would doubtless regard as just another theory [that is, the "natural attitude"]—a little cruder, perhaps, than its more up-to-date rivals but with no more initial plausibility than they can claim. My reply to this objection is that such a categorization of the natural attitude as a primitive theory has little to recommend it. Theories, after all, have to be tested by their application to a field that they do not simply control so that it can only confirm the theses that they propose. . . . A world, self, and others—these are "facts" that the natural attitude presupposes and that every human being must somehow be familiar with because they are implicit in every form of inquiry and in every human practice. No theory could be confirmed unless the field of inquiry were already ordered by the distinctions they imply. My thesis is, accordingly, that unless a theory reconstructs human being in such a way that this kind of familiarity finds a place within it, it hardly deserves to be treated as even minimally adequate to the ostensible purpose.[34]

This is certainly a challenge to the extremes of analytic philosophy. Olafson has in mind the linked doctrines of dualism and reductionism, which pragmatism would of course join in opposing.

But just how telling is the actual thesis? Olafson favors both sides of the dispute: on the one hand, he says he is prepared to accept the possibility that the "natural attitude" is false, though he knows of no compelling argument to that effect; on the other hand, he insists that *his* own "facts" (he calls them "phenomenological facts")[35] are "implicit in every form of inquiry and in every human practice." If the first option holds, then naturalism would be perfectly compatible with the "bare" phenomenological facts adduced in the second; but if the second option holds (as Olafson reads it), then naturalisms of the strongest and most characteristic analytic sort (that is, scientism and reductionism, *not* the pragmatists' version) would necessarily be incompatible with those same "phenomenological" facts; or the phenomenological facts would be indistinguishable from "naturalistic" facts of a nonscientistic sort.

Another way of putting the same point that I find helpful simply reminds us that whatever we take to be an adequate picture of the real world must answer to whatever is humanly "given" in that minimal, unprivileged, unendingly reinterpreted sense that marks the existential nature of human cognition and practical life reasonably assigned to Hegel's *Phenomenology*,

Dewey's *Logic*, Heidegger's *Being and Time*, and (as a courtesy) Merleau-Ponty's "Course Notes" on Husserl's "The Origin of Geometry." If that reading were sustained, we would already have achieved the rapprochement we want. Notice, incidentally, that universality, here, is a matter of faute de mieux considerations, *not* of anything modally necessary. But if that's true, then there is no advantage to be gained by a verbal disjunction between the mundane and the transcendental—an important point I shall return to, which is also the point of Olafson's constructivism.

Pragmatism would prefer to say that scientism and reductionism fail entirely *on their own terms*, without our ever needing to broach Olafson's deeper confrontation. On the first option, Olafson would count as a naturalist of a sort not very different from the pragmatists—in spite of the way he enters the debate; on the second option, he might never be a naturalist of any stripe (though the differences adduced might well be picayune). Husserl's strongest doctrine opposes every naturalism, no matter how moderate, because his doctrine harbors an exclusionary claim about transcendental privilege. The distinguished phenomenologist J. N. Mohanty concedes that there *is* a continuity, within human capacities, between empirical or "natural" cognitive powers and phenomenological inquiry said to yield its own sui generis form of certainty.[36] Nevertheless, phenomenology draws its conceptual data for its own work *from* one or another contingent *Lebenswelt*. Yet if that is so (and it must be so), phenomenology could never vindicate a form of certainty firmer than that of "natural" conviction, unless it also claimed (however doubtfully) a cognizing power beyond the "psychologistic" data on which its favored faculty is practiced. On the concession Mohanty tenders (which he claims to find in Husserl), we cannot possibly identify a confirmed source of phenomenological certainty that we cannot find in natural reason.

In favoring the first option, the facts Olafson adduces cannot be "primordial" in any sense that is demonstrably beyond the competent inquiries of one or another nonreductive science; cannot be "transcendent" in the existentially ontological sense by which Heidegger intends (in his analysis of *Dasein*) to surpass Kant's cognitive a priori: namely, what is sui generis and essentially invariant (but not changeless!) in the being of a human being. But I cannot see why the posit of transcendent *Dasein* cannot be construed as an a priori but *not* privileged *natural* speculation about the cognitive or existential conditions of whatever distinction we claim for ourselves. Some commentators—Mark Okrent, notoriously and problematically—are inclined to read Heidegger as a failed naturalist and pragmatist. I am not one of these.

I argue that a human person or self (as distinct from any mere member of *Homo sapiens*) is a hybrid artifact, an indissolubly emergent, individuated entity possessing "second-natured" powers (speech, reflection, agency, freedom, and responsibility), incarnate in its biological nature, brought into effective existence by the enculturation of the gifted infants of the human species.[37] This is in fact precisely what I mean by "Darwinizing historicity" and "historicizing Darwinism"; but to say so baldly is hardly instructive here. Please be aware of the theme, however, as the argument unfolds.

But if all this is so—in the relevant phenomenological sense (epistemologically, so to say, not ontologically in any separable sense)—"world, self, and others" *are also artifacts* of our having internalized language and culture in the first place; and the very distinction of the human (its duality as *denotatum* and cognizing pole) may indeed be explained, in principle, in emergent (suitably qualified causal) terms, well within the competence of some nonreductive science, without precluding in any way the coherent, principled threat of reductionism (however remote that possibility may prove to be). In fact, to admit the second-natured nature of human persons entails the causal efficacy of human agency, the denial of the "causal closure of the physical world," the limited transitivity of causal explanation—the reverse of what reductionism requires—at the level of emergent culture.[38] (I read this as a thesis akin to that of Hegel's Absolute *Geist*.)

These are doctrines incompatible with any form of analytic scientism (for example, as I've suggested, Kim's supervenientism)—but not with naturalism in general or pragmatism.[39] On the contrary, if a reasonable argument can be mounted in favor of the culturally "constructed" nature of the human self (which I believe is more than merely possible, and which draws on Darwinian resources but also exceeds them), then pragmatism's naturalistic option can indeed eclipse all of Heidegger's (a fortiori, Husserl's) "extranaturalisms."

Olafson may be too hasty here. Heidegger is hardly hasty, but he is certainly arbitrary in dismissing the bare possibility of a naturalistic explanation of the unique capacities of human being. There is no reason why there cannot be a responsible science that respects Olafson's "phenomenological" distinctions, *if* they hold in naturalistic terms as well. After all, science is itself a uniquely human undertaking.[40] All that would be required, which the continentals often miss, is a distinction between two kinds of naturalism—itself required to mark the essential difference between pragmatism and analytic scientism. I see absolutely no reason to think that the naturalism appropriate to pragmatism would be inappropriate to the distinctive work of the continentals, though they of course demur. But—precisely—*that is* pragmatism's advantage.[41]

Olafson's so-called phenomenological regularities confirm the following: (1) we cannot regard "world, self, and others" merely as small-scale empirical theories that can be evidentiarily disconfirmed—notoriously, the gist of Paul Churchland's doctrine;[42] (2) they are, nevertheless, notably stubborn "facts" tethered to our contingent but remarkably regular formation as selves—which seem to be shared by pragmatism and what, in the most generous terms, we may claim as phenomenology; (3) they yield no privileged competence of any detailed or determinate sort (as of perception or thought)—an argument directed, somewhat confrontationally, against the extreme views attributed to Husserl and Heidegger, with or without Olafson's acquiescence; (4) the details of phenomenological reflection *are*, indeed, theory laden in their own way—hence, they go contrary to Husserl's disclaimer, perhaps to Olafson's cautions as well; (5) as we presently understand matters, the human being *is* unique in its encultured competence, which Olafson, following Heidegger, collects within the terms of the *existentialia* of "presence" and "transcendence";[43] (6) the "phenomenological facts" adduced make it impossible at the present time to justify disjoining first-person and third-person discourse and discrimination (as, say, against the well-known thesis advanced by Daniel Dennett)[44] or to justify disjoining, within naturalism's terms, the factual and the normative; and (7) whatever may be regarded as "factual," whether phenomenological or not, is "constructive" in the naturalistic sense.

Joseph Rouse, for instance, who begins his studies of the natural sciences under a considerable debt to Heidegger's "existential" phenomenology, construes Heidegger as an effective critic of Husserl's "antinaturalist conception of necessity" (in effect, Husserl's "phenomenological reduction"); he finds a parallel between Heidegger's argument and Otto Neurath's critique of Rudolf Carnap's conception of necessity. By this and other means that suggest to Rouse how figures as diverse as Quine, Sellars, Heidegger, Neurath, and Wittgenstein all contribute to the dismantling of a pervasive antinaturalism focused on a problem Rouse calls "the problem of manifest necessity," we glimpse some ingenious possibilities of fashioning an antiscientistic naturalism that might even begin to reconcile elements of analytic philosophy and phenomenology!

There are, it must be said, some disputable themes in Rouse's argument: the parallel between Heidegger and Neurath, for instance, indifference to Carnap's later pragmatist tendencies, indifference to Heidegger's own antinaturalistic (or extranaturalist) bias (especially after the *Kehre*), indifference to arguments like Merleau-Ponty's that find a convergence between Husserl and Heidegger leaning in a naturalistic direction (or, nondisjunctively, to something akin to Heidegger's existential reading of the "ontological"—opposed to the "ontical"). But I mention Rouse primarily as another recent investigator—drawn, like Olafson, to continental themes—who is also bent on collecting fresh options for a strengthened naturalism.

Rouse construes the problem of "manifest necessity" as ontological rather than epistemological, which is interesting:

> The problem is this: any attempt to ground normativity in necessity must be able to show how the alleged necessities are both authoritative and binding upon materially and historically situated agents. The issue is not epistemological. The worry is not that we might fail to know what is or is not necessary, but that its supposed necessity would make no effective contact with the normativity it was to explicate. Appeals to necessity would thereby account for normative authority at the expense of normative force [that is, of relevance to actual practices].[45]

Very neat and very useful: that is, apart from agreeing or disagreeing with the textual story.

But the obvious resolution stares you in the face. If realism takes a constructivist turn, then all the normative features of the sciences (say, truth and validity) must be constructivist as well—as, conformably, our moral and political norms would be. But that *is* the pragmatist conception: effectively, the sense, in Peirce and Dewey, that justifies abandoning all substantive or ontological necessity. Hence, at one stroke, norms prove to be easily accommodated in naturalistic terms and can be freed from alleged strong forms of necessity (the kind of necessity claimed—by Michael Dummett, for instance, in Gottlob Frege's name—for the "laws of thought," the "laws of the laws of nature") that would make such a resolution impossible.[46] I gladly adopt all seven adjustments mentioned previously, which I imagine everyone hospitable to the pragmatist orientation will also find congenial.

If you grasp the lesson, you see at once how the objectivity of moral and political norms can be made out in Deweyan terms, "constructively," without appealing to Darwinian reduction or to ideological fiat. The argument would feature pragmatically experimental idealizations of the *sittlich* or paideutic regularities of actual historical life—drawing therefore on Hegelian and Aristotelian inspiration. I mention the plausibility of such a gain because I cannot afford the space to broach the huge topic of normative practice in the present inquiry.

THERE ARE UNDOUBTEDLY MANY WAYS of characterizing the whole of Eurocentric philosophy. From my vantage, the principal quarrels of the twentieth century appear to have taken the form of a three-sided contest increasingly centered on the nature and adequacy of a realism that is (1) constructive or constructivist; (2) naturalistic; (3) nonreductive and nondualistic; (4) fitted and responsive to the sui generis, nearly unique abilities of the human being; (5) persuaded that there are no privileged, transcendentalist, or apodictic cognizing faculties and no unconditional necessities or invariances in reality or thought; (6) opposed to any hierarchized, disjunctive, or modular order at the level of reflexively acknowledged human competences—as between practical and theorizing powers or between perceptual and conceptual powers; (7) Darwinian, in the sense that linguistic and other sui generis cultural competences presuppose and are emergent from and incarnate in the biology of the species, though evolutionary in a sense distinct from, or discontinuous with, biological evolution itself; (8) constrained by conditions of reflexive reportage, hence primarily phenomenological rather than phenomenal, in the sense of being presuppositionless, however causally influenced or horizoned; (9) prepared to concede that the human person or self is best construed as a "second-natured" hybrid artifact indissolubly and emergently embodied in the members of *Homo sapiens*, through having internalized the language and culture of one or another historical society; (10) historicized, in the sense (irreducible to the merely biological or biochemical) in which our conceptual resources are themselves continually formed, enlarged, reduced, altered, transformed as a result of changes in the ongoing formative, communicative, and sustaining processes of cultural life itself; (11) not, therefore, opposed in principle to admitting objective judgments of a relativistic or incommensurabilist sort, should they prove to be (as I believe they are) self-consistent and coherent; (12) prepared to account for the normative features of meaning, logic, validity, justifiability in theoretical and practical matters, knowledge, legitimation, factuality, rationality, communication, and the like in thoroughly naturalistic terms; hence, (13) cast entirely in terms of a self-reflecting (a priori) inquiry that deliberately replaces Kant's or any Kantian-like apodictic pretensions (transcendentalist) originally applied beyond (but now confined, a posteriori, within) the familiar bounds of "nature." Item 13, read in terms of item 9, is the decisive innovation, the linchpin of the intended rapprochement.

I would now, in fact, define pragmatism in terms of just these thirteen commitments. They fit the classic pragmatists surprisingly well, though we are more than half a century beyond their best reception. They also spell out the leanest form of realism that the great philosophical tradition spanning Descartes and Kant and Hegel, the post-Kantians, the analysts, and the continentals down to the beginning of the twenty-first century could possibly support. Of the three movements sketched, pragmatism is the only one that is more or less unconditionally committed (however inadequately at times) to the entire tally. That is indeed a distinct advantage in an age largely becalmed by philosophical nostalgia. Still, no familiar philosophy to this day—at least none that I am aware of—has as yet successfully reconciled with its own assumptions all of the themes just tallied.[47]

Let me isolate, for the sake of a very slim illustration, the key to a pragmatist treatment of a strategic question that catches up the force of the tally just given, focused particularly on how items 7, 9, and 12 might be applied. I have in mind the general problem of how to construe "information" in a manner suited to Peirce's work in the theory of signs and to all the usual problems of communication and the grasp of semiotic content. The matter is entirely straightforward, at least in preparing the ground for all eventualities. "Information" is normally treated as abstract, in a sense akin to the sense in which "number" and "meaning" are abstract. The initial puzzles are all very nicely met by considering only two elementary simplifications.

The first holds that what is "abstract" but real information is always "abstracted" *from* some actual, incarnate, or embodied instantiation, whether, say, in the genome or a conversation; and there, some human paradigm takes precedence over all other semiotically freighted specimens, since, faute de mieux, semiotics is always anthropomorphized. Furthermore, the relation between the behavior of information without regard to content or even abstracted from content is best treated top down rather than bottom up, since information must be incarnate or embodied in some way and since, otherwise, barring a successful reductionism, there is no way to model the transmission, reception, or grasp of semiotized information from physical events alone. (Otherwise, the semiotic would be no more than the causal, in the relationally external sense drawn from purely physical data.)

The second simplification is also uncomplicated: merely treat any incarnate or embodied information belonging to the human paradigm, apt for communication among persons or selves, as the complex, emergent, hybrid, indissoluble "content" of a human "utterance"—adequate for conveying meaning, intention, significance, and the like, as by speech, gesture, sign or symbol, act or action, manufacture, creation, interpretation, and so on. The entire model falls very naturally within the terms of the tally given, and I see nothing that might be wanted that need be omitted or slighted in any way.

Information, then, is easily rendered in naturalistic terms without conceptual distortion or untoward privilege. In particular, "utterance" is not a causal notion as such (or not a causal notion in the externalist sense favored in the natural sciences), since the "relation" between utterer and utterance is *too close for external relations*. Uttering is like raising one's arm, inasmuch as both are open to semiotized attribution and both signify the exercise of agency; raising one's arm is, of course, a "species" of utterance, and standard causal relations can always be specified within the space of utterance itself. But that is as much as we need secure for our present purpose. Also, although it must be embodied, content may be embodied in a variety of things and in diverse ways: animate and inanimate, biological and encultured, determinately and determinably. The questions that remain are unaffected by such adjustments.

Paradigmatically, information and semiotic content are "decoded" (or understood) in some culturally formed or transformed space. The result, on the argument intended, is that information is not, in any primary or paradigmatic sense, abstract, open to a reductionist formulation, or capable of being determinately fixed in any privileged or accessibly certain way.[48] This is the decisive advantage of Peirce's triadic account of signs, although admitting that does not oblige us to rest with Peirce's analysis of meanings—which remains distinctly preliminary. In any event, to begin with information in a contextless and contentless way is already to favor reductionism and bottom-up analyses over top-down ones. But *if* reductionism fails, then the asymmetry of the two approaches will have to be met.

The most daring forms of analytic philosophy favor an entirely different version of naturalism from what has just been collected—one that exceeds pragmatism's constraints and is incompatible with them. I concede that Kant's transcendentalism may indeed be replaced by a carefully confined naturalism, but it would have to yield up all of Kant's modal necessities. I concede as well that, for all its extravagance, Hegel's conception of mind or *Geist* is already naturalistic, even respectful of the small powers of individual human agents, though it would be hard to fashion an explicit account of no more than "merely" human competence confined in precisely the way Hegel intends. There's the pivot of the entire contemporary agon. The viable forms of agency and information fall between the limits of an inaccessible reductionism and the impossible powers of a collective *Geist* that incorporates all the finite manifestations of human intelligence—hence, between the limits of an impoverished naturalism and an overinflated extranaturalism, between what can be shown to be actual and what can never be more than mythic or metaphoric.

Beyond all that, I've added to the tally rendered a number of provocative doctrines that (pace George Mead and Josiah Royce) were never featured by the original pragmatists, though they were aired incipiently during pragmatism's second phase and are increasingly favored now. My thought is simply that the additional items can no longer be ignored—historicity and relativism in particular, an encultured world as well, which is slighted more than ignored—once constructivism is separated from all Kantian (transcendentalist) and similar-minded presumptions (notably, the regressive features of Husserlian "constitution"). The tally is, in this respect, more a proposal regarding pragmatism's prospects than a record of its past achievements. I admit my own preferences. But the tally begins to show why Eurocentric philosophy is likely to bring its strongest views into line with these gathering lessons. Pragmatism will simply expire if it fails to pursue the "new" lines of inquiry just mentioned: mentioning them now reminds us of pragmatism's original infelicities.

Pragmatism, you realize, has only recently come of age. Its best promise is a direct function of the exposed vulnerabilities of analytic and continental philosophy. That cannot be said, in the same sense, of either of the other two "movements" vis-à-vis pragmatism. Pragmatism's great strength lies with its having been eclipsed for nearly thirty years! Whereas the strongest figures in both analytic and continental philosophy have either straddled both halves of the twentieth century (most notably,

Heidegger and Wittgenstein, perhaps also Carnap and Cassirer) or have extended into the second half of the century the main lines of thinking of the first half (Quine and Davidson, among the analysts; the lesser phenomenologists and Heideggerians, among the continentals; even the Carnapians and Sellarsians, among the lesser positivists and unity of science theorists). In an odd but plausible sense, pragmatism exhausted its original program and turned quite naturally (rather weakly in effect) to respond to the seeming strength of the analysts and continentals.

The short life of pragmatism's second wave (viewed chiefly through the work of Richard Rorty) actually bequeathed pragmatism a role defined, quite unpredictably, by the perceived inadequacies of its natural rivals—in a way only nominally linked to the original themes of the classic pragmatists themselves. Its own weakness, therefore, has proved to be the source of its greatest promise, given the important additional fact that, very nearly alone among the English-language movements, pragmatism never completely abandoned its post-Kantian, even Hegelian, commitment. That single commitment redeems the narrow force of pragmatism's very modest beginnings.

Pragmatism began as a distinctly minor and parochial movement, in spite of its being aware of the principal post-Kantian currents in Germany and Britain as those were perceived not very long after their first appearance and reception. Peirce was almost completely unknown though remarkably well informed, and he was both original and unusually daring; James was more of a pop figure than a leading thinker, although reread in the context of the more systematic efforts of Peirce and Dewey, he is often remarkably suggestive (even where he bungles, as on truth, or ventures into analytic thickets, as on reference, where it may be argued James ought not to have roamed); and Dewey, pragmatism's sine qua non, came to his mature reckoning only a short time before the movement began to wane and lose its influence—through the late Depression years, the approaching war years, and their aftermath.

What the pragmatists accomplished (Dewey in particular) could hardly have been grasped until the fatigued philosophies of postwar Europe and the altered fortunes of analytic philosophy—which were refocused at midcentury largely by Quine (more in the United States than in Britain)—revealed in the plainest way their inherent limitations and pragmatism's serendipitous advantage. All of this crested shortly before pragmatism's "second wave," which, unintentionally, obliged all those interested in its better prospects (Rorty and Putnam, for instance) to test their mettle against the visions of the analysts and continentals.

It would not be unfair to claim that "the linguistic turn" Rorty welcomes is little more, in the analysts' hands, than code for a drastically decontextualized formal analysis of concepts that in fact require (according to the drift of the running argument pursued here) the resources of an ample *Umwelt* that the convergence between Dewey's "indeterminate situation" and Merleau-Ponty's "circumscription of an unthought" subtly signify. In short, the ersatz precision of analytic probes of the central concepts favored in the linguistic turn are easily exposed as seriously impoverished by the constraints of their own would-be precision. The bankruptcy of recent analytic accounts of truth (as in Davidson), meaning (as among the positivists), and reference (as in Saul Kripke) yields the unrelenting evidence.

The result has been a much-amplified and altered pragmatism still attracted to the themes of the primacy of the practical, the here and now, the contingent regularities of a fluxive world, the defeat of Cartesianism, the lessons of the Kantian and post-Kantian figures shorn of idealist extravagance, the rejection of extranatural or doubtfully natural conceptual resources, the perceived needs and interests of the human creature that we take ourselves to be, a Darwinian disposition, meaning and truth construed in an openly anthropomorphized way, a preference for the phenomenological over the phenomenal, an anthropocentric realism that acknowledges the inseparability of fact and value, the barest beginnings of historicist tendencies, and a tolerance for the improvisational and interpretive variety of instrumentally useful conceptions of "self, world, and others" in addressing the contingencies of practical life. (Here, it helps to invoke Olafson's least "facts," that is, those he calls "phenomenological.")

Pragmatism also needs to collect all the puzzles local to the systematic programs of the analysts and the continentals that bear on the three-sided agon sketched earlier *and* to fashion new answers and assessments by which to test its viability in these changed times—its capacity to confront the scientisms of the one and the extranatural extravagances of the other. My sense is that if it can do that, if pragmatism can indeed help to fashion a Eurocentric rapprochement involving continental themes and analytic rigor (which is not to deny continental rigor—Husserl's, for instance—but only to insist on abandoning analytic scientism and on holding to whatever rigor remains), we shall find ourselves ready for conceptual inventions that have probably been delayed for at least fifty years by the perseveration of late twentieth-century philosophy.

Closer to home, there remains an unbearable dearth of analysis in Anglo-American philosophy regarding the very nature of the human being, its duality, its historicized and culturally formed condition, the problematic relationship between biology and culture, and the bearing of these considerations on standard philosophical problems (reality, knowledge, norms, mutual understanding). It is an extraordinary fact that there is almost no centrally sustained interest on the part of English-language philosophy in the ontological and epistemological complexities of history conceived in Hegelian and post-Hegelian terms (as in Marx, Nietzsche, Dilthey, Sartre, and Foucault, for example). Its absence in analytic philosophy is very nearly required. Its absence (or, better, its tepid presence) in classic pragmatism is simply a mystery—worse, a scandal. (Why, for instance, do Peirce and Dewey ignore the topic of historicity? Were they simply inadequately informed?) The upshot is that the needed themes are largely collected in Anglo-American "continental" philosophy.

At the present time, philosophers still presume to fashion their accounts of what a human being is, without ever addressing the matter of the historicity or "second nature" of the human condition itself. Though it is widely denied or ignored, it seems impossible to formulate a convincing account of science that never addresses the question of the formation and objective standing of the conceptual resources of human scientists themselves.[49] Admit the gap, and you begin to see the strong convergence, across discontinuous philosophical practices, of the work of figures like Thomas Kuhn and Paul Feyerabend and those, drawn from the continental side, like Nietzsche and Foucault.[50]

The continental tradition has never abandoned the analysis of the human being and never neglected to test the validity of the best work of the period spanning Kant and Hegel. It has its structuralists, of course, retrograde figures like Louis Althusser, who seems to have completely ignored (or who simply never knew) Marx's early critique of Hegel.[51] But the major contributors to continental philosophy have also largely failed to identify what, in a narrow sense, bears on the functional competence of individual persons within the space of their ethos and collective history—or simply within the boundaries of the "natural world."

Here, surely, is the best possible site for an essential confrontation between pragmatism and continental philosophy that has only barely begun to be tested. The irony is that analytic philosophy's hegemony within the Anglo-American world has largely deflected English-language philosophy from pursuing any such recuperative inquiry. It is hard to imagine how, from the pragmatist vantage, there could be any single more productive undertaking than to test how far a naturalistic reformulation of continental analyses of the human world might succeed and with what consequences; or how, from the continental side, to test the presumed inadequacy of naturalistic conceptions of the principal distinctions regarding "self, world, and others" that the strongest European accounts have rendered.

The ultimate question remains: how can we best understand the differences and similarities between being human and being a mere "thing" (or, more probingly, between animate creatures and human persons); or between human individuals and their societies and the artifactual cultural world they produce? But if even this much were attempted, we would be well on our way to fashioning a very different picture of philosophy's questions, a vision that would begin with our present impasse and return us, after two hundred years (perhaps better, after nearly four hundred years), to the intuitions that count as the truly modern beginnings of Eurocentric philosophy. Among the early Hegelians, Marx is surely as strongly committed (in his best efforts) to an unyielding naturalism and historicity and, even more clearly than the pragmatists, to the natural artifactuality of the self.

THE CONTINENTALS FEAR—they have reason to fear—that English-language naturalism has no deep interest *in the human*, if that interest cannot be adequately served by an idiom the analysts deem adequate for describing and explaining inanimate nature and the Darwinian world "below" the level of encultured life. But they confuse too easily the neglect of the human and the advocacy of the natural. The analysts *are* committed to the natural, but they deny that they neglect the human. What they mean, speaking as partisans of one or another form of scientism (though analytic philosophy is hardly confined to scientism: witness Putnam), is that, in whatever sense the human *is* natural, it must eventually yield to a perfectly extensionalist analysis cast in materialist terms.[52] (I remind you again that analytic rigor need not be scientific.) The continentals fail to reckon with the pragmatists, who mean to match *their* (the continentals') every scruple, except that the pragmatists refuse to exceed the outer limits of nature itself. In this way, the analysis of the "natural" now defines the agon of our age.

All three movements may therefore claim to be realist in various local senses, taken singly or in pairs. The continentals and the pragmatists, for instance, tend to be constructivists and antireductivists; the analysts tend to be neither. The pragmatists and analysts are assuredly naturalists, but the continentals are very often not. The analysts and continentals tend to be irreconcilably opposed, whereas the pragmatists steer a middle course between scientism and any would-be extranatural powers or modes of being.

From the analysts' point of view, both the continentals and the pragmatists may actually be "idealists," since they tend to be constructivists and, favoring the empirical, appear to favor dualism inconsistently. From the vantage of the continentals, the analytic forms of scientism are demonstrably incoherent, since they wrongly conflate the human world and the world of "things." From the pragmatists' point of view, the analysts fail to demonstrate that scientism is actually valid, apart from its being coherent; and the continentals fail to demonstrate that (as they very often believe) to admit the unique mode of human being *must* exceed the boundaries of the natural world itself. The most radical analysts tend to cast the natural world in terms confined to what is common to the inanimate and subhuman world. The pragmatists admit a Darwinian continuum but find no difficulty in acknowledging the uniquely human sphere of freedom and reflexive understanding. And the continentals reject the analysts' scientism outright and have the gravest doubts about the pragmatist alternative. Quite an extraordinary three-sided contest!

I have shown that the continental worry (which, following Heidegger, Olafson isolates as "presence" and "transcendence") is simply *not* unconditionally opposed in any familiar respect to pragmatism's concerns. Frankly, I have already tried to recover an analogous space of debate between the analysts and the pragmatists, one that centers on the question of the coherence and viability of scientism itself. Let me remind you of the point of that second question by citing some remarks from Quine.

Quine opens the title essay of his John Dewey Lectures (1968) with a rather nice touch: he says he attended Dewey's William James Lectures on art and experience at Harvard in 1931, while himself a graduate student. Now, he adds, he finds himself giving the first John Dewey Lectures at Columbia! Very neat. He has, of course, a deeper purpose in saying what he says: he moves at once to confirm the sense in which his own view might be thought to be essentially in accord with Dewey's. "Philosophically," he says, "I am bound to Dewey by the naturalism that dominated his last three decades." Quine explains:

> When a naturalistic philosopher addresses himself to the philosophy of mind, he is apt to talk of language. Meanings are, first and foremost, meanings of language. Language is a social art which we all acquire on the evidence solely of other people's overt behavior under publicly recognizable circumstances. Meanings, therefore, those very models of mental entities, end up as grist for the behaviorist's mill. Dewey was explicit on the point: "Meaning is not a psychic existence; it is primarily a property of behavior."[53]

One must appreciate the clever way in which Quine coopts Dewey: the two actually construe behaviorism in very different ways. Quine inclines toward B. F. Skinner's rejection (in evidentiary terms) of the mental altogether; Dewey is unwilling to separate the mental from the behavioral, but not for reductionistic reasons. They are both opposed to the Cartesian forms of private mental states. That is the conceptual lever that both joins and separates them; yet their convergence also fuels the confused presumption that pragmatism and analytic philosophy are already irreconcilably opposed or already "reconciled" in Quine's very smooth way.

This is not the right occasion for a close comparison between Dewey's and Quine's views. But it does afford an opportunity to complete the picture of the three-legged contest that has been sketched here—now with an eye to its possible resolution as well as to the source of misunderstanding between pragmatism and analytic philosophy. Both Dewey and Quine agree with the line Quine cites from Dewey—hence, both accept Quine's inference "that there cannot [as a result] be, in any useful sense, a private language."[54] In fact, Dewey and Quine also agree that (1) meanings are not entities of any sort; (2) meanings cannot be first grasped in what are usually said to be private mental states; and (3) there simply are no private mental states, that is, mental states completely disjoined from bodily states or behavioral events—or as epiphenomena otherwise publicly inaccessible in principle. That's the extent of their agreement and the sense in which Dewey would probably not oppose his being characterized as a behaviorist of sorts. *But they read the line Quine cites in very different ways.* (And they share a larger vision than that of the vaunted "linguistic turn.")

Dewey surely means that the mental *is* real, *is* genuinely "personal" but *not* hermetically "private" (in the epistemic sense in which we first grasp meanings). Though Quine is known for his well-placed ambiguities, he surely means, finally, to eliminate all reference to the mental wherever it does not yield to extensionalist analysis—even if, informally, he might never explicitly deny a run of mental states not yet analyzed in the scientific way. Put in the simplest terms, Quine has no use for the idea that human persons are second-natured creatures, transformed by the processes of enculturation. But then, there's no point to a philosophical rapprochement through strengthening naturalism's hand if naturalism doesn't return us to the analysis of the puzzles of cultural life—which, on the argument offered, accounts for the artifactual emergence of the self as the encultured transform of the primate offspring of *Homo sapiens*. Quine bets too heavily on the cultural legibility of behavioral cues *within our own linguistic practices*, in fathoming the linguistic import of the behavior of agents who speak an alien language. But he has no perspicuous theory of how to fix linguistic meanings in our own language: this, you realize, is essentially the same problem we have already acknowledged in attempting to formulate a general theory of "information."

The ulterior argument, which ranges over Kant, the post-Kantians, Husserl and his phenomenological progeny, Heidegger and his existential progeny, as well as Rorty and Putnam, depends on the decisive demonstration of the reasonableness and viability of a naturalistic replacement of Kant's entire apriorist project. But that is precisely what had already been delivered in Hegel's original critique of Kant and, more pointedly, in C. I. Lewis's pragmatic version of the a priori. Given that much, the field is entirely clear for a pragmatist recovery of the best achievements of continental philosophy. (I shall come back to Lewis, Cassirer, Apel, and Habermas in an effort to explain the strategic importance of providing a thoroughly naturalistic account of the "transcendental turn.")

Let us recall again Merleau-Ponty's pregnant comment on Husserl's "Origin of Geometry": "[A] thought is not *some ideas*. It is the *circumscription of an unthought [ungedachte, impensé]*," a phrasing apparently influenced by Heidegger, which may well be in need of a naturalistic (if contingently a priori) analysis. It is an important intuition of the inadequacy of empiricism applied to culturally informed processes, perceptual as well as reflective; of the inadequacy of construing thoughts as "objects" of a kind that would yield to one or another form of scientism; of the pertinence of what is not expressly thought *in* one's thought but is somehow latent in it, determinably but not determinately, that is, interpretably as far as apt communicants are concerned. It makes reductionism impossible, but it also threatens to afford no articulated sense of how it may be "recovered" in the context of actual social life. That is undoubtedly the key to the often perceived kinship between Merleau-Ponty and George Herbert Mead: for Mead begins to explore the possibility of explicating something akin to Merleau-Ponty's notion in terms of praxis.[55] I must mention again the extraordinary ingenuity of the pragmatist account: the culturally contingent emergence of the hybrid, second-natured human self provides the conceptual ground on which *any* viable successor to Kantian transcendentalism may be cast in naturalistic terms. I take it that the Husserlians' failure to recognize this obvious challenge (which Olafson obviously grasps) accounts in good measure for its continuing adherence to the claims of apodicticity and necessity.

Quine could not have failed to see the decisive difference in his own and Dewey's views: Dewey's theme is given on the very same page from which Quine draws the "behaviorist" line he favors; and on the next page of Dewey's text, we read the telltale clarification: "Primarily meaning is intent and intent is not personal in a private and exclusive sense." This is meant to elucidate what is involved in the example Dewey provides, when, say, "*A* requests *B* to bring him something, to which *A* points [say, a flower]." He continues: "The characteristic thing about *B*'s understanding of *A*'s movement and sounds is that he responds to the thing [the flower] from the standpoint of *A*. He perceives the thing as it may function in *A*'s experience, instead of just ego-centrically."[56] This is the nonreductive and nonscientistic sense in which Dewey would concede that *he* is a behaviorist. Notice, however, that perceiving a flower and grasping the meaning of what is said, or the meaning of a piece of behavior linked to speech, entails the mental, even if the mental is not extensionally reducible to behavior, or even if we make room (as by social convention) for the "ego-centric" (which need not be private in any solipsistic way), as well as for what is pertinently "implicated" (that is, publicly interpretable).

You grasp the full import of this distinction if you contrast the sense in which Dewey and Quine speak of "stimulus" or "stimulation" under perceptual and intentionally qualified behavioral conditions. Here is Dewey's careful formulation: "[N]either the sounds uttered by *A*, his gesture of pointing, nor the sight of the thing pointed to, is the occasion and stimulus of *B*'s act; the stimulus is *B*'s anticipatory share in the consummation of a transaction in which both participate."[57] Dewey might almost be thought to be speaking *after* Quine has spoken in order to correct the drift of Quine's scientism—in particular, to correct *the radical, extensionally reductive sense in which Quine treats perceptual occasions in terms of "ocular stimulation" and intentional behavior in terms of "radical translation."*[58] It is just *this* extreme reading of "behavior" that Quine means to feature; it identifies Quine's reading of the line already cited: "Language is a social art which we all acquire on the evidence *solely* of other people's *overt behavior* under *publicly* recognizable circumstances." The important, rather occluded, discovery is this: the reductionist believes that top-down and bottom-up analyses of human thought (encultured thought, as I say) are distinctly convergent with regard to *any* adequate analysis. But that, precisely, is far from obvious, and it is certainly not Dewey's view.[59] Symptomatically, and systematically, Quine favors a phenomenal rather than a phenomenological account of what may be perceptually identified as "stimulation" in the behavioral setting. Dewey, read as a much-attenuated "Hegelian," cleaves instead (however intuitively) to a Hegelian-like form of phenomenological reportage. There's the difference between their two "behaviorisms"—and their two conceptions of how we understand the cultural dimension of human life.

These remarks are meant to remind us of Quine's extraordinary notion of radical translation and his elimination of intentional factors in understanding an alien people (and, by analogy, in understanding one another). That is precisely what Quine has in mind when he says, rather smoothly, in "Ontological Relativity": "The semantic part of learning a word is more complex than the phonetic part . . . even in simple cases: we have to see what is stimulating the other speaker."[60] The clause "what is *stimulating* the other speaker" is, in Quine's view but *not* in Dewey's, reductive, extensional, atomic, completely free of intentional and intensional complications of just the sorts that arise in Dewey's behaviorist account of what is stimulating *A* and *B* in the example given. Quine's unruffled remark that "language is a social art" is meant to be self-dismissive: Quine is indeed an analyst with a touch of pragmatism about him, especially when he counters the early Carnap and the later Davidson. But he draws the line against concessions that would threaten his own systematically extensionalist tastes. When Dewey identifies the "stimulus of *B*'s act," it's clearly informed by *B*'s having discerned the pertinent import of culturally informed practices. So it does not yield in Quine's direction from the very start.

I've pressed the essential lesson of comparing Quine and Dewey on the analysis of behavior (keeping Merleau-Ponty and Mead in mind) in order to match the point of contrasting Olafson's views (as a continental thinker) with a pragmatist's naturalistic alternative. These comparisons hardly yield knockdown arguments as they stand. But they help to make clear just how promising a prospect it is to work toward an understanding of what still separates the three movements I've been tracking. Too many philosophers, believing them to be utterly irreconcilable, lack patience enough to formulate the essential questions for our time.

In short, Dewey's behaviorism introduces the problem of determining the right successor to Kant's transcendentalism (say, something that may be compared with Husserl's phenomenology); but Dewey introduces it in order to render it adequately in naturalistic terms. Quine makes use of no such reflexive dimension of human understanding. So Husserl, Heidegger, and Merleau-Ponty are right to resist all the forms of scientism: scientism simply lacks resources enough to meet the continental challenge. But they are, perhaps, not clear enough about the difference between a naturalistic account of the successor to Kant's transcendentalism (Hegel's great intuition) and a naturalistic account of the distinctive capacities of a specifically human mode of being that sees no need to count the "successor problem" as insuperable (the point of Hume's charm, for instance, that first revealed to Kant the unexamined issue Kant then recovers in his impossibly gymnastic way).

The fact is that the pragmatists were never entirely consistent in confining the sources of knowledge to whatever might reasonably be characterized as "empirical" (say, as suited to the work of the empirical sciences). Morton White, for instance, argues very compellingly that Peirce, James, Dewey, C. I. Lewis, and Quine (whom White counts as a pragmatist) all concede "dualisms" of empirical and nonempirical knowledge somewhere in their respective accounts.[61] What is important about these concessions is that they betray inconsistencies within the naturalistic constraints of a thoroughgoing pragmatism (among the pragmatists themselves); and, more provocatively, that those inconsistencies effectively obscure the seemingly clear distinction between the naturalism of the pragmatists and the insistence on nonnaturalistic sources of cognition that one finds in continental philosophy. I would add to White's account the evidence that, in developing his ramified version of fallibilism, Peirce clearly construes "abduction" in a way that appears, for all the world, to harbor a priori truths of a distinctly transcendental cast, which he officially eschews. A general charge of cognitive privilege has been made regarding James's and Dewey's emphasis on what is "given" in experience, but I think it depends on an equivocation on the meaning of "given" (phenomenologically): if you read the pertinent texts in Hegel's sense rather than in the empiricists', you cannot fail to see that "given" is likelier to be presuppositionless than privileged.

One cannot escape the irony that not only must we choose between the naturalistic and extranaturalist alternatives of the pragmatists and the continentals but we must correct and extend the work of the pragmatists with regard to their own essential doctrine. By and large, this can be done only, I would argue, by adhering, first, to something like Quine's rejection of a principled disjunction between the analytic and the synthetic (which the pragmatists may have weakly anticipated) and, second, by adhering to a thoroughgoing constructivism with respect to normative (validative and legitimative) judgments (as of moral obligation) applied to empirical and mathematical truths. But to acknowledge the point of such a labor is, effectively, to acknowledge, for our time, the full import of the central challenge of the three-legged contest I've been sketching but have yet to resolve.

Let us cast the matter then, for the record, as a manifesto or promissory note. Eurocentric philosophy in the new century will collect its best prospects in pursuing a rapprochement among the principal strains of pragmatism, analytic philosophy, and continental philosophy wherever it is committed (1) to testing the adequacy or inadequacy of one or another form of naturalism that can escape, in all pertinent sectors of inquiry, the scientistic naturalizing of analytic philosophy as well as the extranaturalist pretensions of the leading strains of continental accounts of "world, self, and others"; and (2) to isolating all viable successors to Kantian transcendentalism apt for answering a priori questions of conceptual "possibility" wherever they arise in inquiries committed to (1), within the bounds of nature and without presumptions of privilege, substantive necessity, exceptionless generalization, changeless essence, or apodicticity of any kind. I view all of this more as the definition of a temperament than of an actual objective. But it does afford a sensible reform of sorts amid increasing scatter.

I must say, emphatically, that I am well aware that these introductory remarks cannot be more than preliminary. I offer them primarily in the way of orienting us to a larger issue I've hardly touched on: pragmatism's role regarding the possible rapprochement among the principal currents of contemporary Eurocentric philosophy. What I've offered cannot be taken to count as a balanced overview of the whole of Western philosophy: I've mentioned only those figures and movements that belong to the story that follows; there's an immense multitude of important thinkers that I haven't touched on at all, of obvious interest to a comprehensive history of Western philosophy, who nevertheless have little, if any, sustained bearing on the questions that have shaped the three-legged contest I've introduced. The entire story depends on the reception of the work spanning Kant and Hegel that sets the problems the pragmatists (Peirce originally and, later, Dewey) first draw on. All the other figures that I've marked for close attention belong to the twentieth-century reception of pragmatism itself: chiefly, Husserl, Heidegger, Quine, Apel, and Habermas and an expanding cohort of others focused through an examination of these and read in a way that bears on the basic comparison wanted between pragmatism and analytic and continental philosophy. Whoever else catches our attention (those most often mentioned include Rorty, Putnam, Sellars, Davidson, McDowell, Brandom; Dreyfus, Okrent, Olafson, Rouse, Blattner; Merleau-Ponty, Zahavi; Carnap, Neurath, Cassirer, Lewis, Wittgenstein, Kuhn; and others) enters and exits in a way intended to fill out the narrative and argument that are before us. I have no doubt that other figures will be favored by other discussants, even if they address the same general problem. But why pretend it could be otherwise?

2

Reclaiming Naturalism

ALL THE THREADS of contemporary Eurocentric philosophy come together in a fractious way to define the meaning of "naturalism" for our time. Definition, however, cannot now be read as a search for incontestable essences: too much depends on meeting the running puzzles of our inquiries while fending off rival challenges doing much the same—all with an eye to possible defeats and reconciliations on the way to the scattered unity of a shared world. The process cannot be easily completed or made to serve a single purpose. We are not likely to find our own intuitions adequately represented in the options the ancient accounts collect—for example, in matching the rationality of the human mind with the intelligible order of nature in the large. The ancient inclusions are too unhelpful for our present needs.

Aristotle's match between the powers of *nous* and the intelligible structure of the physical, biological, and astronomical worlds once counted as a model of the naturalistic kind, but it can no longer do so. The aporiai of first causes, the presumption of one or another essential telos in all that belongs to nature, the very necessity of a changeless order embedded in, or embedding, a changing order of reality, the facultative competence of our cognitive powers assuredly fitted to grasping the inherent structure of the world, the primacy of a teleologized biologism are altogether too problematic and divisive for what we would now allow to fall within an acceptable naturalism, though to resist on all these fronts at once may well entangle our best efforts to resolve other difficulties that now seem more important. Frankly, we are prepared to tolerate certain stubborn antinomies that threaten all otherwise promising versions of naturalism alike, provided that what we now view as our most pressing puzzles can be satisfactorily met for the time being. Unresolved antinomy, for example, may be preferable to confidently accounting for the big bang ex nihilo or to conceding infinite regress—whether according to Stephen Hawking or to Thomas Aquinas.

The least distorting, the most adequate pronouncements on naturalism in our time must rely, I would say, on a distinction the ancients never directly considered—possibly the only modern contribution to the standard philosophical idioms of the West of its size—a "metaphysical" distinction, hardly a disjunction, within nature itself, between physical nature and human culture and what that may entail. That essential difference was never explicitly formulated before the latter half of the eighteenth century, not before the time of Kant's, Herder's, Humboldt's, Goethe's, and Hegel's inquiries and, truth to tell, it has not yet been made sufficiently clear. Nevertheless, Kant and the others mentioned are among the very first to begin to define the truly "modern" modern preoccupation with the issue, though Kant himself never succeeds, in the *Critique of Judgment*, in formulating more than the barest counterpart of Aristotle's account of rational freedom—in which the modern distinction of the cultural pointedly fails to appear:

[A]mong all [man's] ends in nature there remains only the formal, subjective condition, namely the aptitude for setting himself ends at all and (independent from nature in his determination of ends) using nature as a means appropriate to the maxims of his free ends in general, as that which nature can accomplish with a view to the final end that lies outside of it and which can therefore be regarded as an ultimate end. The production of the aptitude of a rational being for any ends in general (thus those of his freedom) is *culture*.[1]

Imagine being thus constrained only a short time before the appearance of Hegel's *Phenomenology*!

To understand Kant's limitation, you must consider what could possibly be meant by his construing human freedom as the pursuit of an end "that lies outside of [nature]." Kant signals a difficulty in his own doctrine that the post-Kantian idealists (including Hegel) never managed to resolve perspicuously, though they had a far better grip on the problem than Kant did. In the *Critiques*, Kant is all but incapable of formulating a coherent picture of the specifically *human* subject or self—a fortiori, he fails to define the cultural world as well. His transcendentalism collects what "lies outside of [nature]."

Naturalism at its most farsighted sets itself the problem of accounting for "human being" entirely in terms of the natural world, though in a way that still collects the distinction between the natural and the cultural. But "the natural world" itself means very different things to different theorists. Problematically, for Heidegger, for instance, as we have seen, no merely naturalistic treatment of *Dasein*, which humans in some sense incarnate, could possibly suffice since what "exists" or is "beyond nature" is precisely whatever captures the uniqueness of the existentialia of *Dasein*—which apply to nothing else; for Kant, the powers of *Vernunft* define certain "subjective" conditions of empirical cognition but cannot themselves be captured by the empirical or natural world we thereby come to know; and, against Kant, Hegel assigns *Vernunft* to actual human beings, but then it appears that the inherent power of philosophical Reason—according to which "the truth of Reason is but one" ("absolute knowing")—cannot be captured by any familiar conception of finite nature. In particular, if "being," with which Hegel begins his *Science of Logic* (*Wissenschaft der Logik*), is in its "simple immediacy" "unanalyzable" qua "simple," then it seems clear that its being simple (also, what Hegel makes of that) is itself a constructive posit that depends on passingly persuasive arguments within the then-current fashions of philosophical thought—and thus becomes an artifactual simple within the complexities of thought.[2] All three accounts are remarkably tenuous.

Hegel's *Geist* is a blunderbuss that hides even more than it explains, though we must admit (in hindsight) that it collects in the most compelling way available to its own age the conceptual threads of any viable resolution of our question. My own suggestion is that we must begin with Hegel but cannot round out an adequate analysis of the cultural world without conjoining Hegel's immense innovation with the new conceptual possibilities made manageable by Darwin's discoveries. That is in fact the relatively inchoate, thoroughly naturalistic intuition of the classic pragmatists. It's also the point of acknowledging that there is indeed a confirmable evolutionary continuum that joins the prehuman primates, the extinct hominids, and the sole surviving species of the genus *Homo* (*Homo sapiens*) to which we belong, within which biological evolution makes possible for the first time a convincing account of the difference between physical nature and human culture.

My sense is that the "cultural" (in all its manifestations) presupposes and depends on certain late biological developments but cannot be analyzed perspicuously in biological terms alone. Hegel grasped that much (in his accounts of *Geist* and *Vernunft*); he lacked a crisp distinction between biological and cultural evolution, though he obviously viewed beauty in the fine arts ("born of *Geist*")—a fortiori, the world of human culture—as, ontologically, "higher than nature." In fact, his own philosophical impulses were, I would say, distinctly naturalistic, though we cannot rest with his extravagant account of *Geist*, which is as much a placeholder for a theory as an incipient guess at an adequate theory itself. There's the promise of the most fruitful post-Hegelian undertakings: notably, though still only incipiently, the promise of the classic pragmatists.

My own solution is that now the most convincing view of naturalism, addressed to the analysis of the human world, construes the human self as a "natural artifact,"[3] an evolutionarily new form of "being" that depends on the sui generis emergence of true language; and the capacity to use language and the cognate cultural resources that it makes possible develop along lines that can no longer be explained in terms confined to the physical and biological—in accord with which, in truth, *we* actually constitute ourselves (developmentally), both individually and specieswide, as selves. In this sense, the recovery of naturalism cannot fail to be essential to the kind of rapprochement within the Eurocentric world that I've been hinting at. The principal evidence in its favor is the sheer impossibility of fashioning an exclusively biological analysis of language and speech—a fortiori, the deep novelty of defining the human "self" itself. Slim though they are, such discoveries mark a mode of argument that cannot have appeared earlier than the middle of the nineteenth century.

By Darwin's time, an evolving naturalism had in effect discerned that the world of human culture could no longer be identified with physical or biological nature alone; the self's mode of being and activity called into play descriptive and explanatory categories that could not be explicated in physicalist terms alone; and, nevertheless, the cultural world evolved completely within an encompassing larger space of nature and was in fact indissolubly incarnated in physical and biological processes.

Yet even this much regarding the sui generis attributes of culture has often been conceded only weakly and grudgingly in our time. Francisco Ayala, for example, a well-known biologist who admits the requisite difference freely enough and who effectively acknowledges much the same argument that Richard Dawkins favors—that is, "human beings are not gene machines"—nevertheless can go no further than to say that "a distinctive characteristic of human evolution is adaptation by means of 'culture,' which may be understood as the set of non-strictly biological human activities and creations."[4] But that effectively papers over all of the important conceptual issues or falls back to unacceptable equivocation: what exactly are these "non-strictly biological human activities and creations"? They undoubtedly feature adaptation by one or another form of "social learning," but that alone is not enough to distinguish between primate learning and the unique form of learning and creation (assigned to selves) that is "penetrated" by language and the cultural resources the mastery of language makes possible. To my thinking, the upshot is plain enough: proceeding thus, we cannot yet overtake the "continental" challenge of theorists like Husserl and Heidegger or confront the reductionisms of "analysts" like Sellars and Jaegwon Kim.

Aristotle's naturalism is incapable of providing conceptual resources apt for resolving disputes of our contemporary kind between naturalists and antinaturalists or between different kinds of naturalists: say, between Rudolf Carnap and Martin Heidegger or between W. V. Quine and Jaegwon Kim or between Wilfrid Sellars and Edmund Husserl. The fact is, Aristotle's faculty of reason, *nous*, has no biological roots of its own. But the essential distinction between the natural and the historical or cultural may be said to have been already implicit in the Greek world, as Aeschylus's *Oresteia* and Sophocles' *Antigone* confirm. The Greeks might indeed have anticipated what must be the most distinctive philosophical contribution of the modern world. You may glimpse the reasonableness of such a claim by reflecting on the poverty of Aristotle's formulation, in the *Physics*, of the meaning of "nature" developed along the following lines, which are obviously of the wrong gauge for what our contemporaries would make of *Antigone*, supplemented now by what may be developed from their own larger cultural resources:

[Nature] is the primary underlying matter of things which have in themselves a principle of motion or change, . . . [or] nature is the shape or form which is specified in the definition of the thing. For the word "nature" is applied to what is according to nature and the natural in the same way as "art" is applied to what is artistic or a work of art.[5]

Plainly, Aristotle anticipates no difficulty in the analysis of what it is to be human, or of the contrast between the physical and the cultural, or between the objective and the subjective; although, of course, the *Physics* leads ineluctably to its own problematic reflections, like that (in book 7) of resolving the paradox of the continuum of motion and causes. In fact, Aristotle's own naturalism leads inexorably to a kind of "super- (or extra-) naturalism" that became the rule for much of the medieval world.

According to a well-known argument, *nature* "must" have had (in the medieval sense) a beginning. Since the power that originally created nature "must have been" beyond nature, medieval "naturalism" (if I may call it that) was already dependent on supernatural sources. Our contemporary forms of naturalism would refuse such an extension—would need to reinterpret in a drastic way the usual causal questions posed by the whole of physical nature. Here, the meaning of "nature" obviously changes—avoids the supernatural and what, in cognitive terms, I am calling "extra-naturalism," namely, what implicates certain privileged but completely derivative human competences capable of discerning something of the changeless verities by way of participating in the divine order itself.

In any event, the most up-to-date naturalisms now begin with the rejection of all such extravagances. The required adjustment is remarkably simple: admit the unresolved antinomies and move on! As far as naturalism is concerned, stalemate about the First Cause, for instance, is *not* an endorsement of the necessary existence of any originative power either in or beyond nature.

The associated lesson regarding the distinction between physical nature and human culture—the threat of conceptual insufficiency more than of metaphysical extravagance—is largely unmarked even in contemporary debates. You will find the threat revived, for instance, in the difference between Alvin Plantinga's regressive return to the supernatural grounding of the natural and Heidegger's sense of the impoverishment of any merely naturalistic account of *Dasein*. Recent pragmatists have emphasized, in more modest ways, the promising convergence between, for example, George Herbert Mead and Maurice Merleau-Ponty (between pragmatism and phenomenology) and between Karl-Otto Apel and Jürgen Habermas and Charles Peirce and John Dewey (between pragmatism and Kantian transcendentalism), but they tend to ignore the question of naturalism's conceptual adequacy.[6] There's the issue before us now.

What I have in mind is the prospect of demonstrating that currently central disputes about the boundaries of naturalism, whether defended or attacked, tend to dissolve in a surprisingly congenial way (not entirely without repercussions, however) when reconfigured in terms of the biological/cultural divide made possible by but hardly derived from Darwin's account of evolution. For instance, privileged cognitive faculties (as in Descartes's rationalism) might count as "naturalistic" within the terms of seventeenth-century philosophy; but they could never be more than insurmountably problematic (affecting, say, the standing of Husserl's faculty of pure phenomenological inquiry) within twentieth-century discussions. Husserl treats pure transcendental phenomenology as exceeding the competence of any merely "natural" or "naturalistic" form of understanding; but he means, in part at least, to dramatize the contrast between the supposed scope of empiricist or psychologistic accounts of experience and what he defines as altogether different, functionally, even if not actually separable from the psychological powers of the mind (as in reflecting on the muddled intuitions of Descartes and Kant, whom he seeks to salvage or supersede). I shall return to Husserl's phenomenological claims later in this chapter.

Darwin's longitudinal picture of the emergence of a gifted species (*Homo sapiens*) provides the essential ground for a deeper conceptual innovation that has still to be fully grasped: the idea of a creature that is "naturally artifactual,"[7] a hybrid of biological and cultural development whose "second-natured" competences evolve in tandem with biological maturation but cannot be explained in biological terms alone or primarily; in short, the constitution of an artifactual self biochemically sustained but capable of functioning in linguistic, lingual, semiotic, and related ways that appear to be largely irreducible biochemically and are even incommensurable (though not incompatible) with the descriptive and explanatory treatment of the latter. If you permit the idea to count as the proper focus of an adequate naturalism in our time, then the most daring claims of Aristotle, Kant, Husserl, Heidegger, and others about exceeding the bounds of nature, about gaining necessary synthetic truths regarding cognitive privilege and apodicticity and the like, suddenly begin to appear entirely arbitrary, impossible to validate, no longer relevant or plausible or legible in terms of the self's artifactual origins.

Darwin brings into play for the first time the robust possibility that the members of *Homo sapiens* might be evolvingly transformed over short periods of time in ways impossible to explain or foresee in terms of the extremely slow processes of biological evolution, manifested in socially stable transmitted practices—all the while remaining open to further, endlessly novel such changes. The entire process is completely sui generis, unmatched anywhere in the animal world: the achievement of a creature whose hybrid "nature" is its own history, causally efficacious in immeasurably powerful and unpredictable ways, unlikely to be regularized under causal laws capable of achieving a measure of closure at the cultural level.

It's obvious that the apodictic pretensions of Husserl's phenomenological *epoché* are likely to be defeated as easily as Descartes's insistence on rational indubitability, in virtue merely of being relocated within the terms of external *Bildung*. The philosophical advantage of admitting the full import of the Darwinian achievement is nothing short of breathtaking: it sweeps out Aristotelian essentialism and teleologism and Kantian transcendentalism at a stroke! I am, I concede, constructing before your eyes a Darwinized reading of Hegel's extravagant innovations trimmed down as far as possible to capture the incompletely explicit nerve of classic pragmatism's naturalistic vision. That is indeed the very engine of Dewey's best vision.

All too plainly, this now exposes the inherent limitation of John McDowell's small but adventurous first step (in *Mind and World*) in the direction of reconciling Hegel and analytic philosophy (by way of Kant and Aristotle, if you can imagine that).[8] Even so, McDowell appears as the exceptional voice of a potential vanguard. The pivot of the needed innovation, however, was, for different reasons, never perceived (or if perceived, never adequately perceived) by figures as grand as Aristotle, St. Thomas, Descartes, Hume, Kant, and the analytic reductionists of the twentieth century. In fact, it was scanted even among those post-Kantian philosophers who caught the deeper innovation of Hegel's critique of Kant's innovation: Hegel himself falls short in some measure, as do Marx, Dilthey, the classic pragmatists, the Husserlian phenomenologists, the Romantic and Heideggerian hermeneuts, the Frankfurt Critical school, and even such splendid but self-isolating figures as Kuhn, Wittgenstein, and Foucault.

The boldest conjecture here relies on the coherence and viability of the stunning idea that the cultural world is a sui generis, irreducible, emergent, biologically dependent, artifactually self-constructed, endlessly evolving world set in motion by the fateful evolution of *Homo sapiens* and the incipience of true linguistic communication, the primate mastery of which entails the full development of the powers of what we now call persons or selves. It is indeed the discovery of the hybrid, artifactual existence of the self that, in my opinion, is the ultimate and decisive innovation that the nineteenth century made accessible just prior to the advent of American pragmatism, which flourished at just the right time to seize the idea's advantage. But the pragmatists slighted both their Hegelian and Darwinian sources even as they joined them productively in their new undertaking.

All this constitutes an utterly new chapter within the bounds of what appears to be the endlessly alterable run of nature—sparked by "plain facts" rather than philosophical ideologies. Aristotle's biologism, Kant's transcendentalism, analytic philosophy's scientisms are dismantled at a stroke by the unique, emergent, immensely effective presence of language, culture, history, and an artifactually autonomous mind or agency formed by evolution and continually transformed by the reflexive processes of cultural history. For nothing is more completely confined to the natural world than the artifactual; and there, nothing is more spectacular, conceptually, than the constantly confirmed truth that the artifactual maturation of the self outruns at an accelerating pace the conventional span of the biological maturation of the human creature itself. We have become the continual re-creation of our own technologies.

The naturalist's reply to Husserl insists that the empirical (or empiricist or phenomenal) and the phenomenological (including whatever Husserl might pretend comprises "pure transcendental phenomenology") are not only continuous at their source (that is, located in "nature" in some generous sense that spans the physical and the cultural) but are inseparable in function as well (and, as a consequence, impossible to treat as incorporating any specifically privileged powers, whether read conjointly or separately). Husserl, it needs to be said, is never more than arbitrary (and inexplicit) in providing a suitable rationale wherever he claims to identify the would-be powers of transcendental reason. Furthermore, no up-to-date reading of Husserl has (as far as I know) found any textual basis for supposing that he ever abandoned his apodictic claims, which the admission of the artifactual self would have contested in the deepest way.

My sense is that claims of cognitive privilege are now routinely dismissed, though they may still count in some notional way as natural or naturalistic. They cannot possibly be recovered, however, given Kant's own argument against the seventeenth-century rationalists and dogmatists and the outcome of post-Kantian objections to Kant's own transcendentalism turned finally against the idealists as well. Indeed, whatever Hegel's grandiose temptations may have been, his having historicized inquiry and cognition (against Kant) and his having removed all presumptions of privileged competence from his account of what is "given" (in his *Phenomenology*) surely apply to speculative *Vernunft* as readily as to what, in the 1931 preface to the English edition of his *Ideas* (1913), Husserl defines as pure phenomenology.[9] The key to Hegel's "revolution" rests with the fact that *Vernunft* is not a faculty of cognition at all but an autonomous, culturally informed interpretive and appreciative aptitude, which presumptive knowledge cannot do without.

Husserl hardly provides a convincing argument for recovering transcendental privilege: his affirmation is little more than an obiter dictum; and Hegel's emphasis on historicity and presuppositionlessness strengthens the thrust of contemporary naturalism, though Hegel's effort appeared too early to have considered the Darwinian lesson. Hegel's radical critique of Kant,[10] therefore, raises the question of whether Kant's transcendentalism (a fortiori, Husserl's) may not rightly be assigned some sort of extranatural standing. It does not oblige us, of course, to adopt a favorable reading of Hegel's extravagant system, though it entails or entrenches a distinct change in the analysis of the logic of predicates and categories, which, to my mind, marks the best possible reading of the sweep of Hegel's influence on contemporary thinking. Nevertheless, Hegel does not fit easily within naturalistic limits.

In any event, the definition of naturalism with a human face is both historically grounded and historicized—and is meant to accommodate within reasonable limits (and without privilege) whatever philosophical solutions addressed to pertinent, now-salient puzzles may strike the champions of contending factions as being sufficiently compelling. Certainly, the very idea of deciding the relative strength of contemporary movements like those of pragmatism, analytic philosophy, and the principal varieties of continental philosophy—preeminently, of phenomenology in the sense in which Husserl and Heidegger must be jointly featured as being in opposition to Hegel, who is of course a very different kind of phenomenologist—could hardly be relevantly explored without redefining naturalism for our time. I suggest that the assessment of naturalism's prospects is the master theme of every pertinent reexamination of what it would take to restore a reasonable sense of the underlying unity of contemporary philosophy, without prejudice to the state of play of its most important disputes. Once you admit that Kant was not a naturalist at all, that Aristotle was a naturalist of a kind displaced by Galileo and Darwin, that Hegel was at best a modern naturalist in the making, you see how difficult it is to draw the lines of naturalism correctly from the conceptual resources of such very different pasts.

We cannot make progress here without grasping the essential discontinuity between the truly "modern" analysis of naturalism (that has come to dominate—was, indeed, largely developed in—the post-Hegelian nineteenth and twentieth centuries) and its more usual puzzles in the rest of philosophy's history, running from ancient times up to the prescient stirrings of the modern (in Vico and Herder).

I suggest the apparent discontinuity is itself rightly perceived as a deeper form of continuity, provided we realize that the older tradition unquestionably failed to distinguish what (by a term of art) I have already called an "encultured" or "enculturing" conception of human nature. Metonymically, the contrast may be neatly focused in the differences between Aristotle's and Hegel's conceptions of humankind's "second nature" (the one biologized, the other historicized and encultured) *and* in the characteristic tendency, in influential contemporary quarters, to conflate the two accounts in unhelpful ways.

Here, we learn from our mistakes: for what is meant by historicity and enculturation is incommensurable with Aristotle's biologism and Kant's transcendentalism; and the distinctive mark of truly "modern" modern philosophy depends on the new conceptual unity made possible (but not yet achieved) by conjoining Hegel's theme of *geistlich* history and Darwin's discovery of the evolutionary process that culminates in the appearance of *Homo sapiens*. *No* mere improvement of Aristotle's or Kant's (or Hume's) characteristic philosophical rigor even begins to approach the larger vision of naturalism McDowell leads us to suppose he wishes to draw from Hegel's innovations—but cannot formulate in terms of the conceptual resources he draws from Kant and Aristotle.

The essential clue is perfectly straightforward. The cultural world emerges from the biological by sui generis processes—primarily by way of the incipient invention of true language (from the forms of primate communication) and its continually improved powers, which, reflexively, entail the matched transformation of the biologically evolved competences of the primate members of *Homo sapiens* into those normal to the artifactually hybrid, enlanguaged and encultured agents we call selves or persons—in such a way as to sustain the orderly transmission of the new competences from generation to generation (linguistic, psychological, agental) as well as their continuing evolution under the conditions of cultural history.

The process requires two very different modes of evolution and development: one, accounted for in terms of genetic, biochemical, epigenetic, and related interactive factors collected in our best inquiries along neo-Darwinian lines, however adjusted by continuing inquiry; the other, embodied and manifested in the first or, further, artifactually, in the materiae of the physical and biological world (as in our technologies, arts, and histories) but accounted for by the transformed, causally efficacious, culturally "penetrated" powers attributed to selves and to whatever they characteristically produce, collected in accord with the paradigm of linguistic meaning or of evolving analogues of the same (symbolic, semiotic, significative, institutional skills), which, by a term of art, I call "Intentional" (whether fully linguistic or simply "lingual," that is, not actually verbal but impossible without linguistic competence: as in baking bread, dancing, committing murder, engaging in war, making love, promising, worshipping, pursuing a career) and which, by various conceptual economies, is able to reclaim (for our best versions of naturalism) whatever of Hegel's exuberant *geistlich* world contributes to a reasonable picture of the human condition.

The pivotal issue concerns the definition of the *metaphysical* differences between the biological and the cultural: the specification of the emergent, novel, sui generis, irreducible processes and attributes of the cultural world that nevertheless remain causally efficacious in distinctive ways. And, indeed, if there *is* such a world, which includes societies of selves and what they are said to be capable of "uttering" (as by the skills mentioned earlier), then we will have already succeeded in providing a rationale for the strategic (straightforwardly naturalistic) innovation of distinguishing between the biological and the cultural: for example, we will have accounted for the "natural artifactuality" of selves or persons, and we will have replaced the classic reductionist forms of the unity of science program with an entirely new unity conception that prioritizes the executive role of artifactual selves and their cultural world. I cannot imagine a philosophical change of comparable power, except a successful reductionism or eliminativism. But there are no convincing essays of the latter sort. (Treat this as a response to McDowell's first step.)

WHATEVER IS DECISIVE for the definitional question, looking forward to the recuperation of the unity of Eurocentric philosophy, lies with the difference between two versions of the relationship between two distinct conceptions (the biological and the cultural) of *humankind's "second nature."* I'm persuaded that the three-legged opposition dividing so-called pragmatists, analysts, and continental philosophers may be greatly simplified—defanged as a source of insurmountable difference—merely by interposing the distinction just tagged and by redefining in its terms those troubling suspicions that have divided Eurocentric thought against itself: that is, by investing them with the transformative resources first put in play by Kant's innovations and by Hegel's profound critique of Kant, because each introduces a new conceptual channel for canonical philosophy.

Kant's transcendental questions loom over the whole of epistemology and metaphysics even after their privileged pretensions have been completely discredited; and Hegel's radical historicizing of a vastly enlarged *geistlich* interpretation of what Kant had unconvincingly restricted to his own privileged questions of transcendental possibility now redefines what might be meant by a merely human grasp of the actual structure of the world we claim to inhabit—and to know under the condition of our being first formed and continually altered historically. This is perhaps as close as we may come to Hegel's conception of "Absolute Knowing," which is itself no more than the infinite asymptotic limit that we forever invoke in our finite attempts to grasp the posited concrete unity of the whole of reality. In any case, it's what McDowell has yet to fathom and what figures like Aristotle and Kant never envisioned and Husserl believed he had satisfactorily tamed.

The cunning of history shows the way here. Because, in spite of its presumed argumentative skills, analytic philosophy remains weaker than pragmatism or continental inquiry in its grasp of the conceptual revolution wrought by Kant and Hegel. All this affords an ample confirmation of just how far—and yet how far short of what is needed—the most perceptive (and courageous) *analytic* forays into the uncertain ground that all "three" movements share have dared to penetrate. I've singled out (opportunistically, for the sake of an instructive economy already bruited) the helpful candor of John McDowell's intention, centered in his relatively recent John Locke Lectures, *Mind and World* (1996), to coopt Hegel's concept of *Bildung* in the service of correcting Kant's transcendental extravagance within the largely ahistorical and pre-Kantian inquiries of the best of contemporary analytic philosophy.

McDowell fails hands down in the Locke Lectures to capture the central theme of Hegel's *Bildung*. But I read the verdict in a generous way, because McDowell succeeds (by failing in his own venture) in drawing our attention to the flat impossibility of benefiting from Hegel's critique of Kant and pre-Kantian philosophy (reaching back to Aristotle), if the analytic movement or we (philosophers of any stripe) fail to incorporate into our conception of naturalism the full meaning of historicity and the difference between a biologized and a hybrid conception of "human nature" that concedes "metaphysical" differences between the biological and the cultural. We lose the decisive contrast between the two conceptions of humankind's "second nature"—implicated in the splendid (but still-inadequate) paradigms offered in Aristotle and Hegel, now dubiously conflated by McDowell. I admit the matter has its comic side, because neither Kant nor Aristotle could have addressed the Hegelian and post-Hegelian contrast between biology and culture and because Hegel's account, often drowned in the excesses of Absolute *Geist*, never rightly isolates the difference needed (though it collects within its hodgepodge whatever distinctions would be finally needed).

I hesitate to plunge in without providing more preparation for what needs to be said. But perhaps I'll not be misunderstood if I draw a perfectly obvious small clue from McDowell's reflections on naturalism (well, ethical naturalism) that nevertheless falls short of what I have in mind. Here's the argument: in "Two Sorts of Naturalism" (1996), McDowell notes that in the *Nicomachean Ethics* Aristotle "stipulates . . . that he is addressing only people in whom the value scheme he takes for granted has been properly ingrained" (as by "ethical upbringing").[11] There's the point! (McDowell offers nothing more expansive.) But *he cannot mean what he says here* unless he means to legitimate what I call "Aristotle's *Bildung*" by way of Hegel's usage, which would rightly require introducing the modern distinction between biology and culture—*which Aristotle lacks* and Kant all but lacks; or he means that Hegel's *Bildung* is essentially the same as the Greek *paideia*—which would be false, since *paideia* construes the normative issue as essentially biologized and conventionally drawn (though idealized) from the prevailing *Sitten* of Aristotle's world. That is, McDowell construes *Bildung* in the same sense in which Aristotle invokes "upbringing"; but *Bildung* poses the question of the origin of selves in a way that *paideia* does not. Failing to mark the difference, McDowell fails in a decisive and telling way.

Hegel's sense of *Bildung* entails the dialectical challenge of the evolving *Sitten* of one's own and of other encountered societies—still "internalist," I concede, in a way that might yet be confused with Aristotle's narrower notion; though it also requires a running assessment of competing norms, however provisionally, within the flux of history (in effect, of historicity). Aristotle's doctrine involves no more than an appeal to upbringing, ordinary instruction, indoctrination fitted to prevailing practices that are simply not construed in terms of any historicized or emergent challenge. And even Hegel's account fails to come to terms with the artifactual standing of all possible *Sitten* viewed in terms of a Darwinized picture of external *Bildung*.

McDowell's failing is clear confirmation of the profound inertia of the best of analytic philosophy: of its remarkably late awakening to the need to bring a command of historicity and historied culture into the space of its most salient forms of naturalism. More than thirty years earlier, Carnap had already expressed his admiration for Thomas Kuhn's draft of *The Structure of Scientific Revolutions*. Kuhn's *Structure* has been massively rejected in analytic circles, but it has surfaced once again, insistently, in a new philosophical surge that bids fair to enlarge current accounts of naturalism along broadly Hegelian lines. In any case, I dwell on McDowell's initiative because, hard as it is to believe, there is at the moment no more centrally placed "analyst" committed to reconciling Hegel and analytic philosophy! (The trouble is that there's almost nothing in McDowell that could possibly serve our purpose.)

According to McDowell, Aristotle conveys the sense—the sense McDowell champions—in which the ingrained spontaneity with which we learn to respond to ethical matters identifies (our) second nature entirely *within* the resources of (our) biology. McDowell says, "Any actual second nature is a cultural product, a formed state of practical reason . . . not something that dictates to one's nature *from outside*." He then adds:

[Where we apply] the rhetoric of ethical realism, second nature acts in a world in which it finds more than what is open to view from the [merely] dehumanized stance [that is, more than what it could possibly gain from the "disenchanted," "naturalistic," Humean-like world we treat as "viewed from nowhere"—as lacking human meaning altogether] that the natural sciences, rightly for their purposes, adopt. And there is nothing against bringing this richer reality under the rubric of nature too.[12]

Fine. But McDowell does not explicitly account for the cultural (or enculturing) transformation of the human that makes "practical reason" and "ethical upbringing" *normatively meaningful at all*, open to genuine normative validation—naturalistically—that is, in the sui generis sense that marks the unique emergence of an encultured world. (Unless, that is, second nature is no more than a selective strand of an ethic identified only in the anthropological sense, which is certainly less than Hegel would require.)

The legitimation of ethical norms cannot be gained by any improved naturalism by merely "reenchanting" nature: that is indeed Aristotle's (and McDowell's) limitation. Think of the matter this way. Aristotle nowhere assures us that the relationship between "potentiality" and "actualization" in encultured and enculturing processes behaves in the same way the paradigmatic processes of human biology do, or that the relationship can be shown to be governed by biologically specified norms of any kind. McDowell could never offer the requisite assurances, since he lacks the conceptual distinction between biological nature and human culture. He cannot even explain the original *acquisition* of ethical norms: in effect, he cannot explain the force of Hegel's or Gadamer's use of *Bildung*.

They, too, lacking or ignoring the import of Darwin's discovery, fail to grasp the longitudinal significance of the prelinguistic achievements of the nonhominid primates, perhaps even the achievement of early humans brought to the very threshold of true speech. But then we, too, have delayed two hundred years too long. McDowell presumes too much in supposing he can accommodate Hegel's *Bildung* by merely reenchanting nature by way of Kant's account of the difference between reasons and causes joined to something akin to Aristotle's ethical instruction.

There's an enormous conceptual gap here, all but invisible to McDowell, that seems likely to miss completely the *metaphysical* difference between physical nature and human culture. I'm prepared to risk the entire argument on a single challenge: if it were possible to redescribe all the distinctive features of true speech and language in physicalist terms alone, I would be persuaded that the difference I now take to be essential to the definition of naturalism could be refused without philosophical penalty. We are at a crossroads here, because the very existence of human selves, history, the entire cultural world is artifactually inseparable from the emergence of true language by way of a sui generis mode of evolution that depends on, but is altogether different from, the biological evolution of *Homo sapiens*, which we now explain canonically in terms of one or another form of neo-Darwinism.

I'm not concerned to provide a satisfactory analysis of the huge distinction I have in mind. (I admit it's absorbed most of my energies over an entire career.) But it bears in a decisive way on the rapprochement of the principal movements of Western philosophy that I'm recommending. I intend only to map in the briefest way the most important conceptions of naturalism struggling for hegemony at the present time that come together on the nature/culture distinction.

There are, I suggest, three master strategies of the naturalistic kind that have occupied us chiefly through the second half of the twentieth century and the opening decade of the twenty-first: first, a reductionism of various kinds, perhaps most compellingly those kinds associated with the classic unity of science program but open to accommodating the emergence or supervenience of the mental and the cultural—perhaps then, also, the stopgap measures of dualism and epiphenomenalism (think here of Kim); second, an emergentism of various kinds, perhaps most promisingly those associated with some form of biologism (narrow gauged or wide) opposed to any mere physicalism as far as the human world is concerned but hospitable to subsuming the mental and the cultural (including linguistic behavior, intelligent action, cooperative commitment, creative and purposive production, and the like) within the terms of a teleologized reading of biological processes (think here of an updated Aristotle); and third, an emergentism involving cultural entities and processes, at once hybrid and sui generis, complex and irreducible, inseparably incarnate or embodied in physical and biological nature, instantiating novel forms of causal efficacy (preeminently, the agency of selves) and subject (for that reason) to causal explanations incommensurable with the classic unity of science canon though compatible with empirically confirmed forms of physical causation shorn of all pretensions of nomological necessity and the causal closure of the physical world (think of Peirce's evolutionary initiatives).

These very large options collect the most inclusive varieties of naturalism in our day, but they also make provision for supernaturalisms and anti- and extranaturalisms. I've listed them in the order of descending professional support—and increasing conceptual resilience. Jaegwon Kim's supervenientism rightly counts as a strong contender of the first sort of naturalism; I've already mentioned John McDowell as a contemporary advocate of something close to the second; and I confess I'm committed to the third, which I judge to be the most resourceful of the three, congenial, especially, to the fortunes of contemporary pragmatism.

McDowell is certainly right in thinking that there cannot be any discontinuity between our grasp of truth and explanation respecting physical nature *and* legitimated norms and reasons applied to human action. Yet the project fails if McDowell will not or cannot press further in the direction of Hegel's very different conception of *Bildung*. For what is natural or naturalistic, as we now understand matters, must account for the radical difference between physical nature and human culture—without meaning by that to prejudge reductionism's prospects. For if reductionism fails (as I believe it must), then what falls within the bounds of nature will need to be sorted in such a way as to admit sui generis "cultural" properties and processes (which I collect as "Intentional"). McDowell's Kantian sympathies and Aristotelian convictions betray him here.

About "acquiring a second nature," McDowell ventures no more (in *Mind and World*) than this: "I cannot think of a good short English expression for this, but it is what figures in German philosophy as *Bildung*."[13] But precisely, that stops short of the deeper theme of *Bildung* or second nature ("external *Bildung*," as explained previously) that McDowell needs but has not probed at all. It's the same naturalism that accounts for the causal efficacy of encultured agency (the self's distinctive causal powers) and the would-be objective norms of theoretical and practical life (the norms of science and morality, say). It's precisely what I mean by "Darwinizing Hegel."

You cannot fail to see that McDowell is aware of the problem, since, on the very next page of his text, after remarking that "we need to recapture the Aristotelian idea that a normal mature human being is a rational animal, but without losing the Kantian idea that rationality operates freely in its own sphere," he explicitly says, "Modern naturalism is forgetful of second nature."[14] Of course, he's right: that's just the point of mentioning the need to recover a full-blooded sense of naturalism adequate to reuniting all the threads of Eurocentric philosophy. But that sense (the *second* sense of "second nature," as it were) *cannot* be drawn from Aristotle, Hume, Kant, or the "modern naturalism" (the disenchanted version) McDowell discounts—or, indeed, McDowell's own proposed improvements. It needs our restoring at least Hegel's innovations regarding history and culture. Quite literally, McDowell brings his own inquiry to a halt by endorsing the very doctrines Hegel dismantles. McDowell never crosses the metaphysical divide.[15] And we, too, cannot cross, unless we produce a suitable account of the "metaphysics" of the self; but we cannot do that unless we oppose McDowell's regressive reliance on the completely contrived, universally assured, utterly abstract use of the faculty of reason Hegel had already dismantled in Kant!

You have only to remember that Wilfrid Sellars (whom McDowell admires but finds it necessary to improve on) had already supposed that we could (if we wished) simply *add* the norms and rational functions assigned to persons (the language of reasons, meanings, explanation, and justification) to the language of disenchanted science (the language of bare physical causes) to capture in effect all that McDowell might require.[16]

Sellars's maneuver utterly fails: persons are already existent "hybrid" entities in the sense I've been sketching, are already implicated in Sellars's speculation (a fortiori, in Kant's). Ethical values are second-natured, *for selves and for selves alone*.

It's hard to believe Sellars could have meant his "addition" to be taken seriously. McDowell keeps to his own improvement: "The right contrast for the space of reasons," he says, "is not the space of causes, but [echoing Kant] the realm of law." It's true, he adds, "that a *merely* causal relation [which nature 'as the realm of law' already exceeds] cannot do duty for a justificatory relation"; but "it is also disputable that the idea of causal connections is restricted to thinking that is *not* framed by the space of reasons. . . . The contrast leaves it possible for an area of discourse to be in the logical space of causal relations to objects without thereby being shown not to be in the logical space of reasons [for 'reasons might *be* causes']."[17] Of course (or, perhaps better, with due care for the unexamined complexities of Kant's own doctrine).

Still, all this skirts the essential issue: what, finally, are the boundaries of the domain of nature that could include and join disenchanted causes and justificatory reasons without yielding to such problematic extremes as reductionism, dualism, or the tinkering of a philosophical *bricoleur*?[18] The answer depends on a *naturalistic account of the hybrid nature of human persons and human agency*,[19] because *if*, following Jaegwon Kim's version of the unity of science argument, we agreed to the doctrine of "the causal closure of the physical domain," we would find it impossible (as Kim himself would say) to extricate ourselves from a reductionism of the unity kind. But if you see the conceptual link between causal closure, nomological universals, and reductionism, you will have grasped the sense in which to attempt to reconcile Hegel and analytic philosophy may well entail concessions regarding the realist status of the cultural world potent enough to oblige us to consider radical changes in the canonical picture of science itself.

McDowell is aware that he must reconcile the causal treatment of physical events with the causal treatment of human actions, say, that incarnate meanings in causally efficacious ways tethered to "explanations by reasons," where, as McDowell adds, "reasons might be causes." In Kim's view, only something like a unity of science reductionism could possibly be reconciled with "causal closure," and even causal efficacy.

I argue, therefore, that there can be no convincing way of escaping Kim's trap if we cannot provide a compelling naturalism of the third kind sketched earlier; for only such a naturalism could possibly vindicate our modifying the closure doctrine in a respectable way: an insult, for example, may cause another's anger and the usual reddening of the face and change of pulse and the like; the closure doctrine may then be admitted to hold for the whole of nature, but that could never validate the presumption that if it held, it must hold in adequately physicalist terms alone or, indeed, in terms that entail strong nomological necessities. Kim, therefore, cannot defend his own position any better than McDowell defends his. Culturally emergent but physically embodied actions—speech acts, for instance—may in principle be made to conform with some as yet unformulated version of the closure doctrine while at the same time it resists reductionism.[20] McDowell nowhere bridges the divide or explains what he means by *Bildung* in a way that might answer a critic like Kim.[21]

IN CHIDING MCDOWELL, I mean to draw your attention to the even more baffling truth that pragmatism has almost completely ignored the frontal analysis of the twin themes of historicity and enculturation, even though, as a "Hegelian" movement, it was always subterraneanly informed by both. Apart from Mead and Royce, chiefly among the continentals these themes are rarely far from center stage.

At the close of his Woodbridge Lectures (1997), almost entirely given over to tracking the Kantian import of Wilfrid Sellars's work, McDowell remarks:

> [Sellars] is unresponsive to the Hegelian conceit of incorporating receptivity within Reason, and I have tried to display this as a blindness to a more soberly describable possibility. Given his conviction that the transcendental exercise must be undertaken from outside the conceptual, Sellars's responsiveness to Kant gives him no alternative but to construe the transcendental role of sensibility in terms of guidance by "sheer receptivity."[22]

This is, to be sure, the key to Hegel's objection to Kant.[23] But it's a lesson McDowell himself cannot rightly draw. McDowell's critique suffers from the same poverty of analytic philosophy's naturalism that he wishes to overcome. For it requires a theory of active reason originally informed by the transformative powers of *Geist* applied to what (in a Darwinian sense) may be called "primate" intelligence at the human level: McDowell exposes the inadequacy of Sellars's option on internal grounds but has next to nothing to say about the other matter, the issue I've been calling external *Bildung*—

within the terms of which alone internal *Bildung*, Aristotle's doctrine of upbringing (according to McDowell's reading), makes any sense at all as the historicized formation of a self rather than as mere indoctrination.

Hegel enlarges our account of *Vernunft* immeasurably by incorporating the distinctive metaphysics of history and culture within a conceptual space that we might easily reclaim as naturalistic; but Kant could never have made such a move—and never made the attempt: it would have utterly subverted the assured closure of his transcendental system and the would-be standing of the changeless categories of understanding (*Verstand*) Kant claims to have discovered. Historicity and universalism are finally incompatible. There, for instance, lies the key to Ernst Cassirer's profoundly Hegelianized Kantianism, which McDowell might have consulted.

My own view is that Kantian transcendentalism is a species of extranaturalism that might have passed for naturalism in its own day but hardly in ours; so are all the forms of cognitive privilege: Descartes's clear and distinct ideas as well as Aristotle's *nous*. (They make us out to be minor gods, though still exceptional.)[24] Invoking constructivism under the condition of historicity, however, entails the complete dismantling of the Kantian a priori and any principled disjunction between transcendental concepts (or categories) and empirical concepts (transiently formed). Hegel's myth of Reason, therefore, profoundly alters the metaphysics of *Bildung*: outflanks at a stroke whatever, by apriorist means, might have stalemated the redefinition of naturalism in the conciliatory spirit I've been advancing.

You realize there's no settled picture of *Vernunft* in Hegel's entire account: Hegel cannot quite free himself from the heady thought that human reason is a fulguration of something akin to the Stoics' divine fire; at the same time, he cannot abandon the thought that knowledge is no more than a human achievement bounded by finitude and horizontal history. Hence, he favors the safety of a certain amount of bombast (benignly in touch with the distinction of the *geistlich*), all the while we glimpse the impossibility of abandoning a thoroughly naturalistic economy.

The appearance of Darwin's innovation and of the data confirming the immensely slow evolution of the various species of the genus *Homo* leading to *Homo sapiens* and (doubtless) Neanderthal (now extinct) forces us to concede that, in acknowledging that the gradual invention of language and speech accounts for the enculturing transformation of the primate capacities of the species—hence, for the emergence of the artifactual self—we find ourselves obliged to abandon Descartes's and Kant's cognitional mythologies and to streamline the excessive extravagances of Hegel's *geistlich* rhetoric. The best first steps in this direction lead through the work of the classic pragmatists and figures like Dilthey and Cassirer, since Marx and Søren Kierkegaard appear too early to have incorporated Darwin. Pragmatism has surged again, so it might well return to the unfinished business of reclaiming its Hegelian heritage within the agon of contemporary philosophy.

The classic pragmatists never completely lost sight of the Hegelian corrective, though their analyses were often remarkably meager, until thinkers like Rorty, Davidson, Sellars, Quine, and Frege had all been puzzlingly treated, at one time or another, as exemplars of the best work of pragmatism itself! In any case, the classic pragmatists were never drawn to Kantian disjunctions or transcendental privilege—all inimical to a viable naturalism: neither Peirce nor Dewey ever hesitated along these lines. In a curious way, then, the pragmatists and continentals have been waiting for someone like McDowell to come along: to attempt to bridge the gap between themselves and the analysts, from the analysts' side. Accordingly, McDowell confirms the depth of analytic philosophy's estrangement and the vagueness of the pragmatists' reading of Hegel.

There are obvious constraints—some oblique, some straightforward—that may be incorporated at once into naturalism's larger proposal. For example, Kant's entanglement with noumena is a blunder that must be completely set aside: it has no useful life at all; it has nothing to do, for instance, with supporting the sensible admission that things may exist even if completely unknown to us, or that what we claim to know we may have good reason to believe exist in the way we claim they do, though independently of all our claims. There is no way to defend the thesis except by "constructivist" means—by positing (for good-enough reasons) a known thing's existing (as we claim to know it) independently of knowing or claiming to know it.

Simply put: noumena literally cannot be discussed at all, and the concept of an independently existing thing is not the same as the concept of a noumenon. But if you see that, you see as well that representationalism in the epistemological sense favored in the seventeenth and eighteenth centuries, favored in the first *Critique* (and, once again, in twentieth-century analytic thought), is little more than the obverse side of noumenalism—a doctrine, therefore, unacceptable to a rigorous naturalism. This is the implied lesson of Kant's admission to Marcus Herz (in his famous letter of February 21, 1772), identifying the fatal link between transcendentalism and noumenalism. To see this is to mark the burden of any viable post-Kantian forms of transcendental inquiry. Transcendental categories (Kant's categories) cannot be shown to fall (for epistemological reasons) within the bounds of nature: *they never*—are never made to—bear directly on what is "given" in experience, or is subject to empirically generated concepts, or depends on the psychologically accessible data on which alone we could possibly build our claims to know the world. (Their a priori necessity depends on a higher, an autonomous, faculty of reason.)

Kant's transcendental distinctions are antipsychologistic: hence, finally, antinaturalistic. The only way to recover their specifically naturalistic advantage requires the defeat of Kant's actual system: "transcendental" categories would have to be empirically generated—dialectically favored, revised from time to time, serially idealized wherever holistically or systematically promising—meant only to provide (by constructive guesses) a provisional a priori rule of objectivity fitted to our present inquiries but ready to be replaced where needed. (In this sense, Kant's system cannot be defended without being displaced.)

This is indeed Hegel's master clue regarding the error of Kant's extraordinary effort to secure the objective standing of the natural sciences.[25] Kant could never have countenanced Hegel's revision of the transcendental undertaking. Hegel insists on it; and in his account of "symbolic forms," Ernst Cassirer provides more than a sketch of how a Hegelianized version of Kant might actually work.[26] But the correction requires that the a priori be, finally, an a posteriori projection; that transcendental necessity be no more than rhetorical contingency; and that, strictly speaking, there simply be no demonstrable transcendentalist categories of Kant's sort. Here you gain a sense of the price of an adequate naturalism for our time.[27]

You realize that realism and idealism cannot be more than "regulative" assumptions—articles of rational hope perhaps, in Peirce's pretty sense—never "constitutive" in the sense Kant explicitly favors (and Hegel advances in his problematic way). Idealism cannot persuade us to accept the thesis that the physical world is somehow constructed or constituted, in part at least, by the mind's activity; nor can Kant's argument persuade us that empirical realism must be construed conformably.

Kant's transcendental innovations introduce the inescapable constructivism of epistemology. But Kant goes too far—fails to grasp the thoroughly constructivist nature of his own postulated faculties and categories.

Kant is too early to benefit from Hegel's revisions just as Hegel is too early for the revisions that Darwin makes possible. They are in a way already anticipated in Marx and the classic pragmatists even before the endorsement of the argument of the *Origin of Species*.

Constructivism remains in force so long as epistemology is needed and so long as it is a priori. But, then, there cannot be a principled disjunction between the empirical and the transcendental or between the psychological and the phenomenological. If you grant the force of Hegel's argument, you see that it must lead as well to the defeat of Husserl's regressive attempt to identify an even more unyielding form of transcendental apodicticity than Kant proposed. All this bears directly on the definition of an adequate naturalism. (I shall return to Husserl.)

Indeed, C. I. Lewis, somewhat in sympathy with Dewey, affirms, in accord with his own "conceptual pragmatism," that "*a priori* truth is definitive in nature and rises exclusively from the analysis of concepts. [Nevertheless,] that *reality* may be delimited *a priori* is due . . . to the fact that whatever is denominated 'real' must be something discriminated in experience by criteria which are antecedently determined. [Yet] the choice of conceptual system for . . . application to 'particular given experience' is instrumental or pragmatic, and empirical truth is never more than probable."[28] Lewis never risks going beyond the bounds of nature (naturalism) in defining the a priori, or what might count as transcendental "certainty" or the "independence of the conceptual" from the empirical:

> The reality of possible experiences in which any interpretation would be verified—the completest possible empirical verification which is conceivable—constitutes the entire meaning which that interpretation has. A predication of reality to what transcends experience completely and in every sense is not problematic; it is nonsense.[29]

Murray Murphey has recently offered the following congruent summary of Lewis's conceptual strategy: "Lewis emphasizes that our categories are historical social products and, although they are prior to any given experience, they nevertheless can, and do, change over time. . . . The test of the *a priori* is pragmatic, and the *a priori* is just that element in [systems of] knowledge that can be changed for pragmatic reasons."[30] This catches up, very nicely, more explicitly than does McDowell or Putnam, the themes that serve to reconcile analytic philosophy and pragmatism in the strongest possible naturalistic terms: demonstrates, in effect (per Dewey and Royce and even Hegel and, by anticipation, even Kuhn, though hardly in Kuhn's terms), the historical replaceability of "conceptual systems" and an underlying commitment to the flux of experience.[31]

There simply is no determinate autonomous space of mind in which transcendentalism can actually distinguish between a priori and a posteriori ("synthetic") truths; hence, the decisive option affecting the definition of naturalism in our time rests with the force of Hegel's critique of Kant and the implied "pragmatist" critique (in Hegel's name) of Husserl's phenomenology (read in the standard way). I see no reason to believe (against the apparent views of McDowell and Putnam) that the achievements of science and logic cannot be reasonably recovered in accord with the flux of experience—or the flux of history (historicity)—if they can be recovered at all; and, accordingly, I see no reason to believe that objectivity in science is, as such, incompatible with one or another coherent form of relativism,[32] if objectivity can be recovered in the constructivist way.

Necessity, Peirce affirms, obtains only in deductive logic: where more is needed "metaphysically," we must fall back to constructivist devices. "Conceptual truths," Hilary Putnam has persuasively argued (in a way that shows us how to harmonize pragmatism and analytic philosophy), are inherently revisable under historically pertinent conditions (as, contra Kant, with the first mention of viable non-Euclidean geometries). What Putnam demonstrates surely suggests a beneficial paraphrase of Hegel's treatment of the notion of historicity, although I doubt Putnam would welcome any such phrasing. Similarly, what he says accords with Dewey's somewhat undeveloped acknowledgment of the flux of history, though he roundly condemns relativism as conceptually irretrievable. Putnam is disposed (mistakenly, I would say) to believe that realism and relativism are incompatible and that (very possibly) the admission of a strong form of historicity or the flux of experience may threaten (as Lewis seems at times to suppose) the quasi-foundational function of scientific knowledge.[33] (They seem to signal pragmatism's continuing weakness.)

Once you abandon cognitive privilege and disallow "necessities of reason" (in accord with Putnam's excellent argument)—otherwise canonically disallowed in spite of evolving experience (think of non-Euclidean geometries)—you will have to concede at the very least, vis-à-vis Kantian questions, that objectivity in the sciences is bound to entail the a posteriori reading of a priori posits. Furthermore, if that be allowed, the compatibility of realism and relativism (within naturalistic bounds) will, wherever relativism proves coherent and self-consistent, follow at once. Viewed this way, Dewey's pragmatism confirms the relativistic proclivities of the Hegelian correction of Kant—and thus enlarges the resources of naturalism. It is also, perhaps, part of the perceived advantage of a Darwinian critique of teleologism.

I mention these qualifications for a number of reasons: partly to illustrate the systematic coherence of certain proposed constraints on a form of naturalism fitted not merely to analytic philosophy but to the whole of Eurocentric philosophy—where, that is, other options, even if equally naturalistic, are demonstrably not nearly as congenial or resourceful; partly because they suggest the considerable difference between pragmatist and analytic versions of naturalism, as well as the ease with which they may be reconciled; partly to confirm that the debate about naturalism need not adversely interfere with the undistorted treatment of other important issues—realism and objectivity, for instance; and partly to hint (before addressing the matter in a frontal way) at how important a decision it is to "ground" (without involving privilege) the naturalism debate in one or another version of phenomenology—where Hegel's conception starts us off on the right foot. When all is said and done, I suggest, phenomenology (read in Hegel's rather than Husserl's way) begins to define the minimal conditions of an inclusive Eurocentric naturalism. But if you think back to Hume's and Kant's impoverishment of the cognizing and active "I" of late eighteenth-century philosophy, you see at once the sense in which the culturally transformed Cartesian *Ego* or Kant's *ich denke* (the puzzlingly weak posit of § 16 of the first *Critique*) is the assured *artifactual* mate (the self-constituting evolving agent of linguistic and allied fluencies) on which naturalism itself finally rests—the same "self" that (rightly) remains invisible in Hume's *Treatise*.

IT WOULD NOT BE UNREASONABLE to claim that the philosophical motley that includes Descartes, Hume, Kant, Herder, Hegel, Peirce, Marx, Nietzsche, Heidegger, Husserl, James, Dewey, Mead, Kierkegaard, Merleau-Ponty, Sartre, Gadamer, Austin, Wittgenstein, and Foucault all depend on one or another version of "phenomenological" reportage. There is no single model that could possibly fit all of these figures perspicuously, but the collection is worth pondering. The lax use of the term "phenomenology" is not a weakness therefore; it's a concession to an important consideration that may be met in endlessly different ways and for different purposes: namely, that every effective philosophical thesis that has any epistemological or metaphysical pretensions in the post-Kantian world must begin by acknowledging some initial (some admitted but not the "first" or any "originary") set of *data* or *données* or "givens" of reportable experience.

I'm speaking loosely here—and must because any prior, determinate, systematic, or reasoned limitation on what to include or exclude from the salient givens of "experience" would violate the spirit of what is provisionally thus collected. The only possible way Husserl could have construed phenomenology in the "methodological" way he does requires yielding to antecedent privilege of some kind—thereby subverting the whole point of phenomenology, as Peirce very neatly puts it, as "a preliminary inquiry," for Peirce was an exceptionally effective (admittedly controversial) phenomenologist in the pragmatist mode.

Peirce follows Hegel—criticizes what he takes to be Hegel's "errors" and arbitrary restrictions (in the *Phenomenology* and *Encyclopaedia Logic*) but follows Hegel faithfully nevertheless—even to the point of idealizing Hegel's "three stages of thinking" in terms of the "universal Categories" of Firstness, Secondness, and Thirdness. Peirce exceeds his own insight here; his pass at a short list of universal categories—in the sense in which he finds Aristotle, Kant, and Hegel all bent on the same effort: "to bring out and make clear the *Categories* or fundamental modes [of things or experience]"—is at best a problematic undertaking if we acknowledge the informal boundaries of the phenomenological and the elastic nature of the would-be Categories. Peirce adds, "Hegel was also right in holding that these *Categories* are of two kinds: the Universal Categories all of which apply to everything, and the series of categories [which Peirce calls 'particular categories'] consisting of phases of evolution [that is, developments that are salient in one phenomenon or one 'kind' of phenomenon but not in another]."[34]

If you allow the distinction, then "Universal Categories" are *also* provisional, though ubiquitous enough (among whatever "appears" to us) to justify being so construed in contrast with "particular categories." In any case, we cannot vouchsafe their necessity, exceptionlessness, or apodictic objectivity; or their confirmation as uniquely valid *within* phenomenology's inescapable informality, unless vacuously, for instance, as a formal consequence of one of Husserl's "discoveries" regarding "transcendental intersubjectivity." Husserl affirms:

Concrete, full transcendental subjectivity is the totality of an open community of I's—a totality that comes from within, that is unified purely transcendentally, and that is concrete only in this way. Transcendental intersubjectivity is the absolute and only self-sufficient ontological foundation [*Seinsboden*], out of which every objective (the totality of objectively real entities, but also every objective ideal world) draws its sense and its validity.[35]

Peirce might easily have favored something of the sort, but he would have meant it in the terms of his fallibilistic idiom: that is, as holding at the end of infinite inquiry. Husserl could never have spoken thus: it would have precluded all his transcendental claims at a stroke.

There are at least three insuperable difficulties that count against Husserl's way of drawing transcendental conclusions, that is, conclusions that claim to be necessary or apodictic or universal: if what is phenomenologically given is not first constrained "transcendentally," inferences of universal scope or necessity will be as uncertain as the boundaries of what is "given" without privilege (on which a transcendental review must reflect); the transcendental will be inseparable from, will depend on, will be subject to, whatever (in changeable and divergent ways) *is* given empirically to natural experience, hence in a way incapable of being transcendentally (exceptionlessly) assured; and, in Husserl's own view, the "transcendental subject" (as distinct from the empirical subject, however loosely or generously conceived) will be "constituted" (in effect, continually reconstituted) within the very process of "constituting the world" in Husserl's special sense: the sense in which he speaks of allowing the world to "show itself potentially" in the constituting process that affects subjects, world, and intersubjectivity together.

The young Danish phenomenologist Dan Zahavi admits that Husserl "never gave a clear answer to the question of whether constitution is to be understood as a creation or a restoration of reality."[36] More to the point, Husserl never gave a satisfactory explanation of the privileged standing of the transcendental factors themselves. There's the *pons* of Husserl's entire project—because necessity and apodicticity are nowhere needed and nowhere assured! Contra Kant, there is no science of science; and contra Husserl, there is no transcendentally assured philosophy of transcendental philosophy.

I concede that Husserl arrives at a perfectly reasonable schema here. But I cannot see that it escapes being more than the immensely quarrelsome posit of an objectively discernible world—a "transcendental non-ego" that, as Husserl himself holds, "presupposes an element of *facticity*, a passive pregivenness without any active participation or contribution by the ego."[37] I suggest we are back at Kant's fatal limitations. I concede that Husserl effectively rejects *that* form of naturalism that disjoins subject and object epistemologically. But so do the pragmatists, the Hegelians, the post-Kantian idealists, and indeed Heidegger—speaking of different subjects and different objects; and Husserl may not really have escaped Kant's decisive problem, since he introduces the "passive pregivenness" of the world within the space of transcendental intersubjectivity. Since Husserl admits a world inseparably bound (in the constituting sense) to coordinately constituted subjects ("I's") and their intersubjectivity, I cannot see how his exertions could convincingly capture anything necessarily objective or apodictic here (frankly, anything bordering on the noumenal) except by circularity or sheer fiat. If we take Zahavi's admission seriously, we realize we cannot confirm the dividing line between subjective passivity and the active autonomy of whatever is implicated in what constitutes world, self, and intercommunicating selves, or indeed what accounts for any such constituting power.

The following is as good as one can find among pertinent efforts (apart from Hegel's own efforts) to clarify the ineluctability and special scruple of Hegel's phenomenology, regarding its "neutrality" in relation to the classic Husserlian way of entering the intended contest: that is, bearing on the scope or amplitude Hegel accords the "given," on his avoidance of all pretensions of privileged standing, on his admission of the continuing influence of natural experience, his rejection of facultative or subjective certainty or any principled link between such certainty and the supposed objectivity of science, metaphysics, or methodology. Peirce affirms—as an implicit opponent of Husserl, also as a rather freewheeling Hegelian phenomenologist:

> [B]efore we can attack any normative science, any science which proposes to separate the sheep from the goats here [Peirce "names three normative sciences: Ethics, Esthetics, and Logic, 'the three doctrines that distinguish good and bad' representations of truth, . . . efforts of will, . . . (and) objects considered simply in their presentation"], it is plain that there must be a preliminary inquiry which shall justify the attempt to establish such dualism. This must be a science that does not draw any distinction of good or bad in any sense whatever, but just contemplates phenomena as they are, simply opens its eyes and describes what it sees; not what it sees in the real as distinguished from figment—not regarding any such dichotomy—but simply describing the object, as a phenomenon, and stating what it finds in all phenomena alike. [Hegel made this his "starting-point" in the *Phenomenology*,] although he considers it in a fatally narrow spirit, since he [Hegel] restricted himself to what *actually* forces itself on the mind. . . . I will so far follow Hegel as to

call this science *Phenomenology* although I will not restrict it to the observation and analysis of *experience* but extend it to describing all the features that are common to whatever is *experienced* or might conceivably be experienced or become an object of study in any way direct or indirect.[38]

Peirce confirms the good sense of the main thrust of Hegel's unconditional informality, although what Peirce adds surely casts "science" as no more than an honorific category.

I have also touched very briefly, earlier in this chapter, on Hegel's problematic use of the notion "being" at the start of the *Science of Logic*. Any such "beginning" must explicate the role of *Geist* in isolating whatever we take to stand at the beginning of any pertinent metaphysical inquiry. But it needs to be said that there is no single or most salient way of beginning and that any solution comparable to Hegel's is, like Hegel's, dependent on its own *myth* of how to validate its findings.[39] For present purposes, our concern lies with querying whether, in the most generous sense of phenomenology, what we find in experience obliges us to acknowledge the conceptual insufficiency of naturalism. (I say, emphatically, that it concedes no such thing.)

That lesson begins straightforwardly enough: in contests between pragmatism and analytic philosophy, the motto I recommend is "natural but not naturalizable"—reading the second term in the scientistic way associated with the proposals of figures like Quine, Davidson, and Rorty;[40] in contests between either pragmatism or analytic philosophy and continental philosophy (represented in the strongest way by Husserlian and Heideggerian phenomenology), the motto might be "naturalism but neither supernaturalism nor extranaturalism," where the second term is liberalized to include transcendental subjects and transcendental worlds manifesting privileged attributes. I take the first motto to be already vindicated; and I take the second to be well on its way, already the principal focus of late Eurocentric philosophy. Both mottos preclude *any* disjunction between the empirical (or natural) and the a priori (or transcendental): they build instead on an intuition that joins Hegel, Peirce, Lewis, and Cassirer in the critique of Kant's transcendentalism and the confirmation of the a posteriori status of the a priori.

A few initial constraints congenial to naturalism suggest how we may separate the least doubtful forms of phenomenology from those that are plainly indefensible or seriously problematic—for example, (1) the given cannot be fixed or shown to be indubitable or cast in terms of separable "subjective" and "objective" sources; can only manifest whatever saliences they are said to exhibit (phenomenologically) as "the-way-things-appear-to-us-to-be"; cannot invoke or entail or explicitly affirm any second-order facultative privilege; cannot pretend to free any such reports or avowals from the contingent contamination of whatever enters into the natural formation of any human agent's ability to report same; hence, cannot be originary or more than contingently posited "in the middle of our engagement with the world"; (2) the given cannot be shown to be merely "passive" or undistorted or uninfluenced by whatever is alleged to enter "actively" or from the side of reflexive avowing, *in* whatever is said to be thus given; and cannot, conversely, be shown to be a "pure" active contribution from any subjective vantage, as if by way of reason opposed to sensation or by way of experience unalloyed in any such way; (3) whatever is taken to be given in senses (1) and (2) includes elements of experience, perception, feeling, emotion, thought, conception, or reason that, as given, appear to be inherently enlanguaged, penetrated by language, belief, theory and the like; that is, given as linguistically and reflexively reportable but not decomposable into subjective and objective factors—paradigmatically human in the most ordinary ways; so that (4) all speculation or inference regarding what is given in the experience of sublinguistic animals and children is ineluctably anthropomorphized, meaning that such characterizations are informally modeled on the human and uttered from the human vantage speaking in the name of sublinguistic creatures, with whatever degree or kind of qualification may be needed to preserve a semblance of objectivity; and (5) phenomenological reports and avowals, often transient and accidental, are not inadmissible for that reason or diminished in any sense in conveying what is given. In short, what Husserl (and Heidegger) treats as phenomenologically constituted (whether cognitionally or existentially)—that is, as what "shows itself as what it is"—is not entitled to privileged standing but gains whatever standing it may claim contingently, provisionally, by diverse and divergent means, replaceably, constructively, by second-order reflections on what is admitted to be given.[41] But if *that* is true, then even Peirce's "Universal Categories" cannot, faute de mieux, be more than provisional.

Arguably, Kant advances a phenomenologically indefensible option, because he treats what is given through the senses as entirely passive—contra (2); and Husserl's mature version (or at least the standard version of his mature account) is similarly indefensible, because he treats pure transcendental phenomenology as capable of yielding certainty or essentiality regarding the analysis of concepts; because he fails or neglects to explain the bearing of the contingency of whatever such putative certainty depends on, or how pure phenomenology escapes the effects of such contingencies—contra (1)–(3).

The point of these caveats is to suggest—perhaps to demonstrate—that versions of Hegel's phenomenology are bound to be more easily defended, more congruent with naturalism's project, than any alternative that might favor Kant's or Husserl's classic options (as just construed). In any event, the economy brings us to what may reasonably count as a first pass at reconciling the entire sweep of Eurocentric philosophy ranging over pragmatist, analytic, and continental undertakings. But if so, then the entire diversity of the Eurocentric world may yet prove to be manageably convergent along naturalistic lines.

THERE ARE DECISIVE CONSEQUENCES to be drawn from all this. As already suggested, the best phenomenological paradigm must be closer to Hegel's model than to Husserl's. Hegel's emphasis is not centered on a preferred philosophical method of analysis or of reportage or methodology of any kind (though Hegel has his preferences), or on the selected findings of any such method or methodology. Instead, it features *Erscheinungen*: that is, whatever may be reported or avowed as perceived or experienced—"lived through," as Husserl often says—by subjects or agents, naturally, "second-naturedly" (as we may now say): subjectively, as conscious "subjects" capable of reporting the appearings-of-the-world-to-us without invoking antecedent presumptions of any kind regarding what, finally, is given and what inferred, what subjective and what objective, what first order and what second order, what perceived or experienced or felt or thought or imagined and what the meaning of any of that may be, what transient and what essential, what a priori and what a posteriori, what accidental and what universal, what reality may be thought to require and what conforms or does not conform with same, or anything of the sort.

The phenomenological is relatively "innocent" then, but not (for that reason) determinately neutral or certain in any assuredly objective regard: the given is changeable, often ephemeral, subject to diverse and uncertain influences of all sorts, valuable in that it includes what, as best we can tell at any moment of judging, we are least likely to ignore or deny as salient or familiar in the way of what "appears"—as well as what we would not exclude (if queried) however marginal it may seem. This is, in fact, very close to Hegel's notion of "being" (*Sein*) invoked at the start of the *Science* of *Logic*;[42] it also confirms the sense in which Hegel's phenomenology—straddling the *Phenomenology* and the *Logic*(s)—is essentially naturalistic in the most problem-free way. It's the key to the daring scruple of what Hegel means by "concrete" actuality.

In emphasizing what is reportable, we implicate the provisional saliencies of the verbal and reportorial skills of what we ordinarily call selves, persons, agents, second-natured subjects, ourselves—without prejudice to what we may theorize *is* a self or subject (or, for that matter, without prejudice to whether such entities actually exist or are only formally or functionally posited); without prejudice as well to what may be counted as the range of experience of prelinguistic animals and children; without prejudice to individual or aggregated or "intersubjective" or historically diverse avowals at the level of ordinary human competence; without prejudice to what is thus avowed or reported and to what (at any putatively higher level of scientific or philosophical analysis) may be sorted as empirical or transcendental or the like. I take these to be the characteristic, most preliminary features of a constructivist account of objectivity in the realist sense.

In *Philosophical Investigations*, Husserl constrains any "egologically" determinate account of subjective experience as merely empirical (stream of consciousness), contrary to what he himself features as belonging to any genuinely a priori analysis of consciousness and experience. But he risks thereby violating the naturalistic continuity between the empirically a posteriori and any "higher-order" phenomenological analysis in a way that invites comparison with Kant's own problematic disjunction between the empirical and the transcendental. Hegel's account in the *Phenomenology* makes it impossible to distinguish in any principled way, finally or apodictically, between "empirical" and "transcendental" (or between experientially avowed and facultatively privileged) reports of what is given—because the would-be invariances and necessities of a priori self-understanding are themselves contingent artifacts of encultured experience (that have "succeeded for a time"), continually sedimented within the evolving givens of phenomenological reflection in ways that invite endlessly inventive, newly minted, further a priori posits.

Once we admit, effectively with Hegel—or even if we assume (mistakenly, in my opinion) that Hegel was seriously tempted to find a way of escaping the flux of historicity—that the a priori is an a posteriori posit (artifact or construction) meant to accommodate the demands of evolving experience, we cannot distinguish, except horizontally, between the contingent and the necessary or between the empirical and the transcendental. Whatever we there concede affects as well the pretensions we invariably find in Husserl and later phenomenologists (in Scheler, for instance, in Heidegger, in Sartre, in Merleau-Ponty) that cling to the methodological reliability of a disjunction between merely natural or empirical and a priori faculties of analysis, even where disputes arise regarding what the a priori reveals.[43]

Husserl, in the *Investigations*, *Cartesian Meditations*, and *Ideas I*, plainly views phenomenology as a discipline that claims to analyze a "recovered" range of "primordial" experience that cannot be disclaimed within the competence of human reflection though it exceeds the bounds of any naturalistic inquiry. I see no compelling evidence that recent "corrections" in the reading of Husserl in the direction of reclaiming a robust sense of intersubjectivity (notably, in Dan Zahavi's readings) qualify Husserl's apriorism in any significant respect. The decisive key is not intersubjectivity itself, however holistically joined to plural "subjects" and "world," but the import of any such complex viewed as implicating the inseparability of the empirical and the phenomenological at *any* "level" of reflection. Husserl, I suggest, is a philosophically regressive figure, viewed in terms of transcendental privilege—just as Kant is, viewed from the vantage of Hegel's critique. We lack in principle sufficient grounds for confirming any compelling *human* recognition of either Kant's or Husserl's essential disjunctions.

In the interests of textual accuracy, we must distinguish between Husserl's views regarding the subject of experience in his own early and later work and his views about the difference between empirical (or naturalistic) and transcendental reflection vis-à-vis the structure of experience itself. Zahavi makes a convincing case textually (but hardly philosophically) for construing the ego of transcendental phenomenology as non-egological (that is, as not identical with the empirical self or subject of any naturalistic reflection or the "owner or bearer of experiences, but simply [as identical with] the experiences [themselves] in their totality"). Regarding this extraordinary claim (which obviously risks incoherence), Zahavi reports Husserl as holding, in the introduction to the second part of the *Investigations*, "that when we engage in a phenomenological description of experiences we should seek to capture them in their essential purity and not as they are empirically apperceived, namely as the experiences of humans or animals." Zahavi glosses Husserl's theme as follows:

We should not focus on sensory physiology or neurology, that is, on the empirical conditions that must be fulfilled in order for *Homo sapiens* to be conscious; rather, we should aim at analyzing the fundamental structures of consciousness, regardless of whether it belongs to humans, animals, or extraterrestrials. In other words, when investigating the experiential dimension, we should aim at essential descriptions of the experience, and . . . such descriptions will precisely exclude any reference to their empirical bearers.[44]

To be candid, I see no way to construe Husserl's *epoché*—in effect, the rejection of the adequacy of the "natural attitude"—as anything but conceptually ungrounded, vacuous, utterly arbitrary, inescapably self-serving, and impossible to reconcile coherently with any of the givens of (egological) experience on which transcendental reduction is said to work its separate magic.[45] I understand the correction intended: the "world" transcendentally encountered is said *not* to be encumbered egologically, remains accessible nevertheless for objective description without reference to any empirically generated distinctions. But I find this impossible to take seriously: every would-be pertinent test would seem to be privileged in a circular and question-begging way. Husserl has no grasp of the import of what I have labeled "external *Bildung*." What could Zahavi mean by "analyzing the fundamental structures of consciousness [among] animals or extraterrestrials"?

I cannot see how the structure of consciousness could ever be effectively disjoined from considerations about how consciousness is itself embodied—the entire discussion of "other minds" and "intersubjectivity" (in Husserl and Zahavi—and Wittgenstein for that matter) depends on it; I can't see how the consciousness of infants, animals, or extraterrestrials could possibly be studied, except under the constraints of anthropocentric reflection and theoretical cues drawn from the developmental history of such organisms; I can't see how the phenomenological or pure analysis of consciousness could be distinguished, in principle, from empirical or naturalistic inquiries.

Surely, the transcendental must be relativized to what is said to be given in experience; and, surely, what is thus given is continually qualified (reportorially) by whatever (for a time) is thought to be operative a priori. (Recall Putnam's discussion of "conceptual truths.")[46] Nevertheless, I don't deny that there is an important difference in reporting what we experience and in conjecturing about what makes such experience conceptually "possible"; and I don't doubt that Zahavi presents Husserl's views accurately—perhaps more accurately than accounts that rest entirely on texts like the *Investigations* and the *Meditations*. But Zahavi's qualifications are not meant to weaken the standard transcendental claim (may in fact make it more problematic and resistant to revision); and Zahavi's own qualifications seem to entrench the cognitive privilege of consciousness's "content" (not weaken it), without strengthening the grounds for any such confidence. Notice, also, that Zahavi's line of thinking has nothing to do with establishing Husserl's non-egological view of consciousness, as expressed, say, in Husserl's Fifth Investigation (in *Logical Investigations*); on the contrary, the non-egological view *presupposes* the distinction between the empirical and the transcendental mode of the phenomenological itself (through all the classic variations of the latter).[47]

On its own showing, transcendental phenomenology must be aware of the empirically generated categories that apply to the givens it claims to analyze in its privileged way. I take that to be a *reductio*. Put in the briefest terms: wherever we admit action and responsibility (as well as perception and the intelligent use of perception in directing action), we admit agency; wherever we admit agency, we must (as far as anyone has argued) admit the individuation and reidentifiability of individual agents; and wherever transcendental agents reflect (or must reflect) on what is empirically given, such agents and the egological agents of experience must, in effect, be one and the same. *Any* principled disjunction here, must, accordingly, be incoherent; but to admit the formal point is not yet to say what the "nature" of empirical and transcendental "egos" is.

It's entirely possible—even convincing—to suggest that effective agency depends on more than can be assigned to any ego (any single mind or brain, for instance), since what among second-natured agents depends on "information"—accessible in some ambient cultural space (as, in different ways, Hegel, Husserl, and Heidegger all admit)—may require, or concede, informational sources external to the consciousness of any particular ego. The complications of *Geist*, *Lebenswelt*, *Mitsein* surely implicate a plurality of human agents; but what these categories collect also includes what, whether biologically or culturally, qualifies the nature of the selves or agents we admit.[48] Furthermore, except for resurrecting privilege, it is difficult to see how to avoid a constructivist account of objectivity: but surely, that means favoring some form of naturalism.

My point is a double one: first, if the phenomenological description and analysis of conscious experience (pure or transcendental) cannot be disjoined from the empirical or naturalistic description and analysis of egological experience, then Husserlian phenomenology will finally depend on something close to Hegelian phenomenology (whether it admits the fact or not). In that regard, the Hegelian conception will be more fundamental and (in my opinion) less doctrinaire, less problematic, in fact superior and more inclusive. And, second, if that be admitted, then the entire project of transcendental phenomenology will be placed at considerable risk vis-à-vis a naturalistic phenomenology, whether one admits the existence of a determinate subject of experience or not (that is, regardless of what our options are or may be). As I've already remarked, the entire counterargument can be made absolutely clear by simply reading Husserl's preface to the English edition of the 1913 German original of *Ideas*, which betrays the completely regressive, undefended nature of Husserl's enterprise—regardless of the fortunes of the analysis of such categories as "experience," "ego," or "intersubjectivity."

Consider the following lines, therefore, meant to explain "transcendental subjectivity," without holding Husserl to his own early "idealism" or his tendency to disjoin the contribution of the transcendental (or "philosophizing") ego from the supposedly inseparable contribution of the non-egological world, though these and similar considerations do indeed belong to the preface of *Ideas*, where Husserl affirms:

Transcendental Subjectivity does not signify the outcome of any speculative synthesis, but . . . is an absolutely independent realm of direct experience that becomes available only through a radical alteration of that same dispensation under which an experience of the natural world runs its course, a readjustment of viewpoint which, as the methods of approach to the sphere of transcendental phenomenology, is called "phenomenological reduction."

In the work before us transcendental phenomenology is not founded as the empirical science of the empirical facts of this field of experience. Whatever facts present themselves serve only as examples. . . . In this book, then, we treat of an *a priori* science ("eidetic," directed upon the universal in its original intuitability), which appropriates . . . the empirical field of fact of transcendental subjectivity with its factual (*faktischen*) experiences, equating these with pure intuitable possibilities that can be modified at will, and sets out as *its a priori* the indissoluble essential structure of transcendental subjectivity, which persist in and through all imaginable modifications. . . .

I am no longer a human Ego *in* the universal, existentially posited world, but exclusively a subject *for* which this world has being, . . .

I now also become aware that my own phenomenologically self-contained essence can be posited in an *absolute* sense, as I am the Ego who invests the being of the world which I so constantly speak about with existential validity, as an existence (*Sein*) which wins for me from my own life's pure essence meaning and substantial validity.[49]

I cite this extended passage partly to assure you of Husserl's extraordinary hopes for phenomenology; partly to suggest that, although he changed his views about realism and idealism, about the status of the egological and transcendental subject, as well as about the inseparability of "I's," world, and intersubjectivity in both naturalistic and transcendental space, Husserl does not seem to have retreated from his strongest transcendental presumptions under the terms of later doctrinal revisions; and partly to confirm that the arbitrariness of Husserl's entire undertaking changes hardly at all through his enormous output and unpublished reflections. But if so, then, at least so far, phenomenology is not likely to withstand a thoroughgoing naturalistic challenge—along, say, Hegelian, if not pragmatist, lines.

In all of this, I find an insuperable vulnerability in Husserl's conception. I have always been struck by the peculiar but philosophically prudent impoverishment of the "I," the subject or self of Hume's and Kant's reflections. My own conjecture about the self suggests that the reflexive functions we nominally assign the individuated human self themselves evolve as the artifactual (second-natured) powers of the equally artifactual, emergent (but all the same genuine), socially formed and entrenched subject that the well-formed aggregated cohorts of selves of different societies come to recognize as they come to recognize themselves as selves.

To speak this way is, effectively, to recover George Mead's dialectic of the "I" and the "me" in terms of the overlapping but very different processes of formation that belong to instantiations of the different kinds of emergence made possible by the mechanisms of biological and cultural evolution that I sketched earlier in my argument. Hume and Kant could not have answered in the biologized and enculturing terms that were hardly accessible before Darwin's contributions (and, of course, Hegel's contribution). But Husserl could not have proposed his doctrine of the Transcendental Ego without being aware of the need to explain its provenance. There's the point. Husserl's confidence regarding the apodictic possibilities of the phenomenological *epoché* depend completely on the standing of the Ego itself. But if the Ego is a culturally contingent (though regular enough) artifact, as I would argue, then it's child's play to mount a *reductio* of Husserl's thesis. But if so, then Husserlian phenomenology can hardly hold the line against a naturalism "of the third kind" (already introduced). In fact, the gathering argument makes it perfectly clear that the single most decisive thesis in favor of contemporary forms of naturalism—collecting Darwin and Hegel along the lines I've termed "external *Bildung*"—is indeed the doctrine of the culturally generated artifactuality of the self.⁵⁰

AS FAR AS I CAN SEE, the contest between pragmatism and analytic philosophy on the one hand and between pragmatism and continental philosophy on the other pretty well comes down to the question of the adequacy or inadequacy of a naturalistic account of subjectivity—and the form that subjectivity must therefore take. Such a summary is already an extraordinary economy. Nevertheless, there's a price to pay for endorsing naturalism's adequacy, though its gains are entirely straightforward. Let me offer a small tally of what would be essential to any satisfactory account of naturalism, drawing largely on what has already been admitted or confirmed or is obviously entailed by what has been confirmed.

Consider the following items as part of a reasonably well-formed, hardly strenuous compendium: (1) subjectivity (in all its graded variety) may be ascribed sui generis to whatever "is" or "has" a mind, the content of which is directly reportable at some paradigmatically human level of functioning or is taken by plausible analogy to be reportable, where attributed to sublinguistic animals; (2) experience, in the phenomenological sense, is, or is embedded in, what is intentionally structured, whether reported at the human level or imputed to human or animal manifestations of mind; (3) paradigmatically, the human mind is also profoundly "encultured" or "Intentional" (my preferred term, meaning its being profoundly enlanguaged and encultured, "penetrated" and "transformed"), so that the whole of human experience functions significantly and bears its own burden of determinable significance; and is, for such reasons, perspectived (or horizoned) as well, second-natured (or hybrid or artifactual), inherently and fluently reportable, publicly intelligible among similarly encultured subjects (who share a common ethos as their aggregated second-natured nature); (4) the mental appears to be irreducible in current physicalist terms (though it may indeed be treated as completely physicalist as such), preserving all of its admitted distinctions, and would then be conceptually intolerable among the sciences if characterized dualistically; it must therefore be biologically emergent (as well as prone to cultural transformation by way of the contingent penetration of its own natural competences, as in infancy), and, qua emergent, it must be indissolubly embodied or incarnate in one or another suitably developed, possibly quite diverse, physical or biological process; (5) the admission of sentient organisms, human or subhuman, to which suitably graded, suitably qualified experiences are aptly ascribed, even if not linguistically or reflexively reportable, requires, faute de mieux, admitting a relatively unitary site of internal common reference (in effect, the paradigmatic human self or some suitable sublinguistic analogue) regarding intentionally qualified subjective awareness, understanding, purpose, a measure of rational coherence fitted analogically to the distinct aptitudes of this or that species, purposive and experientially informed action, and the like—apart from whether the "site" thus acknowledged is merely formally or functionally assigned (grammatically, as it were) or construed in some more substantive way; (6) experience, responsibility, rationality are all holistically interrelated, appropriately affirmed or denied or analogically imputed along graded lines among the different species, normatively qualified, predicatively ascribed at each such site; furthermore, regarding such attributions, there seems to be no competing model of comparable flexibility and adequacy; (7) encultured human beings, second-natured as selves, serve as the Intentional paradigms of the sites admitted in (3) and are even more robustly construed when treated as the sites of specifically enlanguaged thought and experience or of rational response and purposive action; in fact, being a self or agent is actually experienced phenomenologically in self-referential thought (though not phenomenally, as Hume observes, as by sensation or perception), regardless of what we may think to be the true nature of the self; (8) as encultured or second-natured, selves share, through their own artifactual careers, historically formed, concrete, collectively predicated practices and traditions that define their Intentional competences; (9) the Intentional world (which includes, as in painting and architecture, parts of mere physical nature transformed, made hybrid by one or another form of human "utterance") is encultured and enlanguaged at a level "adequated" to the powers of agency (or creativity) of its member selves or subjects, through intelligent responses, purposeful action, feeling and emotion, perception and thought, concern and commitment, choice and deliberation, creativity and openness to evolving experience—in the sense in which the former (practices and traditions) constitute the second-natured public niches within which the equally second-natured aptitudes of the latter (thought and action) are first formed and, as a result, function suitably and well; consequently, each changes coordinately with changes in the other, and as a result, human selves may be said to "have" histories rather than natures (or to "be" histories), or to have hybrid natures that are no more than histories; (10) selves (or agents) must be denumerably individuated and reidentified, as the operative sites of perception, thought, action, and rationality, at every level of functioning at which such competences are ascribed; and (11) there is no reason to think that the items tallied as (1)–(10) and others like them need exceed the conceptual resources of any plausibly ample naturalism.[51]

It is certainly true that we do not yet understand the biological conditions under which consciousness and the prelinguistic modes of sentience, perception, and mentation arise. It's also true that the paradigmatic features of human subjectivity are sui generis, however suggestive the proto-cultural and communicative competences of sublinguistic creatures may be. But nothing so far admitted exceeds (or need exceed) the conceptual space of naturalism; and the insistence that what is paradigmatically human, or what human selves may be thought to share with possible "higher" beings (as yet unknown), viewed (still) as sui generis at its most advanced level of manifestation—which may indeed qualify Heidegger's conception of *Dasein*—has yet to demonstrate that no such admission could be accommodated or reasonably paraphrased within the space of nature.

I fully admit that "natural*izing*" (that is, physicalist reduction) and dualism (construed naturalistically) are philosophically problematic and, thus far at least, entirely unconvincing options. But it is one thing to say that scientism is a failed or inadequate naturalism and quite another to insist that the human *Dasein* cannot be satisfactorily construed in naturalistic terms. Regardless, Heidegger's phenomenology may be the best-known specimen of what may be counted as the final objection to a thoroughgoing naturalism. My sense is that, in meeting its challenge, we are greatly favored by arguments mustered against all the forms of cognitive privilege, a priori powers, extravagant or impossible, extremely vaguely defined or mysteriously potent, uncanny or even quasi-divine competences. For instance, Aristotle's account of *nous* in the *De Anima* (which suggests no biological basis) exceeds nature as we understand it. So does Plato's account, in the *Phaedo*, of the immortal psyche. So does Levinas's prioritizing existential encounters with *l'Autrui* before the applicability of rational categories of individuation and identity.[52]

Heidegger's phenomenology of *Dasein* (for instance, in *Being and Time* and *The Basic Problems of Phenomenology*) I find more illuminating, less abstract, more compelling than Husserl's various accounts of subjectivity, though the convergence between Husserl and Heidegger, once given the reclamation of Husserl's reflections on intersubjectivity, is striking enough. Still, Heidegger writes in a way that favors the existential uniqueness of *Dasein* more than the confirmation of the apodictic necessities of aprioristic inquiry. He remains an antinaturalist of course, but he speaks primarily against scientism and the treatment of selves as mere objects. That is surely the point of the "onto-ontological" doublet that is *Dasein*; the point of speaking of *Dasein*'s "existing"; the contrast between the universal "categories" of ontic analysis (applied to the human *Dasein*) and "existentialia"; the rejection (at the existential level) of the separability of one's own *Dasein*, the *Mitdasein* of others, and the world they share existentially; the meaning of "care" and the anticipation of death.[53]

Let me, therefore, place before you a specimen passage from *Being and Time* that catches up the spirit in which Heidegger offers his characteristic account—which confirms, almost instantly, the "protected" sense in which he distinguishes between categories and existentialia, the methodologically soft sense in which he means to feature the "primordial" transcendence of *Dasein*, and as a result, the ease with which his entire intent may be captured "naturalistically," if we but admit the uniqueness and unique openness of human existence.

The decisive adjustment favoring naturalism belongs to the Hegelian, post-Kantian, and pragmatist corrections of the excessive pretensions of Kantian apriorism (as promisingly sketched in Ernst Cassirer's and C. I. Lewis's proposals). It belongs also to countering scientism. I cannot see how Heidegger could possibly mean more; or, if he does mean more, why his findings would not be as problematic as Husserl's or Kant's alternatives. At his best, Heidegger is a naturalist manqué: in effect, once we accommodate Heidegger's existential themes (according to our own lights), it no longer matters whether we favor naturalism or what I've dubbed "extranaturalism": they come to the same thing substantively, though they diverge rhetorically.

Here is the passage from *Being and Time*:

The disclosedness of the *Mitda-sein* of others which belongs to being-with means that the understanding of others already lies in the understanding of being of Dasein because its being is being-with. This understanding, like all understanding, is not a knowledge derived from cognition, but a primordially existential kind of being which first makes knowledge and cognition possible.[54]

No more than three small observations are needed here. First: "knowledge and cognition" at the paradigmatically human level of comprehension presuppose the mastery of a language and home culture, which cannot (then) be "primordial" or innate or independent of the natural rearing of human infants; at best, they presuppose the enculturing (natural) transformation of the infant members of *Homo sapiens* into fully formed second-natured selves. The aprioristic rendering of this condition as primordial is simply the tautological elevation of a known part of the natural history of selves *as* (problematically) a sui generis, nonnaturalistic, necessary, transcendentally existential condition of whatever is characteristic of the empirically describable lives of humans (in effect, the "ontic") *and* of what is valued *there* (by Heidegger) as what is most essential and most arresting in the human world (in effect, the "ontological"). Second, psychological studies of neonates amply confirm that the linguistic achievements of infants presuppose innate, remarkably determinate prelinguistic social aptitudes of a communicative and playful nature that facilitate the rapid mastery of a home language (and associated culture) *and* the coordinate formation and maturation of an entire population of artifactual selves.[55] This, too, supports the adequacy of a naturalistic rendering of Heidegger's (as well as Husserl's) formulaic extravagances. Third, once we grasp the strategic importance of the fact that Kant's transcendentalism effectively "revived" an oblique version of the same Leibnizian and Wolffian rationalism Kant had already justifiably rejected, *our* continuing to invoke the "transcendental possibility" of any form of human cognition or understanding (under any guise) must be a "constructivist" (now, a naturalistic) posit drawn from the actual saliences of human life and experience.

The fate of Kant's view of the transcendental necessity of Euclid's geometry affords the classic confirmation (contra Kant) of the a posteriori standing (of any seemingly privileged version) of the a priori.[56] But then, all three considerations either defeat or achieve a provisional stalemate affecting the antinaturalistic pretensions of the entire play of Husserlian and Heideggerian phenomenology. You have only to bear in mind that the term "a priori" is pertinently used in two entirely different, irreconcilable ways in relation to our reading of the "transcendental": in one, we admit—with Kant, the post-Kantians, Hegel, Husserl, Heidegger, Cassirer, Sartre, Lewis, Apel, Habermas, and others—that *any* speculation about the conceptual conditions (the "possibility") of our powers of knowledge and understanding may be fairly called a priori, that is, as no more than what we are prepared to posit or postulate or presuppose as *their* "prior" enabling conditions, but without affirming any supposedly necessary synthetic truths about the matter; in the other, we are to believe—with Kant and Husserl preeminently, but not with Hegel and not with the Cassirer of "symbolic forms" or the Lewis of the "pragmatic a priori"—that the first sort of a priori leads inexorably to the discovery of what is said to be apodictic, unconditionally necessary, universally binding on the correct use of certain of our privileged powers of cognition, understanding, or reason. Here, neither Kant nor Husserl—nor Heidegger, Sartre, or Apel—offers any reason (beyond an obiter dictum) to treat the second sense of the a priori as demonstrably valid in any regard that compares favorably with the supposed validation of the first.

There is no such argument to be had: all known efforts are plainly arbitrary, vacuous, and self-serving. On the contrary, if we grant the advantage of Hegel's way of construing phenomenology over Husserl's, that is, conceding the complete informality and lack of privilege regarding what "appears," or refusing to favor (in Husserl's way) any "extranatural" method or criterion for first identifying what is genuinely "given" relative to Husserl's *epoché*, we cannot fail to see the completely question-begging nature of the transcendentalist form of the a priori.

I foresee no additional barriers of comparable importance against the prospects of reinterpreting the whole of the Eurocentric tradition in naturalistic terms. I find the intuition entirely persuasive, but it's also true that the argument in its favor is surprisingly straightforward. The human is not less than unique for all that, nor less impressive in its distinction. Yet what I find even more intriguing is that the philosophies of the Asian world—which we must surely join with our own in some relatively near future—have also been exploring in their own ways other forms of naturalism's economy. Given the example of the history of the physical sciences, I see no reason to doubt that the acceptance of naturalism may require an enrichment of what we should mean by the "natural," partly at least because it will also require an enrichment of what we should mean by the "physical."

3

Vicissitudes of Transcendental Reason

THERE'S A TOUCH OF UNGUARDED ANNOYANCE in one of Hilary Putnam's remarks, close to the end of his much-admired little book *Reason, Truth and History*, that captures what may be the fatal *pons* of the book's entire labor—possibly an even deeper lesson, if we probe a little more patiently. Countering a criticism of Richard Rorty's, which appears in Rorty's Presidential Address before the American Philosophical Association (1980) and which urges us to abandon all absolutes and accept the fact that "there is only the dialogue," Putnam asks:

Does this dialogue have an ideal terminus? Is there a *true* conception of rationality, a *true* morality, even if all we ever have are our *conceptions* of these? [Rorty says there is "only the dialogue"; there is "no ideal end" to our inquiries about truth and right conduct.] But how does [this] differ from [a] self-refuting relativism?

The implication is that there must be "a true conception of rationality" (even if we cannot locate it or say how it may be shown to be necessary); but there is nothing in the entire corpus of Putnam's publications to tell us what it is or must be. Putnam answers his own question this way: "The very fact that we speak of our different conceptions as different conceptions of *rationality* posits a *Grenzbegriff*, a limit-concept of the ideal truth."[1]

This *seems* to mean—it's the only plausible reading—that the denial that there is a *Grenzbegriff* (of truth, say) is incoherent or self-contradictory. Although Putnam (and Rorty) offers examples of self-contradictory forms of relativism, Putnam nowhere demonstrates that a self-consistent, coherent version of relativism is impossible, or is impossible wherever it pertinently addresses the well-known paradoxes generated in the ancient world (by Plato and Aristotle) or the putatively minimal requirements of systematicity anywhere in rational thought. The point at stake is not to hurry to endorse relativism but to ferret out what may be said for and against Putnam's problematic claim.

If Putnam were able to show that relativism was inherently self-contradictory or self-refuting in all of its seriously championed versions, that would certainly spell the end of a well-known industry; but I must frankly say I am unaware of any knockdown demonstration—though I've heard the charge often enough—and I cannot believe Putnam was persuaded by his own specimen cases to draw the general finding. He does not say precisely what he means by a "limit-concept," but I take him to mean a concept of a certain sort (particularly, the concept of truth, knowledge, or rationality or, in practical matters, of moral obligation, possibly even of human value or worth) that must take a universal or universalized form that can be shown to be true or valid or unavoidable as such by way of a dialectical analysis of the unacceptable paradoxes, incoherences, and self-contradictions generated by its denial. Putnam believes that relativism cannot fail to produce such consequences, though, again, I've never seen an argument (advanced by him or anyone else) that states and demonstrates precisely *what* a recognizable form of relativism must be committed to in virtue of which *any* relativism that effectively denied its opposed *Grenzbegriff* would, ipso facto, be self-refuting.

Rorty seized on Putnam's somewhat informal charge (since Putnam had also rejected "externalism" or "metaphysical realism" as indemonstrable) to charge him with being a relativist himself. I don't believe either Putnam or Rorty managed to shake the other's claim effectively—I don't believe either could! In fact, I think it is a vestige of an ancient prejudice that has ceased to be compelling, that an ampler pragmatism will surely find a way of surpassing.

Let me also draw your attention to the potential mare's nest of advancing the following tangle of separate doctrines, each of which strikes me as mistaken but which in context and in accord with other remarks of Putnam's, Putnam himself very likely believes: first, rational discourse of the sort Putnam mentions requires determinably ideal *Grenzbegriffe*; second, to deny that this is so commits us to "a self-refuting relativism"; third, relativism is, in any familiar form, self-contradictory; fourth, disallowing *Grenzbegriffe* commits pragmatism to relativism and hence to self-contradiction and/or incoherence; fifth, Rorty is therefore a relativist and (ineluctably) not a consistent pragmatist; and sixth, a consistent pragmatist must be committed to pertinent *Grenzbegriffe*—hence, to abandoning or severely modifying pragmatism itself. I don't believe I've seen any of Putnam's texts in which he actually opposes, denies, or rescinds any of these condemnations—all of which, as I say, strike me as false. Putnam clearly takes himself to be a pragmatist of a reasonably robust sort. But I doubt that he would reject as false all of the claims I've just tallied, and I don't know precisely how or whether he would now defend any of them as true. I don't see how, if *Grenzbegriffe* are meant to harbor anything like transcendental truths of the Kantian sort or "conceptual truths" of the sort Putnam has himself so tellingly challenged, or if *Grenzbegriffe* are no more than provisional signs of improvisational coherence and consistency, he could possibly treat as certain any of the findings just collected. But if he yielded on the contingency of conceptual truths (as his account of one of Euclid's theorems seems to signify), then it might well mean that he's abandoned the doctrine of the *Grenzbegriff* and then (as far as I can see) he would have to treat the self-refutation of relativism in an entirely different way from the burden of the remarks just cited.

Now, I do think Putnam *is* right in linking the denial of there being a "true" *Grenzbegriff* for rationality, morality, objective science, or the like and an implicit endorsement of some form of relativism, whether relativism proved to be "self-refuting" or not. Rorty does no better, but *Rorty's* "postmodernist" version of "pragmatism" protects him: he's not obliged to defend relativism, though he, too, nowhere shows that it must fail—and, of course, he has no intention of claiming that "dialogue" without *Grenzbegriffe* is actually self-refuting.

Let me begin again a little more slowly. There's a great deal that hangs on this seemingly minor skirmish. Putnam's worry is rather startling if you take it on its face: it poses the possibility—perhaps even the conviction (Putnam calls it a "philosophical temperament")—that the denial of an "ideal terminus" regarding truth and right conduct is, effectively, a commitment to a "self-refuting relativism." If true, that would be a very strong philosophical discovery. Nevertheless, as noted, Putnam opposes (or opposed, at the time of writing *Reason, Truth and History*) what he terms "the perspective of metaphysical realism," "externalism," "a God's Eye point of view"—what, elsewhere, he and others have called "objectivism."[2] The "perspective" he defends (defended at the time) he named "the *internalist* perspective, because it [was] characteristic of this view to hold that *what objects does the world consist of?* is a question that it only makes sense to ask *within* a theory or description." Putnam continues:

> "Truth," in an internalist view is some sort of (idealized) rational acceptability—some sort of ideal coherence of our beliefs with each other and with our experiences as those experiences *are themselves represented in our belief systems*—and not correspondence with mind-independent or discourse-independent "states of affairs." There is no God's Eye point of view that we can know or usefully imagine; there are only the various points of view of actual persons reflecting various interests and purposes that their descriptions and theories subserve.[3]

What Putnam says here is not particularly perspicuous, if we suppose that realism is not equivalent to, or does not entail, one or another form of idealism. I'm more or less sure that what Putnam means is at least that internalism is unwilling to admit any (Kantian-like) noumena—a stand I find more than reasonable, though it's very nearly irrelevant to the defense of realism. Garden-variety realisms *are* normally prepared to hold that true statements "correspond" to "mind-independent" states of affairs, which are not taken to be noumena: if only (1) "correspondence" is not thought to have any criterial force, and (2) what are mind-independent "states of affairs" may be validly determined by the use of some sort of critical or rational posit or construction. "Noumena" and "mind-independent states of affairs" are not, normally, treated as synonymous or coextensive terms. *Per impossibile*, noumena are the true objects of a God's-Eye point of view, a "metaphysical realism"; whereas mind-independent objects or states of affairs are vouchsafed as real on constructivist grounds, though they are not for that reason deemed to be constructed.

Beyond this more than verbal caution, it is certainly not clear that we *ever* have "a theory or description" of the whole of reality (except notionally). Putnam himself is quite insistent: "There is no God's Eye point of view that we can know or usefully imagine." Just so. I take the piety (if that is what it is) to be philosophically important. I have myself been impressed with a stronger expression of the same doctrine (without much in the way of piety) in Nicholas of Cusa's arguments. But I take Cusa's lesson to entail the indefeasibility of a viable relativism if, independently, relativism is at least coherent and self-consistent. In short, I take Putnam to have contradicted himself: either true *Grenzbegriffe* are impossible to grasp or recognize or they are themselves provisional artifacts internal to a "theory or description": hence, compatible with the adoption of one or another form of relativism. For if the "totality" of all that may be "given" in experience—in accord, say, with something akin to Hegel's phenomenology (in effect, "the Absolute")—cannot be grasped by finite thought, then some form of relativism (if relativism may otherwise be coherently and self-consistently formulated) will be an ineliminable option for realists of every viable stripe.[4] (So Rorty is right, after all.)

It's in the spirit of such distinctions that Putnam famously rejects "the 'Brain in a Vat' hypothesis [in effect, completely contextless truths] . . . as a mere linguistic construction and not a possible world at all." He explains that "the supposition that there could be a world in which *all* sentient beings are Brains in a Vat presupposes from the outset a God's Eye view of truth, or, more accurately, a No Eye view of truth—truth as independent of observers altogether."[5] Furthermore, when, more recently, Putnam repudiated the "internal realism" thesis, he nowhere affirmed (as far as I know) that he meant to abandon the minimal "internalist" postulate that "truth [*is not*] independent of observers altogether" or, as a corollary, the claim that metaphysical realism *is not* true.

But then, we are left dangling as to whether the doctrine of the *Grenzbegriff* is, as Putnam believes Rorty insinuates, the admission of a closet relativist. If truth is not "independent of observers altogether," there would seem to be no obvious reason why the dependence must be (or even can be) uniform in any universalist or objectivist way: no reason, for instance, if, as Putnam has himself maintained (at least recently), there are undoubtedly truths that are humanly impossible to verify; or if humans could never know the totality of all that is true.[6]

For, if *some* truths, on the contingent evidence we have, are impossible for humans to verify—or, as with the belief prevailing just before Michelson's successful measurement of the speed of light, which held that light could not be measured by any known method and very likely could never be measured at all—we could never be sure (1) that any presently formed body of science was not erroneously skewed in a way that might be "corrected" by further discovery (which would itself remain at risk in the same way: think of Mendeleev's achievement, despite a mistaken anticipation of what was to become the atomic model of the periodic table of elements); or (2) admitting (1), that we could ever overcome, completely and irreversibly, all nonconvergent, relativistically opposed explanatory theories, descriptions tethered to such theories, or strategies and methods of confirmation and disconfirmation that permitted such stalemates to persist.

But if all this is true, then Putnam's rejection of metaphysical realism, read in the light of his having reversed himself on his former adherence to a seemingly pragmatist version of antirealism, would seem to support a "relativized" view of *Grenzbegriffe* or at least an acknowledgment of the probable viability of some form of relativism.

Putnam may well have misread Peirce's well-known conception of fallibilism. Putnam claims that Peirce and Apel are committed to a "wrong theory of truth." In Putnam's account, Peirce holds that "*it is metaphysically impossible for there to be any truths that are not verifiable by human beings.*"7 But this misreads in a peculiarly wooden way the perfectly clear sense of Peirce's doctrine. For what Peirce means (it's possible Apel does not view the matter this way) is that—in that sense that Putnam himself endorses: namely, there are truths it would be impossible for humans ever to verify (in any literal sense of verifying)—it still makes good pragmatist sense to bring the idea of *un*verifiable truths into line with the pragmatist model of truth, even where, as with "infinite inquiry," verification is literally impossible. (The issue will take on a more pointed meaning when we turn to Jürgen Habermas and Karl-Otto Apel.)

In Peirce's hands, fallibilism cannot count on the verifiability of every well-formed belief; Peirce's doctrine holds that the conjectured, infinite extension of critical inquiry (which we can never reach by finite means) may yet, through rational *hope* (but hardly verification), construe what we suppose would be believed "in the long run" *to be, ideally, congruent with* our best conception of what can now be validated. To read this correctly is, effectively, to grasp the sense in which Putnam's own idiom of an ideally universalized *Grenzbegriff* can be no more than a "fallibilist" variant of the same insight that a more relativistically minded fallibilist (myself, for instance) would construe in an idiom that more explicitly supports what Putnam is plainly drawn to in his own analysis of "conceptual truths." I cannot see how Putnam can escape the import of his own excellent argument.

Consider, further, that it is hardly an incoherent possibility that there may be a number of flourishing, reasonably well-grounded moral visions incompatible with one another but capable of incorporating enough common ground to be fruitfully debated. I would say that Kuhn's and Feyerabend's speculations lead to a similar conclusion regarding the natural sciences. As I read the issue, what needs to be grasped, against the anti-Protagorean doctrine of the *Theaetetus* (*and* what seems to be Putnam's implied charge against relativism as such), is simply that "P is true" cannot, in the relativist's best sense, be read as "P is true-in-L" (for any particular language, world, set of social practices, theories, or the like). With that single adjustment, I think it's fair to say that both Peirce and Dewey (though in rather different ways) construe pragmatism as open to relativistic claims, though open as well to verifiability and warranted assertibility (short of verification). Note, please, that what, bivalently, may be found true or verified "in L" (but, say, not "in L'") is not equivalent to being "true-in-L."

The interesting fact is that Putnam and Rorty each denied that *he* was a relativist; each accused the other of being a relativist; and each failed to demonstrate that he himself escaped the other's charge. Quite a piece of work.

Furthermore, Putnam does say with assurance (and some satisfaction)—in his Carus Lectures (1985), four years after the publication of *Reason, Truth and History* and nine years before his Dewey Lectures (in which he abandons "internal realism" without quite saying whether he abandons "all" of it)—that "the idea of a 'point at which' subjectivity ceases and Objectivity-with-a-capital-O begins has proved chimerical," a thesis he explicitly defends as part of "the essence of 'internal realism.'"[8] But if you conjoin *this* demurrer and the charge against the "Brain in a Vat" thesis, it looks very much as if Putnam *cannot* demonstrate that there must be a *Grenzbegriff* (apart from not being able to "locate" it, or invoke any privileged powers of transcendental Reason by which to prove, pertinently, that there must be one). And if that's true, then it looks as if Rorty is right to suggest that Putnam *is* a closet relativist[9]—and the concession itself suggests we are right to think that Rorty is also a relativist. It needs only to be said that relativism is *not* the principal issue at all: it's the unavoidability of treating realism as a contingent constructivist posit wherever cognitive privilege is rejected. Also, Putnam's argument may signify that he cannot be a pragmatist in anything like Dewey's sense.

The story has gotten muddled very quickly. I hasten to add the following considerations to keep our options clear. First, if we hold that *Grenzbegriffe* are unqualifiedly mind independent, then we *are* unredeemed "objectivists" pure and simple; and if we hold that they are mind dependent in some sense even if independent in another, then we must be "internalists" of some sort *and* will have implicitly admitted the (as yet unsecured) possibility of an adequate and self-consistent relativism. But second, Putnam will have placed himself in double jeopardy, because he will not yet have demonstrated that there are any "ideal" *Grenzbegriffe* either dependent on, or independent of, mind, or that denying that there are genuine *Grenzbegriffe* must commit us to a "self-refuting relativism."

If so, then, third, internalism will surely take two entirely different forms: a subjectivist form (Kant's, notoriously, according to Hegel's critique and that of other post-Kantians); and a form in which the subjective and objective aspects of phenomenological experience are indissolubly linked from the start (which, as we have in effect seen, would stalemate, post-Kant and post-Hegel, any and all disjunctive oppositions between realism and idealism in the epistemological sense, without ever yielding to Kantian subjectivism and without endorsing idealism in the metaphysical sense). But if that is so, then Putnam has simply confused and conflated options akin to Kant's subjectivism and Hegel's commitment to *Erscheinungen*—a mistake analogous to that of conflating noumena and mind-independent things. In any case, the fate of relativism would no longer depend on the prior fate of *Grenzbegriffe*. Their fates would be seen to be different sides of the same issue.

I take the liberty of mentioning again that I have always admired Cusa's splendid scruple in holding (in *On Learned Ignorance*) that "absolute knowledge" belongs to God alone; effectively, human speculation proceeds, in a practical way, without any grasp of the inclusive boundaries of God's Creation (knowing which would have been tantamount to sharing God's absolute knowledge); and as a consequence, all human inquiry must (as we might now suppose) be relativistic, at least in this regard. It follows directly, for Cusanus, that we cannot establish in a principled way the numerical identity of what, under relevant conditions, appears to be one and the same thing.[10] But if that is so, then the *Grenzbegriff* proposal must fail utterly; and then, Putnam's preference for some sort of "pluralism"—really, a "plurality" of ways of formulating *the same or equivalent truth-claims*, *not* a way of admitting the objective validity of a diverse plurality of metaphysical claims that on a bivalent model of truth (but not now) would be deemed incompatible among themselves when read in realist terms—may have to leave unsettled the matter of whether the latter sort of plurality must yield "somewhere" (to invoke Aristotle's idiom but to speak with Putnam) in the direction of a uniquely idealized limit-concept. I see no way that the *Grenzbegriff* can guide us here: it cannot possibly identify what Putnam claims we must rely on.

Let me add, therefore, several small bits from Putnam's texts to strengthen the puzzle's force—and draw out its lesson. First, Putnam concedes (in the Carus Lectures): "Whether we want to be there or not, science has put us in the position of having to live without foundations. It was shocking when Nietzsche said this, but today it is commonplace: *our* historical position—and no end to it is in sight—is that of having to philosophize without 'foundations.'"[11] I take this to "concur" with Nicholas's thesis—and with my appraisal of the meaning of Putnam's relying on his *Grenzbegriff*.

Second, Putnam declares, in *Reason, Truth and History*, that "truth is an *idealization* of rational acceptability."[12] I cannot deny that one would, *ideally*, want such an idealization to rest on a unique limit-concept; but I don't see how it can be guaranteed, and I don't see that it would be incoherent, under the conditions Putnam concedes, to restrict the play of relativism as much as possible without actually precluding it altogether.

It's true that Putnam's formulation (joining the two remarks just cited) is, according to the account of *The Collapse of the Fact/Value Dichotomy*, an antirealist doctrine that Putnam now eschews. So I would not want to rely too heavily on this sort of formulation. Nevertheless, I find no clear answer in Putnam as to how truth in the realist sense is to be conceived, if it ranges over truths impossible to verify. Peirce, you remember, rather cannily noticed that even his fallibilistic argument held that, though truth remains independent of the opinions of "you and me," it cannot be altogether independent of human opinion as such. If that's antirealism (and Putnam thinks it is), then I'd say Putnam cannot escape antirealism (which, of course, is not in the least incompatible with accepting realism).

Putnam also admits "we cannot really attain epistemically ideal conditions, or even be absolutely certain that we have come sufficiently close to them"—although, he also claims, puzzlingly, that "we can approximate them to a very high degree of approximation." But to admit the relativistic threat posed by the problem of the *Grenzbegriff* is *not* (as Putnam seems to think it is) tantamount to allowing that "both a statement and its negation could [then] be 'justified'"—a possibility regarding which he adds: "even if conditions were as ideal as one could hope to make them, there is [there would be] no sense in thinking of the statement as *having* a truth-value."[13] I think you cannot fail to see how the quarrel between Rorty and Putnam sidles into Peirce's grand puzzle regarding finite and infinite inquiry and the distinction between realism and idealism—and, now, relativism. Putnam *assumes* the inviolable restriction of bivalence here, but I don't find the clinching argument in anything he says. His difficulty suggests, I may as well add, the relativistic tolerance of Dewey's notion of "warranted assertibility."[14]

The best Putnam might say is that, under a relativistic reading of how to construct a *Grenzbegriff* (which would set limits to the effective scope of bivalence), we might simply have two statements to appraise that, assuming a standard bivalent logic—*but not now*—would, *effectively, be or entail negations* of one another. *Now*, under a laxer rule of truthlike values, they might easily be entitled to count as no more than (let us say) "warranted" or "unwarranted" (rather than "true" or "false" in the standard sense). Here, without paradox or contradiction, our statements might still be evidentiarily supported in a rigorous way. I cannot see how Putnam means to defeat such a possibility. (To admit relativistic values is, trivially, to admit more options than bivalent truth-values can afford.)

Putnam returns to the topic again in his Hermes Lectures (2001) to pursue two further considerations: one amounts to a benign aside on plurality and relativity; the other introduces a significant advance on the topic of "conceptual truth," which, on my reading, enormously strengthens the relativistic option applied (in effect) to Kant's reasoning about the transcendental necessity of Euclid's geometry. The first issue comes to this: Putnam shows very clearly that we can, if we wish, count or describe the contents of a room in two different vocabularies in such a way that the descriptions would be "cognitively equivalent (in the sense that any phenomenon whose explanation can be given in one of the optional languages involved has a corresponding explanation in the other), but which are incompatible if taken at face value (the descriptions cannot be simply conjoined)." This, Putnam now labels "conceptual relativity," emphasizing the optional standing of the vocabularies in question (relative to cognitive equivalence, whether, say, with respect to description or counting), without permitting such usage to claim any substantive ontological force for the *different* descriptions.

The situation would be entirely different, he adds, if we attempted to describe the contents of a room in terms of its furniture and also in terms, say, of "fields and particles" (which vocabularies do *not* appear to be incompatible and are not cognitively equivalent). About the second scenario, Putnam says: "That we can use both of these schemes without being required to reduce one or both of them to some single fundamental and universal ontology is the doctrine of pluralism. . . . [W]hile conceptual relativity implies pluralism, the reverse is not the case."[15]

It's clear, therefore, that cognitive equivalence (among Putnam's examples) depends on a prior logical convention that precludes incompatibility just where incompatibility (in description, interpretation, appraisal, or something of the sort) is bound to arise (for a bivalent logic)—as among relativistic claims. So the analysis does not yet bear on the puzzle regarding Putnam's *Grenzbegriff*. (It's not meant to, of course.) In the second scenario, Putnam offers a very trim proposal about delimiting pluralism. But the constraints are such that pluralism now proves to be compatible (thus far) with both objectivism and relativism—and not more easily with one than with the other. So pluralism cannot yet be invoked to defeat relativism. (But perhaps it, too, is not meant to be used that way.) The trouble is that Putnam does not quite see that the defense of the *Grenzbegriff* has still to be supplied.

Putnam's discussion of conceptual truths is, I would say, spectacularly strong. He is not concerned to limit his account to Quine's analytic/synthetic distinction but favors instead "an older view, one represented by both Hegelians and pragmatists at the beginning of the twentieth century." (I think he must have had at least C. I. Lewis in mind, but he doesn't mention him.) In any case, Putnam's argument shows very clearly that one must give up "the idea that *every* truth can be classified as either a conceptual truth *or* a description of fact." The analysis can be brought to bear in a particularly effective way on transcendental a priori arguments—in particular, on Kant's account of Euclid's geometry (which profoundly affects the systematic pretensions of the first *Critique*) and of every other strong form of transcendentalism. Putnam explains:

What makes a truth a conceptual truth, as I am using the term, is that it is impossible to make (relevant) sense of the assertion of its negation. This way of understanding the notion of conceptual truth fits well with the recognition that conceptual truth and empirical description interpenetrate; for when we say that the denial of a certain statement makes no sense, we always speak within the body of beliefs and concepts and conceptual connections that we accept, and it sometimes happened that a scientific revolution overthrows enough of those background beliefs that *we come to see how* something that previously made no sense *could* be true. A by now familiar example is the discovery that there actually exist triangles whose angles add up to more than two right angles.[16]

In a nutshell: anyone who would have ventured to say what Putnam offers (about triangles), *in 1700*, "would have been speaking gibberish."[17] So Kant's well-known view of Euclid's geometry ceased to be a conceptual truth as a result of historical developments in mathematics! What was once a reasonable candidate for the status of conceptual truth ceased to be one in due course. I think we have here the briefest *reductio* of transcendental necessity that we could possibly imagine. But why wouldn't it be reasonable to treat Putnam's conjecture about his own *Grenzbegriff* as another would-be conceptual truth—one that has been effectively overthrown by Hegel and Nietzsche and the pragmatists—and his own more recent reflections?

You realize that Peirce's realist account of his own fallibilism has the effect of muting the relativistic possibilities inherent in his evolutionism. The exposé of Peirce's equivocal account of realism and idealism (in the post-Kantian sense), therefore, greatly enlarges the conceptual resources of a pragmatism drawn to effecting a rapprochement of the whole of Eurocentric philosophy. Here, relativism makes sense only if confined to finite inquiry; but if so, then it comes to much the same thing as Peirce's commitment to rational Hope: "Absolute" Hope, let us call it, to invent a Hegelian-like idiom that exceeds the possibility of finite knowledge (though, in the *Phenomenology*, Hegel speaks of its ancestral form as "Absolute knowing," which is itself a form of interpretive conjecture about the meaning of what we believe we know rather than an occasion of confirmed knowledge in its own right) extended (by Peirce) to the infinite continuum (the "long run") of inquiry. You now begin to see the sense in which, per Hegel (however Peirce may have gained his knowledge of Hegel), Peirce's commitment to rational Hope counts as an a posteriori alternative to Kantian transcendentalism.[18]

I FIND IT UNLIKELY that, in responding to Rorty's charge, Putnam was not aware how difficult it would be to support his *Grenzbegriff* thesis on pragmatist grounds. He risks too much on a mere obiter dictum; he cannot have supposed that the clinching argument was self-evident or would be conceded on no more than his say-so by an opponent like Rorty—or by readers open to respectable persuasion. Something akin to what he says does indeed appear in James's lax idiom, but you cannot (I'm prepared to guess) find any plausible support in the more careful efforts of either Dewey or Peirce—and the doctrine cannot possibly be vintage pragmatism. Is it perhaps a synthetic a priori truth?

Putnam remains one of the most perceptive contemporary discussants of these matters, but he seems to be in the grip of an ideology here. It's actually contrary to his usual practice to dangle such a claim without the least sketch of its supporting argument. I single Putnam out, therefore, not to batter his views but to isolate the most telling clues we have confirming the apparent futility of recent efforts, particularly among the friends of pragmatism, to secure any would-be principles of "universal reason" or "common sense," whether in practical or theoretical matters, of a gauge appropriate to validating *Grenzbegriffe*, rules of universal morality, or conceptual or transcendental(ist) truths of any sort. There *is* no faculty of Reason; there are no transcendental faculties of any kind. There are transcendental questions; but there are no reliable or constant or necessary truths of Reason that could possibly direct us, ampliatively, in science or morality. If there were, pragmatism would be utterly untenable.

Putnam himself has shown the way: his own account of conceptual truths demonstrates as conclusively as anyone has that such would-be findings rely on faute de mieux grounds that are normally overtaken by evolving historical or empirical discovery. Hegel's critique of Kant's first *Critique*, the doubtful autonomy of Husserl's *epoché*, Peirce's abductive intuition of transcendental Hope, Cassirer's constructed "symbolic forms," C. I. Lewis's "pragmatic a priori," Kuhn's "paradigm shifts," the admittedly ideological status of John Rawls's "lexical" principles drawn from the "original position," even the supposed nativist fixity of Chomsky's "universal grammars" and the near-vacuity of Wittgenstein's *Lebensform* (treated as an elusive source of a priori truths) confirm in a variety of ways the general futility of believing otherwise: informally described, all are variant forms of would-be conceptual or transcendental truths, the conformable targets of the exposés intended or the gist of the exposés themselves.[19]

You cannot fail to see that Putnam's advocacy of *Grenzbegriffe*, his defense of pluralism, and his dismissal of relativism are versions (or corollaries) of one and the same doctrine—I say, one and the same dogma—affirmed but nowhere vindicated.

Our remarkable appetite for the dictates of Reason, which already appears at the beginning of Western philosophy, is a dreadful trap that has siphoned off our energies from the better prospects of what to believe and do under the conditions of practical life. Putnam is the victim (it seems) of a deep longing that apparently will not subside, that takes the form (in him) of worrying whether our grip on objectivity could possibly survive admitting any form of relativism. At the very least, it is a little startling to find that he senses no incongruity between the ideal function of his *Grenzbegriff* and the standard pragmatist resistance to invariances of any kind. I mean to justify a conjectural leap from Putnam to Jürgen Habermas and, by that, to compare the recent German and American uses of pragmatism. Bear with me, please.

By "Reason" (written with a capital *R*), I understand a would-be blunderbuss faculty apt for discerning or judging what, invariantly, universally, or necessarily, is true or right—or rightly constrains whatever may be judged to be true or right. Putnam is no partisan of Reason conceived so baldly, but his question leads inexorably in Reason's direction: he offers no qualification of any kind.

He opposes any cognitive faculty thought to guide us in choosing the best of all possible conjectures vis-à-vis the ideal laws of a perfected natural science.[20] He plainly takes such notions to be false leads, and he counters with a pluralist proposal. But with the best will in the world, one cannot say precisely where Putnam stands on the issue of realism. As we know, he rejects "the *externalist* perspective," "a God's Eye point of view," objectivism—which claims that "the world consists of some fixed totality of mind-independent objects. There is exactly one true and complete description of 'the way the world is.' Truth involves some sort of correspondence relation between words or thought-signs and external things and sets of things."[21] He rejects this view all right; and he rejects what he calls the "*criterial* conception of rationality," according to which "there are institutionalized norms which define [as by necessary and sufficient conditions] what is and what is not rationally acceptable." He associates the second doctrine (somewhat tenuously) with Wittgenstein, with the positivists, and with the Oxford ordinary language philosophers. He finds the idea fraught with insuperable difficulties. Nevertheless, precisely in saying all that, although he thereby undermines the prospects of his own *Grenzbegriff*, he *does* affirm the *Grenzbegriff* but offers no conceptual grounds for his conviction. The question nags therefore: Are there any favorable arguments to call on? I confess I know of none that are compelling. In fact, I feel sure that Putnam's attack on objectivism converges with the force of Theodor Adorno's excellent *mot*, "The whole is the false."[22]

What I mean is that although the argument in favor of the *Grenzbegriff* may have been a mistake, Putnam clearly means to hold to a strong realism that would at least preclude relativism at the same time it would escape objectivism (the God's-Eye view). What I suggest instead is, first, there is no obvious incompatibility between realism and relativism, though such a union would rule out any realism that would unconditionally disallow limitations on the principled adequacy of a bivalent logic; and, second, it is quite improbable that a pragmatism, qualified in the ways Putnam admits obtain in our time, could fail to yield in the direction of a conjunction of realism and relativism—possibly, then, also a union of realism and historicism and/or incommensurabilism. And if that were true, then just as any transcendentalism of Kant's or Husserl's sort would now be challenged out of hand, Karl-Otto Apel's and Jürgen Habermas's late attempts at universalism are bound to fail as well. The argument begins to take a heterodox turn. I should perhaps mention the possibility that Putnam may wish to distinguish additionally between objectivism and the God's-Eye view by qualifying the first, but not the second, by the adjustment he now calls pluralism—although pluralism seems to be largely occupied (even for Putnam) with conventions of descriptive convenience rather than with metaphysically consequential theories addressed to foundational issues.[23]

But if you go this far, if you support the regulative function of *Grenzbegriffe* in the defense of a realism that rejects the God's-Eye view and falls back to pluralism, then you must construe realism in constructivist (contingent) terms; and you must also separate the defense of the indissolubly conjoint functioning of the subjective and objective sources of our cognitive competence from any idealist ontology, all the while admitting that, post-Kant and post-Hegel, epistemology and metaphysics are, finally, one and the same discipline. The only possible solution entails acknowledging the incoherence of noumenalism and the insuperably conjectural nature of whatever we posit as a fair picture of the independent world. But then the argument forces us (and Putnam) to concede that if relativism could be made coherent and self-consistent, we would be unable to rule out the compatibility of realism and relativism; and then to advocate *Grenzbegriffe* (in Putnam's way) would be as illicit a version of noumenalism as (metaphysical) representationalism has been shown to be.

A congruent conclusion, we may infer, was already latent in Hegel's critique of Kant's first *Critique*. It counts as a genuine piece of philosophical progress, but it is certainly not an apriorist pronouncement. So, when

Rorty returns toward the close of his career to a version of the presidential remark (*his* remark) that originally provoked Putnam's advocacy of his thesis about the *Grenzbegriff*, Rorty exposed the philosophical arbitrariness of *his own* labored disjunction between the "postmodernist" innovation of "philosophical conversation" and the patient fine-tuning of the epistemologies and metaphysics of those he had earlier derided.[24]

Putnam's avowal rests on an uncertain compromise, which he now presses in the direction he calls pluralism: "We must have criteria of rational acceptability to even have an empirical world . . . these reveal part of our notion of an optimal speculative intelligence."[25] Here, Putnam ventures a kind of conceptual or transcendental truth. (Conceptual and transcendental truths behave quite similarly and are vulnerable in similar ways, but they are not necessarily the same. Kant, you remember, argued transcendentally that space and time were "pure" forms of intuition, though he was well aware that prominent figures of his day opposed his doctrine—took space and time to be objective features of the world.) Put in the slimmest way, Putnam's *Grenzbegriff* and Habermas's appeal to Reason risk being irreconcilable with any legible form of naturalism—broadly speaking, for the same reasons: that is, because no one can rightly define just how they are supposed to be distinguished and tested, or how they are to function in ordinary discourse. There is, of course, a role for "speculative" criticisms of whatever we might contend is rationally necessary or best—but "an *optimal* speculative intelligence"? No. Not until we are able to confirm Kant's transcendentalism *or* convert Charles Peirce's "transcendental Hope" into something more robust in the Kantian manner.

I add, as a sort of forewarning, that neither Habermas nor Apel, who are certainly friends of pragmatism and who have labored very hard to explain the sense in which pragmatism and transcendentalism are compatible—or more—have absolutely no argument to offer stronger than or even as strong as the account of the *Grenzbegriffe* Putnam is prepared to provide. Hence, to have shown the inherent weakness of Putnam's account is to anticipate the failure of their alternative as well. (I've been reading Putnam as a stalking horse.)

Husserl, you recall, was pleased to find an anticipation of his method of "eidetic variation" in William James's *Psychology*, embedded in empirical cases. He had a point, though James was never systematic in Husserl's way. But if Putnam, as a late pragmatist drawn to James (who, as I say, invokes the term *Grenzbegriff*), ever intended to reproach Rorty in a Jamesian spirit akin to Husserl's, we might claim here the unexpected advantage of a pragmatist simplification of both by way of a benign a priori constructivism (that is, the a posteriori posit of an a priori condition) to replace all versions of Kantian and Husserlian transcendentalism (for example, by "abductive" means!).

That would be an enormous leap. It is certainly true that C. I. Lewis's account of the "pragmatic a priori" speaks in an idiom close to James's but in a manner incomparably stronger and more assured, in a way that remains "Kantian" and "Peircean"—and realist—and, given Husserl's conjecture about James, possibly phenomenological as well. All in all, Lewis's forceful rendering of the a priori along pragmatist lines anticipates the recoverable lesson of Putnam's original critique of Rorty—except that Putnam hardly seems to have in mind a pragmatist reading of his *Grenzbegriff*.

The point is that pragmatism affords a model of a priori improvisation (abduction, let us say) that is at once naturalistic, constructivist, fitted to the realist and consensual interests of human inquiry, not in the least essentialist or privileged, centered on the continuity of the a priori and the a posteriori in terms of historicized and tolerable contingency, satisfied with conceptual truths of the sort Putnam concedes, and as much concerned with the existential a priori as with its specifically cognitional form. All this is already present in James and Peirce—and Lewis. (I shall delay airing Lewis's treatment of transcendental reason until I turn to Habermas.) But all these themes come together in a surprisingly simple and compelling way in the following relaxed passage from James's *Psychology*, which, to my mind, shows deeper affinities with Heidegger's transcendental speculations than with Husserl's:

> The *fons et origo of all reality, whether from the absolute or personal point of view, is . . . subjective, is ourselves. . . . [A]s thinkers with emotional reactions, we give what seems to us a . . . higher degree of reality to whatever things we select and emphasize and turn to* WITH A WILL. *These are our* living *realities. . . . Reality, starting from our Ego, thus sheds itself from point to point—first, upon all objects which show an immediate sting of interest for our Ego in them, and next, upon the objects most continuously related to them. . . .*
>
> The world of living realities as contrasted with unrealities is thus anchored in the Ego, considered as an active and emotional term. That is the hook from which the rest dangles, the absolute support. And as from a painted hook it has been said that one can only hang a painted chain, so conversely, from a real hook only a real chain

can properly be hung. *Whatever things have intimate and continuous connection with my life are things of whose reality I cannot doubt.*[26]

If I read James right, our a priori categories are, in effect, constructed posits—they may be tacitly habituated—of what, according to our lights, promise to set out in coherent order what, provisionally, is best counted (here and now) as "real" and "unreal" with regard to our description and understanding of our "natural" experience of a common world. None of this is thought to be invulnerable to pragmatic revision. We remain subject (in the pragmatist's way) to the flux of the world, the contingencies of evolving experience, changed convictions, and consensual solidarity. As a result, the a priori and the a posteriori are no more than perspectival opposites abstracted within the course of inquiry itself—each drawing, dialectically, on the other in a way distinctly (though distantly) informed by Friedrich Schelling's and Hegel's sense of the reciprocal influence of the natural and the transcendental. In this extremely promising sense, pragmatism—more palpably in James and Peirce than in Dewey—shows us a way of saving the contribution of the a priori without invoking the extranaturalist presumptions of Kant and Husserl.[27]

I must note that the most sustained effort to "naturalize" Kantian transcendental arguments in the pragmatist way belongs to Sami Pihlström. (The choice of term is Pihlström's, which, all to the good, does not at all conform with the scientistic reading of "naturalize" favored by Quine and Donald Davidson. I myself restrict the term "naturalize" as signifying a reductive version of naturalism; otherwise, I speak of "naturalistic" renderings, which impose limits of their own but are not reductionistic.) Pihlström joins Christopher Hookway in noting Peirce's critical appraisal of transcendental arguments: this is at least part of what he means by demonstrating "how the perspectives of transcendental argumentation and pragmatism can be synthesized in late-Wittgensteinian philosophy of language." I find Pihlström very plausible here: he's right to note that "realism" (in the familiar sense favored in the standard literature of the philosophy of science) cannot capture Peirce's subtlety or indeed the inherent constraints of transcendental arguments.

Nevertheless, if what I've just remarked about the quarrel between Putnam and Rorty holds, then I cannot quite agree with Pihlström's constructivism (which he admits is tantamount to an idealism). I suggest that Pihlström needn't have characterized matters in the way he does: "transcendental idealism" holds only insofar as epistemology and metaphysics are treated as indistinguishable (as well as inseparable) *and* strongly Kantian; but since pragmatism is not transcendental*ist*, it need not be ontologically idealist in the Kantian way. Here is what Pihlström says:

> Pragmatism, at least in the (re)transcendentalized form I defend it here, is in a way a form of transcendental idealism, albeit (or so I shall claim) a (non-reductively) naturalistically acceptable one. It retains the basic idea of Kant's idealism, viz., that the world is, in some sense, *our construction* and dependent on us regarding its ontological constitution and cognizability. We *normatively (de jure) determine*, through our practices, what the objects of our world must be like.[28]

Pihlström equivocates—unnecessarily—on the epistemological and ontological aspects of the issue: a "naturalized" transcendental "idealism" of the classic pragmatist sort (in Pihlström's idiom) need not, perhaps cannot, support an explicitly idealist ontology. Pihlström has gone too far here.

It was just for this sort of reason that I began with Putnam. I was persuaded to regard the advantage of isolating the failure of Putnam's appeal to his *Grenzbegriff* as a quick clue to identifying a similar weakness in Habermas's related exertion.[29] The flaw they share may be put this way: first, what each seeks is flat-out incompatible with the pragmatism he embraces; and, second, the argument each favors founders at a deeper level as the result of a lacuna (that must, but cannot, be filled) that threatens to reinstate what each is at pains to disallow. The very nature of the "contingent a priori" each requires comes easily into focus then: Kant's full-blown transcendentalism simply overshoots its resources—must fall back to what James calls the *fons et origo* of the second-order "possibility" of our "natural attitude" and powers. But what *is* second-order here, as well as a priori, may be admitted only if we abandon all presumption of reflexive, facultative privilege, whether cognitive or ratiocinative.

There's the common ground sketched by James and Peirce and Lewis—that reaches back to Hegel and forward (problematically) to Heidegger, Merleau-Ponty, Sartre, Dewey, Putnam, and McDowell, and now Pihlström. Perhaps the questioning that is genuinely needed (which Kant obviously discovered but misjudged—magnificently as well as indefensibly) should no longer be called "transcendental," since the epithet conveys (when applied to Kant) an irresistible insinuation of privilege: Heidegger affords the knockdown evidence, and Habermas wrestles with the clear knowledge that Apel violates the spirit of Peirce's retreat to the resources of "transcendental" Hope. Perhaps the emerging discipline might be better named *autoréférence* (as has been recently signaled) to draw attention to its Kantian lineage and transformed use as distinctly conjectural (though a priori) beyond the entire post-Kantian tradition still occupied with Kant's specific transcendentalism.[30] (You may glimpse here the possibility of a deeper reading of James's contribution to pragmatism—in the use of his leaner idiom in our rendering Heidegger's discoveries in surprisingly compliant naturalistic terms, in the service of a generous rapprochement of the whole of Eurocentric philosophy.)

Before proceeding further, let me offer another clue from an American source—from Donald Davidson's criticism of Thomas Kuhn, which has the merit of sketching a minimal argument of precisely the sort Putnam and Habermas must be seeking—which Davidson realizes would, if confirmed, reconcile at a stroke the contemporary forms of objectivism that descend from Descartes (without explicit appeal to epistemic privilege) and the play of historically contingent, divergent beliefs that would otherwise scuttle the arch objectivity the first intends to secure. It's a clue drawn from what Putnam calls the "externalist perspective." Here is what Davidson says—I leave it unanalyzed; I offer it only to leaven what I shall shortly say about Putnam and Habermas (though I have analyzed it in some depth elsewhere):

> The dominant metaphysics of conceptual relativism, that of differing points of view, seems to betray an underlying paradox. Different points of view make sense, but only if there is a common co-ordinate system on which to plot them; yet the existence of a common system belies the claim of dramatic incommensurability [that is, betrays, on Davidson's reading, the unintelligibility of incommensurable "conceptual schemes"].[31]

This is a notorious, even cleverly worded, charge that Davidson nowhere shows bears directly on *any* well-known philosophical position or any well-formed vision of relativism or incommensurabilism—say, to be specific, the views of Thomas Kuhn and Paul Feyerabend. I ask you only to bear in mind the similarity between what Davidson says here and what Putnam says about his *Grenzbegriff*. The two agree (with almost nothing in the way of argument) in affirming that relativism is (must be) incoherent. But Davidson explicitly affirms that if (impossibly) relativism *were* viable, it could be defended only by reference to a "Cartesian" conceptual grid that would permit us to plot *all* nonparadoxical conceptions together!

Read in the sense Davidson intends, that would be completely incompatible with the conditions of conceptual relativism's or incommensurabilism's ever being eligible at all. I see in Putnam's *Grenzbegriff* an abbreviated appeal to something similar. The extension of the argument I have in mind is caught in the same Cartesian (or Kantian) net: each pretends that *there is* (in place) or that we must rationally suppose *a closed system* of essential concepts that we may not be able to master. But you have only to recall Cusa's intuition about God (or, for that matter, Hegel's constraint on Absolute knowing) to fathom Davidson's unearned advantage.

In any case, neither Putnam nor Davidson seriously considers the viability of relativism at all: once we set aside the presumption of the *Grenzbegriff* and the "common co-ordinate system" Davidson invokes, we grasp at once the bankruptcy of current analytic attacks on relativism and incommensurabilism. It's hardly more than a step from there to see that Habermas's appeal to the faculty of Reason is another obiter dictum by which, without the least labor, we might outlaw relativism and incommensurabilism within the pale of pragmatism and related European movements. The imputed fate of relativism exposes at a stroke the partisan ideology of Davidson's attempt at a privileged form of *autoréférence*: it hardly defines the principal goal of efforts to compose a valid philosophical system. On the contrary, pragmatism remains unbounded just where Davidson and Putnam suppose it must be closed.

THE PRINCIPAL POINT TO GRASP about Putnam's and Davidson's different treatments of relativism is that they pursue the same grand argument that has threaded its way, in endlessly diverse forms, from the very beginnings of Western philosophy down to our own time—which I've caught in midstream, so to say, labeling it (as it often is) "Cartesianism" or "Cartesian realism" or "Cartesian rationality," possibly because modern philosophy finds its most memorable manifestation in the interval spanning Descartes and Kant. But it could also have been drawn from the interval spanning, for example, Parmenides and Aristotle: namely, the alleged necessity of some ineliminable invariance in thought and/or reality ranging over all intelligible change—so as to give flux its due but not more, and to entrench bivalence. Both Davidson and Putnam acknowledge the flux of history and the flux of experience: they straddle these themes without actually linking them in a single sustained analysis. Putnam's contest with Richard Rorty and Davidson's warning about the incoherence of Kuhn's and Feyerabend's historicizing science are first cousins to one another and second cousins to Habermas's conviction.

What Putnam and Davidson isolate in their different ways is an argument of Reason masquerading as a reasoned argument: an argument that, in a more candid age, would have required a privileged faculty at least; that is, to confirm the bona fides of the *Grenzbegriff* and Davidson's "common co-ordinate system." Peirce palpably hovers behind Putnam and Habermas (and even Davidson), but none of them can match Peirce's "autoreferential" skills.

Peirce straightforwardly abandons Kantian transcendentalism, which he admires but is aware he cannot defend in a literal way. He prefers a regulative Hope (transcendentally invoked but lacking cognitive pretensions of any strong modal kind), which proves so robust, however, in his hands (so tempted by the deliverances of abductive Reason), that we ourselves are inclined to doubt Peirce's literal demurrer. One way or another, something stronger than transcendental Hope persists in Putnam, Davidson, Habermas—and Peirce and Karl Popper—though not in Dewey. Peirce brings abduction close to a "Cartesian" confidence but saves it as a persistent instinct on which cognition cannot count in any directly evidentiary regard. Davidson and Putnam venture privileged truths they cannot defend; and Habermas dithers on the same count in an extraordinarily transparent way.

It is hardly strange, therefore, that Habermas, per Apel, who provides the first sustained European appreciation of Peirce's immense labor (out of Frankfurt Critical sources),[32] should occupy a somewhat Deweyan-like role (relative to Apel—and to Peirce). Not quite, since Reason claims strong (even if uncertain) facultative powers in Habermas, though not in Dewey, and since Peirce never permits himself any specifically privileged claims. Habermas would have been delighted to gain the advantages of transcendental(ist) Reason by pragmatist means, but he could never make the argument convincing, and he himself effectively outflanks Apel's apriorist temperament. Of course, it could never have been sustained by either Dewey's or Peirce's strategies. Indeed, Peirce shows us how to draw the line—very cleverly—which he "crosses" only in Hope, never by way of Reason as a determinate faculty. That is, he never permits his abductive "principles" to exceed their regulative (rhetorical) function. Nevertheless, he's tempted along realist lines that do indeed threaten to exceed the resources of Hope itself, and he's drawn others too far in that direction.[33]

Here, for instance, is a passage from Peirce's well-known "A Guess at the Riddle" (c. 1890), which confirms as well as any short passage can Peirce's equivocation in bringing together in a pragmatist spirit a Cartesian-like treatment of realism (if I may characterize Peirce's effort in this way) and the insuperable contingency of natural inquiry. Bear in mind that, for Peirce, "Law is *par excellence* the thing that wants a reason" (1891); and "A reason has its being in bringing other things into connection with each other [firsts and seconds, in Peirce's idiom]; its essence is to compose: it is triadic, and it alone has a real power [that is, either as law or thought]" (1909).[34] Hence, Peirce's reasoning entails a transcendental ingredient. Can it possibly be confined to the resources of regulative Hope? I have argued elsewhere against such a possibility if Peirce is to be read in his strongest realist manner.[35] Peirce makes this proposal:

> Nature herself often supplies the place of the intention of a rational agent in making a Thirdness genuine and not merely accidental; as when a spark, as third, falling into a barrel of gunpowder, as first, causes an explosion, as second. But how does nature do this? By virtue of an intelligible law according to which she acts. . . . [W]hat makes the real forces really there is the general law of nature which calls for them, and not for any other components of the resultant. Thus, intelligibility, or reason objectified, is what makes Thirdness genuine.[36]

If you read this in the spirit in which Peirce specifically says he favors "objective idealism," according to the formula "matter is effete mind" (1891),[37] you see at once the sense in which Peirce's reasoning occupies a twilight zone in which it is almost impossible to decide whether the passage is a Schellingian hope or a Schellingian truth. Peirce never quite betrays any literal adherence to the excesses of post-Kantian idealism: he regularly retreats to a human form of Hope. Yet he teeters on the edge of reclaiming a more constitutive transcendentalism. He resists the literal doctrine, but the temptation is there. It infects his fallibilism and draws him away from Dewey's leaner intuition. In any case, his clarifications are too ambiguous to be fully trusted: he would have needed to be more explicit about his abductive powers, his phenomenological "principles," his idealist commitments, and, most pertinently, his answer to the question whether the laws of nature are or tend to be exceptionless on grounds firmer than rational Hope or a fallibilism pitched to the telos of infinite inquiry.

Peirce is never a full-blown apriorist in Kant's sense; but he may have made it too easy to elude the letter of the Kantian law. Apel is pleased not to resist the call; Habermas resists but not convincingly. Dewey will have none of Peirce's temptation; Davidson is an out-and-out objectivist (whom Rorty palms off as a pragmatist and who turns against his own best-known claims, slowly and without adequate explanation); Putnam seems not to have quite grasped the deeper import of his having advocated his *Grenzbegriff*. None of these engaging figures—running from Peirce to Rorty—is committed to the spare strength of a thoroughgoing, evidentiarily contingent, constructivist form of realism. Had Peirce favored such an option, he would have anticipated Dewey, seen the advantage of James's (often muddled) theory of truth, approved of Lewis, and escaped the ambivalent "Cartesianism" of his own account of Thirdness. We are, therefore, still at risk!

I COME NOW TO A COMPLICATED PART OF THE STORY, because it is nearly impossible to characterize Habermas's conception of rationality without comparing its treatment with the treatment rationality receives in American pragmatism and in Kant. In fact, one cannot rightly understand Habermas's thesis properly except as a modification of Apel's; one cannot understand Apel's except as a distinctly regressive analogue of Peirce's account of the relationship that holds between the logical, ethical, and aesthetic forms of goodness; one cannot understand Peirce's account except as an intended improvement on (a critique of) Kant's analysis per Schelling and Hegel; and one cannot understand the entire sequence except in terms of the remarkable similarity between the differences that hold between Peirce and Dewey on the one hand and between Apel and Habermas on the other.

I economize here, because I have already sketched very lightly the attitude of the classic pragmatists toward transcendental sources, and because Apel (a fortiori, Habermas, at a remove) commits a fatal mistake in reading Peirce—not a textual mistake, though it is at least that—for Apel strays into a non sequitur that defeats his pragmatized version of the Kantian theme he and Peirce address. The result is a gap in Apel's argument that Apel does not see. The analysis calls for a bit of patience. But the quickest way to identify the flaw in Habermas's account is to review Apel's argument about rationality; and the quickest way to isolate the flaw in Apel's argument is to recall what Peirce says more carefully about the same matter. All of this should be viewed in the spirit of considering whether pragmatism can be reconciled with transcendental*ism* in any form, or indeed whether it must admit some transcendentalist foundation or principle (comparable at least with Putnam's presumptive *Grenzbegriffe*) or Pihlström's idealism. The answer, I've been urging, is flatly no.[38]

In "The Three Kinds of Goodness," the fifth of seven lectures on pragmatism given at Harvard University in 1903, possibly the most influential of Peirce's papers in forming Apel's pragmatized (or semiotized) account of Kant's treatment of normative practical reason, Peirce argues that just as there are necessary laws of nature (if there are!), there are necessary normative laws ensuring the "conformity of things to ends"—which are never more than synthetically linked to phenomena, are never directly derivable from any perceptually grounded sources (are "not within those phenomena").[39] Peirce means that *if* the scientifically factual, the ethical, and the aesthetic *were* transcendentally grounded in terms of theoretical or practical reason, there *would be* necessary laws to be discovered: it's here that Peirce substitutes a purely regulative Hope for the legitimating power of the conditions of experience, which Kant posits as the constitutive ground of cognition itself.

About ethics, Peirce says:

> [E]thics is the normative science *par excellence*, because an *end*—the essential object of normative science—is germane to a voluntary act in a primary way in which it is germane to nothing else. For that reason I have some lingering doubt as to there being any true normative science of the beautiful. On the other hand, an ultimate end of action *deliberately* adopted—that is to say, *reasonably* adopted—must be a state of things that *reasonably recommends itself in itself* aside from any ulterior consideration. It must be an *admirable ideal*, having the only kind of goodness that such an ideal *can* have, namely esthetic goodness. From this point of view the morally good appears as a particular species of the esthetically good.[40]

It's here that Apel goes astray. For Apel makes a point of approving Peirce's remark: "The only moral evil is not to have an ultimate aim"—that is, an end that is "possible," "ultimate" (at least in the sense specified as "esthetic"), "absolute" (that is, "what *would be* pursued under all possible circumstances"), and not such as might (contra Kant) be "reduced to a mere formalism."[41] Peirce means to hold to the general Hegelian objection to Kant's formalism in ethics. He *does not* mean to reclaim any apriorist constitution of moral judgment: there's no necessity in having "an ultimate end," though it is still "evil" not to have one, according to the purely regulative (never necessary) function of transcendental Hope. Apel reads the notion as *a pragmatically necessary constraint on practical reason*. But that is neither Peircean nor anywhere secured. Without the missing argument, Apel's entire theory collapses. In fact, it is nowhere supplied. I don't believe it can be—or can be under pragmatist colors.

Peirce held that an "ultimate end" entails an "infinite hope"; yet, although he obviously believed that "we all have" that hope ("that what is Best will come about"), *there can be no evidence and no conclusive reasons for so believing*! Infinite *hope*, Peirce says, "is something so august and momentous, that all reasoning in reference to it is a trifling impertinence."[42] Just so. There is no necessity in phenomenal and phenomenological matters, and one can only hope that there are necessities in ethical and aesthetic matters. (In fact, there are no necessities there either!) True necessity obtains only in the space of strict "logical goodness" (in effect, in deduction);[43] and infinite Hope raises practical difficulties similar to the theoretical difficulties of the "long run" in the sciences.[44]

If you grasp the limitations Peirce imposes on "ethical science," you see at once the extraordinary simplification Dewey produced in his own ethics and aesthetics, relieved, as in *Art as Experience* and *Human Nature and Conduct*, of any teleologism or evolutionism or constitutive transcendental Reason.[45] In Peirce's view, Dewey would have had to count as an "anthropologist" of sorts.[46] But Apel means to restore (and improve) Kant's transcendentalism by way of Peirce's pragmatist eclipse of Kant himself.[47] Extraordinary!

The whole of Apel's fatal error—not merely in the textual sense but in the way of advancing a transcendental argument—is adumbrated in the following pronouncement:

> Anyone who engages in argument automatically presupposes two things: first, a *real communication community* whose member he has himself become through a process of socialization, and second, an *ideal communication community* that would basically be capable of adequately understanding the meaning of his arguments and judging their truth in a definitive manner.[48]

The phrase "automatically presupposes" clearly signifies that we are (in the second clause) in the presence of a constitutive transcendental condition that is not merely "postulated" in Peirce's sense,[49] but affirmed by an exercise of Reason (that is, the "autonomous cognitive faculty" of Reason). Unfortunately, we have the dictum but not the supporting argument.

Apel wrongly interprets Peirce's dictum—"logic presupposes ethics"[50]—as a definite transcendentalist constraint. Peirce himself always concedes that "an ultimate aim"—truth or rightness, say—may well be "essentially *unattainable*";[51] hence, in Peirce's sense, also impossible to approximate. (Recall Putnam's opposed account of the *Grenzbegriff*.) In any case, it cannot be discerned by any would-be faculty of Reason. Apel's claim fails therefore: Apel nowhere supplies the supporting grounds he requires. (I draw your attention to the fact that Apel's would-be reflexive argument is a standard illustration of what has been suggestively characterized as an "autoreferentially" necessary second-order form of argument that includes, but need not be restricted to, Kant's paradigm instances of specifically Critical reasoning. But that's to say that Apel offers us a moral ideology, not a transcendental truth.)

Note finally that we are already members of "a real communication community" on the flimsiest of biological grounds: we are simply, as infants possessing a distinctive primate intelligence, born into a society of selves, without any thought at all of universal conditions of intelligibility; and we seem to be spontaneously able to understand whatever any normally competent speaker (of our community) elects to say, without any evidence of ever having agreed in any way to common principles of meaning. Universalism seems an entirely unnecessary extravagance here.

Turn, now, to Habermas. In the early 1980s, at the time of the translation of his *Transformation* volume, Apel was certain that he and Habermas held similar views regarding the pragmatic grounding of "communicative competence."[52] Both accepted (for different reasons) the validity of Habermas's important essay "What Is Universal Pragmatics?" as well as the successor arguments of "Discourse Ethics" and *The Theory of Communicative Action*.[53] Habermas's early formulation clearly shares the difficulties noted in Apel's doctrine; and even his more recent formulations tend to do little more than affirm the need for a transcendental (or a "transcendental-pragmatic") grounding of the constraints proposed.

Apel and Habermas have now, however, diverged more and more in their reading and rereading of Habermas's published views; and Habermas himself never quite divests his thesis of the transcendentalizing cast of Apel's influence. Nevertheless, there is good reason to think that pragmatism and Kantian transcendentalism remain completely incompatible, and certainly Habermas has tried to free the "pragmatic" necessities of "argumentative" discourse from the doubtful authority of transcendental Reason. But there is nothing in all of Habermas's immense output to compare, say, with Lewis's faute de mieux demonstration of the simple defeasibility of the Kantian reading of a priori necessity—on which both Habermas and Apel depend. The fact is that Habermas has never made his case.

In a rather complex, strategically motivated essay, "A Genealogical Analysis of the Cognitive Content of Morality," designed to distinguish his thesis from Apel's, Habermas offers the following somewhat tortured observation—we need the full text for a proper sense of Habermas's caution:

> The point of . . . a justification of the moral point of view is that the normative content of this epistemic language game [moral discourse] is transmitted only by a rule of argumentation to the selection of norms of action, which together with their moral validity claim provide the input into practical discourses. A moral obligation cannot follow from the so to speak transcendental constraint of unavoidable presuppositions of argumentation alone; rather it attaches to the specific objects of practical discourse, namely, to the norms *introduced* into discourse to which the reasons mobilized in deliberation refer. I emphasize this when I specify that (U) [that is, the principle of universalizability] can be rendered plausible in *connection with a* (weak, hence nonprejudicial) *concept of normative justification*. . . . With (U) we reassure ourselves in a reflexive manner of a residual normative substance which is preserved in post-traditional societies by the formal features of argumentation and action oriented to reaching a shared understanding. This is also shown by the procedure of establishing universal presuppositions of argumentation by demonstrating performative self-contradictions, which I cannot go into here.[54]

Habermas obviously means to distance himself from Apel's formulation, in spite of the fact that he admits the "so to speak" transcendental constraints (the would-be universal—the unavoidable—presuppositions) that remain *at the level* of "argumentative" discourse: that is, at a level at which whatever form of discourse we acknowledge to be intelligible and capable of being effective (moral discourse, for instance) already submits responsibly and rationally to the universalist norms *of discourse itself* (let us say) *as they apply to* its own domain, without reference as yet to the "normative justification" of its own specialized norms (that is, specifically moral norms, in our imagined specimen).

Habermas clings to the notion of "unavoidable presuppositions" directly affecting moral discourse, the admission of which would be sufficient to justify invoking "performative self-contradictions" *within* such discourse—that is, a palpable breach of *discursive* universalizability. But then, our objections to such a piece of discourse would rest on a presupposition of discourse in general rather than on the violation of a specifically moral norm: hence, hardly freed from the would-be transcendental sources Habermas himself plainly worries may not be demonstrably compelling or convincing to rational speakers challenged *at the discursive level itself*. You realize that this idea—that of the rationally necessary universal norms of discourse, which Habermas now admits must, if they are to be sustained, rely on something more than their rational self-evidence—was actually Habermas's original and most important contribution to the theory of transcendental reasoning, which he and Apel shared. (I trust you see here, once again, the pertinence of Putnam's *Grenzbegriff*.)

When, however, Apel transcendentalizes Peirce's dictum—affirming that "logic presupposes ethics"—Apel means his reading to impute apriorist (or categorical) force *to moral judgments directly*. That is, *on Apel's* reading of Peirce's dictum—a textually erroneous reading (as I have shown) but a reading that also fails to deliver the transcendental demonstration needed—the *same* constitutive *moral* conditions of practical reason apply directly (but dependently) to general discourse and to specifically moral discourse alike. So there is a substantial difference, after all, between Apel's and Habermas's analysis of the transcendental defense of moral universalism.

If I have this right, Apel believes that, effectively, Peirce shows us a way to improve on Kant: the analysis of the conditions of "possibility" of rational discourse is itself *already a moral matter*: a rationally responsible discursive community is already a moral community. Habermas argues only that rationally responsible *moral* agents are already committed to the universal or universalizable norms of *rational discourse*—because they are rational before they are moral. The difference between Apel and Habermas may then be put this way: since, in Apel's account, "logic presupposes ethics," there may in principle be valid ethical universals that are not *derived* from the normative universals of discourse when applied to the moral matters we acknowledge—for instance, the obligation at once to favor universalized "ends" rather than to universalize whatever ends an autonomous moral agent happens to acknowledge. As Habermas sees matters, he is not obliged to admit the transcendental validity of any universalized moral norms or obligations (qua moral) viewed apart from the import of mere discursive constraints *applied* to specifically moral ends.

Both Apel and Habermas, therefore, are open to serious challenge in the worrisome sense in which "the linguistic [or semiotic] turn" may prove to be an insufficient or inapt basis for judging *moral* universalism, because it challenges *discursive* universalism! Both have risked their accounts on what, quite implausibly, they claim (or may be claiming) is an unconditional constraint on *discourse* as such. Consider only that there is no obvious pragmatic or "performative contradiction" in admitting an irreducible plurality of traditional norms of practice issuing from the ethos of different peoples; and surely, there is no obvious performative contradiction that directly renders unintelligible, unacceptable, or unviable all otherwise recognizable instances of ordinary discourse. (Furthermore, all natural languages manifest bilingual competence, and there appears to be no principled difference between interlinguistic and intralinguistic intelligibility—a thesis Quine was very pleased to champion in *Word and Object*.)

Moral universals, judged in purely formal terms, are easily led into paradox (as Hegel famously demonstrates against Kant's Categorical Imperative); discursive universals are even weaker when judged only in terms of the formal aspects of practical or effective communication. Apel viewed Habermas as undermining the Kantian account of rationality by disjoining the logic of discourse and the logic of morality; and Habermas viewed Apel as risking too much by advancing the dubious claim (textually untenable in any case) that discourse already presupposes the moral law. Furthermore, if we speculate along these lines, we will have exceeded any familiar version of "pragmatic" constraints (that might be drawn from Peirce or Dewey), and we will have re-Kantianized pragmatism itself.

The essential point is this: there simply are no obvious, antecedent ("rationally" or transcendentally or normatively binding, a priori) constraints on the effective *intersubjectivity* of mere human discourse or practical life; so there are no obvious or demonstrably universalizable norms of validity regarding judgment and commitment that rationally bind either or both discourse and morality that can be drawn from the bare (the Kantian "possibility" of the) intersubjectivity of human life. Apel and Habermas construe the transcendental relevance of intersubjectivity in terms of the "dialogic" constraints of discourse; hence, they reject "monologic" (or solipsistic) reflection, which they find in Husserl's phenomenology and Rawls's theory of justice. The phenomenologists rightly counter (whether on Husserlian or Heideggerian grounds) that the reflections of a "solitary" or single rational agent need not be the reflections of a solipsist; and that, as a consequence, the actual processes of dialogue themselves presuppose existential conditions that do not (or need not necessarily) yield Apel's or Habermas's Kantian-like abstractions and oppose giving pride of place to the dialogic over the existential (in the narrow sense Apel and Habermas favor).[55]

So, for instance, on existential grounds, whether transcendentally construed or construed in accord with some version of the "natural attitude" (favored, say, by Rawls, Robert Nozick, Michael Sandel, or Roberto Unger), implicit forms of intersubjective consensus might be all that is needed for effective discourse or, for that matter, for any prima facie ethos or ethical practice.[56] But then, the Kantian thesis would be lost. There is nothing inherently irrational about privileging the norms of one's own society over the norms of other societies. Doing so need not conflict with the requirements of consistency or reason or universalizability (in a merely formal sense—terminological consistency, say); and "universal consensus" is never literally or actually invoked. (Think here of Rawls's profoundly circular, question-begging Kantianism.) Speculating along these lines, we cannot fail to undermine the stringent claims Apel and Habermas are known to champion. If you add considerations already adduced from the side of the classic pragmatists, from Cassirer, Lewis, Putnam, and others regarding the logic of transcendental reasoning and would-be conceptual truths, the philosophical naiveté of Apel's and Habermas's entire Kantian or Kantian-like venture becomes increasingly transparent. Mafioso tribalism, for example, is hardly irrational or obviously self-contradictory; and the legal shenanigans surrounding the Reichstag fire demonstrate (if there was ever a need to demonstrate) that every piece of self-serving privilege can masquerade if it wishes in universalist forms. There seems to be no basis at all for fearing that *anything* uttered in any human community and taken to be meaningful could not be grasped by the speakers of any other human community—if, as is obviously true, specieswide bilingualism holds. Furthermore, once we admit Darwinian considerations—the implications of what I've called "external *Bildung*," for instance—the alleged need to embrace universalism in order to ensure discursive (or moral) *intelligibility* utterly founders.

Apel is closer to Kant, in virtue of his mistaken reading of Peirce. Habermas seems to follow Apel at first; but he becomes increasingly uneasy about doing so, since he is unable to explain the difference between the "transcendental" and the "pragmatic" within the sphere of "practical" life itself. He risks more than Apel, because he concedes that the generic universals of argumentative discourse are insufficient to ensure that there *are* ethical universals, or that we can give a purely transcendental account and defense of the universalized features of moral reasoning (for instance, categorical obligation). Habermas himself is not entirely persuaded that a transcendentally a priori justification of moral universalism is convincing, and he is also uncertain—understandably so—that a consensual approximation to universalism can be sufficient for moral universalism.

Frankly, the entire line of transcendental necessity is a dead letter: I see no advantage in favoring either Apel's or Habermas's version of the transcendental analysis of moral reasoning. Both must have been aware of Peirce's having replaced Kant's transcendental thesis, as well as the arguments in James and Lewis and Dewey. They must have been aware that they would need a stronger argument than a mere obiter dictum. But they offer none.

You may claim that no one has ever demonstrated that there are no transcendental necessities to be had—and that is certainly true. But the burden of proof surely rests with transcendentalism's champions. At the risk of a self-defeating paradox, the argument against transcendentalism must be a form of faute de mieux reasoning—always open ended and piecemeal, never conclusively necessary or indefeasible. But there are no successful transcendentalist counterinstances to consult.

It may help to consider an alternative account of transcendental reasoning offered by the most Kantian of the American pragmatists, the logician and moral theorist C. I. Lewis, which, by its very coherence, demonstrates the force of a faute de mieux challenge to Habermas's and Apel's line of reasoning. Lewis advances something of an a priori reading of the Peircean notion of abduction construed along the lines of transcendental Hope. The decisive clue is entirely straightforward: in effect, it catches up the master themes of Peirce's system as well as (without attribution) the master themes of Hegel's critique of Kant's system. (Also, as I read it, it anticipates Putnam's argument regarding conceptual truths.)

Here is Lewis's best shot, pursued in the light of the historical facts bearing on relativity physics' replacing the notions of absolute space and time—a perfect example of the pragmatist force of faute de mieux reasoning applied to familiar specimens of a priori necessity:

> [T]o that mind which should find independent space and time absolutely necessary conceptions, no possible experiment could prove the principles of relativity.... And

the only sense in which it could be proved unreasonable would be the pragmatic one of comparison with another method of categorical analysis which more successfully reduced all such experience to order and law.

At the bottom of all science and all knowledge are categories and definitive concepts which represent fundamental habits of thought and deep-lying attitudes which the human mind has taken in the light of its total experience. But a new and wider experience [relativity physics, for instance] may bring about some alteration of these attitudes, even though by themselves they dictate nothing as to the content of experience, and no experience can conceivably prove them invalid.[57]

Lewis's interpretation of this knockdown argument—that is, the argument that shows the inherent vulnerability of Kantian and Kantian-like transcendental reasoning—is just as elegant as the faute de mieux demonstration itself. Lewis concludes that

neither human experience nor the human mind has a character which is universal, fixed, and absolute. . . . Our categories and definitions are peculiarly social products, reached in the light of experiences which have much in common, and beaten out, like other pathways, by the coincidence of human purposes and the exigencies of human cooperation. Concerning the *a priori* there need be neither universal agreement nor complete historical continuity. Conceptions, such as those of logic, which are least likely to be affected by the opening of new ranges of experience, represent the most stable of our categories, but none of them is beyond the possibility of alteration.

Mind contributes to experience the element of order of classification, categories, and definition. Without such, experience would be unintelligible.[58]

I cannot see how either Apel or Habermas could possibly overcome, by "pragmatic" or other contingent means, this implicit challenge to their respective argumentative strategies. In Lewis's view, even with respect to "the laws of logic," but in any case, with respect to the triadic interrelationship between "our categorical ways of acting, our pragmatic interests, and the particular character of experience," "the dividing line between the *a priori* and the *a posteriori* . . . is only a difference of degree."[59] I cannot imagine a sparer "naturalization" of Kant's transcendental contribution (along Pihlström's lines) or of Hegel's corrective (very possibly per Josiah Royce). A fortiori: to admit the force of Lewis's argument *is* to provide a pragmatist defeat of Habermas and Apel. The deeper lesson of this agon rests with the ease with which norms (and the supposed necessity of valid norms) can be accounted for in naturalistic terms. (The phenomenologists, like the Frankfurt Critical theorists, are also inclined to demur, but they lack a compelling counterargument—or so it seems.)

Let me venture a final observation about the entire sweep of the puzzles that collect the "empirical" and the "transcendental" in the contemporary post-Kantian spirit: the point of Lewis's pragmatist interpretation of the Kantian a priori is to refuse any principled or fixed disjunction between the empirical and the transcendental, while cleaving to the rule that the a priori and the analytic are one and the same. As a consequence, the analytic is in some sense a stable, deep-seated ingredient structure *in* our habituated experience of the experienced world; yet the history of that experience may well lead us from time to time to revise, for "pragmatic" reasons, for reasons that collect the world (under descriptive and explanatory revision) in seemingly more perspicuous ways (think here of Kuhn), under which condition what had previously counted as a priori is systematically replaced by another a priori "system" fitted to what we take to be the same world.

If I understand Lewis correctly, what is here replaced is not shown to have been mistaken (as Putnam would very probably say, thinking of Kant's reading of Euclidean triangles). The decision is pragmatic, which is to say holist regarding the internal, "intertwined" relationship between the empirical and the a priori. I find this quite plausible but not sufficiently articulated to compel our assent. Still, it catches up the deeper contest between, say, Quine and Carnap, which has yet to be adequately spelled out. My own suggestion is that inquiries of this sort are profoundly constructivist—interpretive rather than disjunctive in the Kantian sense. In short, Lewis's venture is "Hegelian" in a sense that collects Peirce and Royce as well—and figures like Michael Friedman and Putnam in ways neither might be willing to admit, and Ernst Cassirer, who would be perfectly comfortable with such an admission.[60]

Habermas continues to affirm the *necessity* of the normative "universals" of "argumentation and action oriented to reaching a shared understanding." But moral norms as such are, he admits, freely "*introduced*" into this or that discourse from contingently relevant considerations—to which, then, indissolubly, the would-be transcendental conditions of rational discourse are *applied*. Habermas has never quite found a convincing label for his pragmatic universals of discourse; but the true reason may be that the would-be "pragmatic contradictions" said to be produced by *their* violation are less than compelling wherever they are taken to be logically or normatively inviolable.

Certainly, Habermas has never satisfied us on that score: very possibly, all the pertinent arguments are circular or question begging. Admit the postulate of an ideal and inclusive community of rational agents: pragmatic contradiction then and thereupon signifies no more than the violation of *that* postulate; challenge the postulate itself: the contradiction dissolves. Also, of course, it's exceedingly rare that apt speakers of a language cannot understand one another even where they are pitted against one another in their normative convictions—whether about discourse itself or about the public forms of morality. Habermas's and Apel's arguments are simply unconvincing: partly because the very idea of a universally accepted system of norms (of either discourse or morality) seems improbable, and partly because they seem to suppose that to be a part of an actual discursive community already entails their rational commitment to some invariant set of *ideal* discursive norms.

The adjustment between the discursive and the moral is meant to mark an additional improvement on Apel's and Kant's original moral conception.[61] Plainly, by this time, Habermas and Apel no longer agree. The difference between them now rests on a division between (1) the pragmatically necessary presuppositions of argumentative communication, the violation of which is said to yield "performative self-contradictions" (Apel); and (2) reasonably "introduced" universalizable norms apt for "possible" practical agreement by "all" in this domain or that, which draws on (never more than pluralistically or "weakly") pragmatic analogues of the "strong" universals of the first kind, now defined as moral proposals or instantiations of the second kind (Habermas). Even this demarcation proves uncertain, if we may judge matters pertinently by way of Habermas's replies to a series of objections (revolving around apriorism and its alternatives) posed by critics like Apel and Herbert Schnadelbach.[62]

It is not easy to reconcile Habermas's mounting replies in a single statement. But it is clear that Habermas opposes Apel's strong disjunction between a priori and a posteriori (or *lebensweltlich*) reason. Habermas has yet to answer on two scores: what kind of rational necessity his "unavoidable presuppositions" may claim, if they are not themselves bona fide transcendental conditions of "possibility"; and what kind of categorical standing can be assigned his universalizable moral prescriptives (even if they are inseparable from discursive necessities) *if* there are no substantive moral norms that take precedence over merely formal considerations. On the first, the would-be presuppositions strike me as utterly vacuous or worse—think of what the commitment to truth or validity comes to if either commitment is treated relationally or operationally (as it must be), or what sincerity comes to, if sincerity, like loyalty, is never more than a dependent virtue. On the second, universalizability is known (surely known to Habermas) to be endlessly manipulable in support of diametrically opposed maxims. (This is, in fact, the point of Hegel's critique of Kant's moral formalism.)[63]

There is no evidence that moral intuitions need be, or can be, plausibly strengthened (in standard cases) by being viewed as universalizable or actually universalized—or that there is even a robust practical sense in which "all" persons "affected" in any given instance could actually be consulted. The reference to "all rational agents" (or, "all rational agents affected") is no more criterial in practical matters than is "all possible worlds" in theoretical matters.[64] In fact, it raises the well-known problem, associated with the work of the British philosopher R. M. Hare, of distinguishing between universalizability construed in terms of verbal consistency alone and in terms of universal or exceptionless extension. (No one has done better than Kant, and Kant's argument is ultimately tautological—in being no more than a straightforward deduction idealized from the imputed nature of "practical reason.")

The short argument comes to this: There is nothing Habermas provides that is adequate for securing any form of normative universality or pragmatic necessity that Apel has not already failed to secure by a priori means. Habermas's "egalitarian universalism,"[65] which exceeds mere consistency of usage, adds nothing that can be counted on. Think of the possibility (which Habermas does not attempt to disprove) that rationality is itself a social construction of some sort, hence hostage to the same normative quarrels Habermas would have it judge. (You see the parallel with Putnam's *Grenzbegriff* and Husserl's *epoché*.) What, for instance, of the possibility that relativism and incommensurabilism (regarding rationality in moral matters, or even truth and validity in science)[66] might prove coherent and self-consistent and pertinent to particular quarrels—and viable and even helpful and instructive? You have only to think of the factions of Northern Ireland or the Middle East, or, indeed, the behavior of political parties anywhere in the world, to see the ideal's faulty charm. Habermas has no answer. He has effectively abandoned the pertinence of historicist and constructivist objections (contexted objections) *by* insisting on universality and universalizability. For they bind him to a Kantian resolution even where he means to resist transcendental fixities.

What both Habermas and Apel miss is the full significance of Peirce's account of fallibilism: Apel fails to see that Peirce transforms synthetic a priori truths into articles of transcendental *Hope*,[67] by which he subverts every epistemic form of Kantian necessity; and Habermas fails to see that fallibilism applied in short-run practices cannot approximate to any universal or necessary long-run norms beyond the constraints of admitted formal consistency.[68] (Think here of Peirce's early emphasis on the lifting of genuine doubt.) In that plain sense, pragmatism cannot be reconciled with any Kantian-like project, whether aprioristic (as in Apel) or *lebensweltlich* (as in Habermas).

Here is another passage that helps to pinpoint Habermas's shortcomings more precisely:

> We understand the expression "justify" [in grounding all argumentative discourse] when we know what we have to do in order to redeem a universal, i.e. trans-spatio-temporal and in this sense unconditional validity claim by deploying reason. This can be the case just as much with regard to the truth validity of an assertoric statement as it can with respect to the validity a normative statement has as being right. We understand the term "justify" when we know the rules for an argumentational game within which validity claims can be redeemed discursively. . . . Justification must always be provided in one and the same place—there are no meta-discourses in the sense that a higher discourse is able to prescribe rules for a subordinate discourse. Argumentational games do not form a hierarchy. Discourses regulate themselves. . . . The fallibilist meaning of an argumentational game takes into account only that universal validity claims have to be raised factually—namely, in our respective context, which does not remain stationary but rather will change. . . . The presumption of fallibilism refers solely to the fact that we cannot exclude the possibility of falsification even given convincingly justified theories which are accepted as valid.[69]

This is as clear a statement of Habermas's recent views as I have been able to find. (We need the entire text.) But you cannot fail to see the telltale traces of the insuperable defects already adduced: first, "universal" (or "unconditional") validity invokes the term "all" only in the sense of consistency of usage—it has nothing whatsoever to do with obligating "all" rational participants in any actual discourse (hence, fails to secure the ground that's needed);[70] second, on a Wittgensteinian reading of the "lifeworld" (which Habermas appears to favor), there are, in following the "rules" of "validity," literally no determinate rules that we follow (which is, of course, Wittgenstein's point but not Habermas's[71]); and third, on

Habermas's rejection of the "hierarchical" disjunction between "final" (or a priori) justificatory reasons and any local, provisional validation of first-order (practical) claims under real-time conditions, the first two findings preclude the recovery of universalized or necessary pragmatic constraints per fallibilistic approximation. In effect, universalism or universalized validity turns ad hoc. Habermas fails in the same way Rawls fails: universality is built into the "original position" of each, though each would deny it.

But to admit all this *is* to defeat both Habermas's and Apel's Kantianisms—certainly, any presumption in favor of detecting "pragmatic self-contradictions" robust enough for the substantive work of moral discourse.[72] To be candid, it is hard to see how (U)—the universalizability principle—could possibly provide, in any operationally convincing way, a necessary condition for the validity of any substantive norm in practical life or theoretical inquiry; or, alternatively, how norms that are *"generalized, abstracted, and [literally] free from all limits"* or capable of answering to "the interests and value-orientation of *each individual* could be *jointly* advanced by *all* concerned without coercion."[73] I leave the matter there, without touching on the enormous question (at once Marxist and Freudian) of recognizing moral self-deception and the true interests of human agents.[74] It is perhaps enough to say that no purely formal account of Reason could reassure us on that score, or that if we presumed to vindicate such a principle, we would not (by that same effort) have violated the limits of naturalism or pragmatism. Nevertheless, there are no such assurances to be had.

In dismissing apriorist or transcendentalist strategies of the Kantian sort, I see no reason to disallow transcendental or "autoreferential" questions (however they may depart from the Kantian paradigm) or abductive claims or claims about "conceptual truths" (in Putnam's sense) or truths of a "pragmatic a priori" nature (in Lewis's sense), or anything of the kind, so long as they are advanced in a posteriori ways or in ways that admit that whatever "necessity" or "universality" or "essentialist" standing they are accorded, they may be defeated under conditions of evolving experience. In this sense, pragmatism and Kantian transcendentalism are indeed incompatible: but now, it's transcendentalism that offers the dubious option.

Epilogue
Pragmatism and the Prospect of a Rapprochement within Eurocentric Philosophy

IT HAS TAKEN NEARLY THE FULL SPAN of the Western philosophical tradition to challenge effectively its most ancient assumptions: what is real is, or includes, the changeless; and what is real in the changing world depends, unconditionally, on what is changeless in the real. These are hardly completely defeated doctrines even now, but their authority has been profoundly shaken. They fit, almost without exception, the more than two thousand years that link Parmenides and Kant. After Kant, with the rapid rise to prominence of the concept of historicity and its remarkable penetration of all the seeming invariances of the accepted canon, what may fairly be termed the "doctrine of the flux" has gained a measure of parity so compelling that the ancient canon has had to look to its own defenses in an entirely new way. Philosophy has been bifurcated ever since in a way that was never possible before. Furthermore, if we divide the post-Kantian tradition along "pragmatist," "analytic," and "continental" lines—perhaps oversimplistically, though not for that reason inaccurately—then pragmatism, nearly alone among the principal movements of our time, has embraced the flux four square, without clinging to subversive loyalties of any kind harking back to would-be older invariances.

The old longings continue to plague us, however—even to instruct us in a useful way. You find them in Peirce, Horkheimer, Habermas, Cassirer, Merleau-Ponty, Gadamer, Kuhn, Popper, Reichenbach, Quine, Strawson, Putnam, McDowell, every bit as much as in Hegel, Marx, Kierkegaard, Nietzsche, and Heidegger. Occasionally, they cross the divide too late in philosophy's career and too zealously to gain back the innocent standing of the pre-Kantian world that beckons Kant, for instance in figures like Husserl and Apel and, more quarrelsomely, in some of the others just mentioned. The most forthright recent reckoning of the general issue appears in a late comment by Thomas Kuhn, who became reconciled toward the end of his career to the troublingly discontinuous contingencies that define the grand success of his *Structure of Scientific Revolutions*—which he himself initially found too difficult to embrace with conviction and which his analytic contemporaries tended to dismiss as self-contradictory or incoherent. Regarding what in his final period he calls the "standard locution developed within the tradition" of the philosophy of science—namely, that "successive scientific law and theories grow closer and closer to the truth," about which Kuhn unhesitatingly affirms that "at present it's not even clear what is being claimed"—he "reasserts" the following "tripartite conviction," which brings him into accord with what had originally worried him in his early work:

First, the Archimedean platform outside of history, outside of time and space, is gone beyond recall. Second, in its absence, comparative evaluation is all there is. Scientific development is like Darwinian evolution, a process driven from behind rather than pulled toward some fixed goal to which it grows ever closer. And third, if the notion of truth has a role to play in scientific development, which I shall elsewhere argue that it does, then truth cannot be anything quite like correspondence to reality. I am not suggesting, let me emphasize, that there is a reality which science fails to get at. My point is rather that no sense can be made of the notion of reality as it has ordinarily functioned in philosophy of science.[1]

I doubt we can do better than this. Kuhn is summarizing a fundamental conceptual change in philosophy's orientation, a version of the largest, most important directive of the last 250 years. His remarks capture in the leanest possible way the essential critique Hegel levels against Kant, without invoking any of the baggage of Hegel's own fandango. Kuhn's charge *is* Hegelian all right, and also pragmatist—*and* it is more than either, since it spells out in the idiom of our own day the implicit nerve of a potential rapprochement capable of collecting all the principal movements of our age congenially. Notably, it yields up without a murmur any and every version of the idea that the intelligibility of the world implicates harboring some stratum of real invariance.

Kuhn makes objectivity a historicized construction, denies every dream of neutral knowledge, retires the God's-Eye view of science, goes completely contingent and transient in evaluations of any kind, rejects teleologism in biology and progressivism in the most careful inquiries, opposes correspondentism in truth and noumenalism in our grasp of reality, and disdains canonical philosophies of science altogether. He hints at how all of this is strengthened by Darwin's achievement. But in the end, he collects once again the fragmented lessons of his own splendid book, albeit with more confidence than before, but without venturing any grander thesis that might conceivably thread together the separate pieces of a still-inchoate fabric, raised up finally as a fresh philosophical vision. He sees no way of drawing on the resources of the revolution set in motion by Kant and Hegel and its natural linkage with the very different kinds of evolution that span Darwin's discovery of the origin of species and the origin and development of true language and culture—and science—which he himself is on the point of discovering.

That, I've been arguing, *is* the missing executive clue embedded in the whole of "modern" modern philosophy that could indeed quicken the rapprochement of its largest late twentieth-century movements in the direction of a genuinely new beginning—possibly (if you don't mind the extravagance) a transformation that might count as a Hegelian "negation" of a very large sort. I mean no more than the simple thesis we seem driven to accept: the human self as a "natural artifact," the naturally emergent construction of the evolving site of self-reference, freedom, agency, self-consciousness; the cultural penetration of our biological aptitudes; the conjunction of the forces of external and internal *Bildung*. Seen this way, every reflexive avowal of our experience of the world could be reclaimed as a potential ingredient of a new "transcendental" approach to what we mean by knowledge or science. So much, then, for the initial grandeur of Kant's first *Critique*.

Kuhn's straightforward pronouncement signifies that we have, finally, been able to conceive, without recoil, the negation of the principal would-be Parmenidean and Eleatic "conceptual truths" that remain in play:[2] that is, we can actually now formulate, without palpable absurdity or meaninglessness, a picture of the real world that no longer requires admitting any indissolubly necessary linkage between the changing and the changeless! Our conceptual possibilities have evolved to an extraordinary degree. That fact alone is infinitely more important than any continuing dispute as to whether the posit of an invariant order is more fruitful than its denial in this or that context of debate. *Dispute* already concedes the point, since it's already on *this* side of the new divide; Kuhn is speaking out of his new conviction, out of *his* sense of eclipsing and fulfilling the pragmatist half-measures of Carnap and Popper and even Quine—and the classic pragmatists themselves. Our age has enlarged our options in an extraordinary way and, in doing that, has propelled philosophy to a new level of invention the Eurocentric tradition has somehow failed to recognize for what it is. We've actually changed the relative weightings among the seemingly best and most salient conceptual truths that confront us collectively in our evolving experience: we have the evidence of the historicized transformation of our thinking.

That, I daresay, is the principal source of pragmatism's otherwise puzzling importance—a certain discipline and promise—through its classic phase and its unforeseen revival through its second life: it has indeed found rigor and resource enough in the changing regularities of a changing world for all its conceptual needs. But in reaching this plateau, it views innovations in terms of philosophical gains, not as Rortyan reasons for outflanking philosophy altogether.

Nothing that was ever feared regarding the ineluctable consequences of abandoning the supposed invariant structures of the real world has come to pass. Pragmatism's unmarked adherence to the flux confirms in a natural, remarkably modest way the sheer viability of conceptual economies larger than its own, prepared to dismantle what had always been thought to belong to "perennial" philosophy: that is, the necessarily changeless nature of what is most fundamentally real and the assuredly foundational standing of the facultative competence by which we discern the fact. That *is* the conceptual confidence that has dominated Western philosophy for nearly the whole of its history; viewed thus, pragmatism remains the single most convincing experiment and demonstration that no part of the Eleatic Truth was ever truly indefeasible. Its immutable assurances were never more than the false buttresses of philosophical dogma.

Our conceptual stones have remained in place for as long as they have, but none has remained forever—none has remained unchanged within the drift of human understanding. The ideal of the modally changeless is utterly beyond the pale of passing evidence: a piece of superstition as far as anyone can now tell. No one has ever shown that to admit no more than the stabilities of actual change is nonsense or self-contradiction. But it's taken more than two thousand years to make the required leap. The result is that much of the history of philosophy is now debris—not to be merely discarded in Rorty's postmodernist way but genuinely and painstakingly superseded nonetheless.

My own conviction is that the lesson was already embedded in the radical possibilities of Hegel's critique of Kant,[3] regardless of what, disputatiously, we now care to make of Hegel's famously opaque doctrines. In any case, the pragmatists have drawn the radical lesson from Hegel, and Kuhn has focused its power in a particularly memorable and daring way by uniting a version of the continuum of inquiry that joins Kant, Hegel, Peirce, Carnap, Popper, himself, and Feyeraband with an acknowledgment of the historical appearance of discontinuous "paradigm shifts" and their concession of intelligible incommensurabilities. You cannot fail to see in this a budding energy of an entirely new philosophical age that probably cannot be strengthened if it cannot engage all the stalemated movements of the present Eurocentric world.

Analytic and continental philosophies, which draw their continuing strength from the same post-Kantian and post-Hegelian sources, have always divided their energies unequally between invariance and flux. Analytic philosophy oscillates between pragmatist impulses and the extremes of scientism (as among Russell, Carnap, Wittgenstein, Quine, and Sellars);[4] and continental philosophy (if you include the Fregeans, the Marburg Kantians, the Husserlian phenomenologists, the Heideggerians, the Frankfurt Critical school)[5] has always been similarly divided, reluctant to abandon the saving stabilities of presumed invariance.

Apart from having evolved from these same (proximate) sources, all the principal movements of Western philosophy have, as it happens, been uniformly damaged by the immense traumas of World War II, the cold war, and an unending series of barbarous wars down to the second Iraqi war. I think *that* actually accounts in good measure for the distinct isolationism and fatigue of the whole of Eurocentric philosophy and its penchant for endlessly recycling, largely without convictions of conceptual adequacy, the once distinctly compelling visions of the first half of the twentieth century. Pragmatism was itself palpably exhausted by the 1940s and 1950s, had all but expired as the result of its growing lack of comprehension of the original lesson of the great transformation effected in the interval spanning the work of Kant and Hegel—which is to say, the lesson of its own beginnings. It lost the edge of its upstart purpose, which, it must understand, it still can, and must, recover.

Put in the simplest way, the lesson comes to this: Kant successfully demonstrated that the problematic nature of knowledge invites and requires a transcendental discipline, an a priori construction of its posited sources of assurance; Hegel demonstrated, in turn, that the Kantian presumption that the transcendental itself required privileged sources was patently arbitrary, inaccessible, uncompelling, ultimately self-deluding and that, accordingly, Kant's invention of his a priori method was never more than an a posteriori posit—though not for that reason unsuited or inadequate for the questions of a suitably diminished task. Pragmatism, then, is that strand of the Hegelian critique that remains transparently committed to a thoroughly naturalistic reading of the a posteriori standing of a derivative of Kant's original apriorist strategy, which now adheres to the doctrine of the flux—and the "Darwinian" lesson of what I've been calling external *Bildung*.

I take this to be the single most important lesson of the entire interval of "modern" modern philosophy, which spans the middle of the eighteenth century and the present time and finds its most immediate objective in the rapprochement of Eurocentric philosophy, that is, the reconciliation of pragmatist, analytic, and continental currents: *aufgehoben*, let us say, in Hegel's manner. Both analytic and continental philosophy are obviously tempted by one or another form of Eleatic invariance: the analytic, by the excessive economies of scientism and reductionism; the continental, by the extravagances of extranaturalism. Pragmatism's advantage lies with its advocacy of a moderate naturalism in tandem with its commitment to the flux and its own reading of the Hegelian critique. I see no prospect of a more compendious or promising summary of the last 250 years of modern philosophy.

All of this is barely more than obliquely discerned. Kant rejects the cognitive privilege of the rationalist tradition he himself transforms along transcendental lines. But he somehow persuades himself that the would-be universality and certitude of transcendental reflection need not be refused so long as it is not directly applied in validating cognitive claims about the real world—where, that is, claims about the cognizing subject, the Transcendental *Ich*, are not about any part of the cognized world. To the modern mind, such presumptions would have to be won afresh if they were ever to be taken as decisive, once we admitted the arbitrariness of construing reason as a cognitive faculty of any kind that might bear in a substantive way on deciding the validity of the truth-claims of one or another science or cognate inquiry. (Nevertheless, I remind you that, in the *Tractatus*, Wittgenstein subscribed to a variant of the Kantian thesis.)

Once we agree that there is no assured prior "science of science," once we view our cognitive powers as the encultured transformation of the extended evolution of the native gifts of *Homo sapiens*, Kant's actual system (the system of the first *Critique*) fails utterly, without yet discounting Kant's brilliant intuition that we cannot legitimate science's labor except by constructing what, given what we suppose our sciences accomplish, amounts to a reasoned guess at the a priori conditions for such an a posteriori success—effectively, for human knowledge. So the exercise is insuperably contingent, even though it seeks to approximate to a would-be conceptual truth about what is reliable in the sciences and cognate forms of understanding.

Hegel saw this much at once in the analysis of historicity: that is, in the analysis of the idea that thinking is itself historied, the idea that reason changes over time in its determinable a priori intuitions about how, effectively, to extend its continuing grasp of the full truth about the world—beyond any provisionally closed body of science. Perhaps it must proceed discontinuously (as Kuhn believes and as Peirce never quite refutes), but always in accord with its own evolving lights—with the dawning sense that the a posteriori forms of the a priori will never capture, and have never captured, Kantian necessities or universalities.[6]

In this precise sense, we begin to grasp—without ever needing to subscribe to Hegel's extravagances regarding the objectification, or the necessities, or the would-be telos of *Geist* itself (though each of these ideas remains perfectly capable of being interpreted in the same carefully circumscribed way Hegel applies to Kant)[7]—the sense in which all the currents of modern Western philosophy are the beneficiaries of Hegel's radicalized continuation of the Kantian revolution.

It's in this spirit that I claim that pragmatism is, still incipiently, the leanest variant of Hegelian philosophy formed within the bounds of the Eurocentric tradition of the last two centuries, quickened by Darwin's discovery of the continuum of animal evolution. Hegel speaks of the ahistorical, changeless truths of Reason; but I take that to be the effect of a special rhetoric, in accord with which human thought that exceeds the finite order of things and guesses at the infinite—what future history may yet yield: within the space Hegel collects as "Absolute *Geist*"—is, very nearly definitionally, changeless! But that has nothing to do with what, *in that sense*, actually proves to be true or needs to be altered to fit our evolving world.

Things proceed the other way round: the "Absolute" continually makes way for the evolving "givens" of actual experience, which cannot rightly claim any cognitive privilege but nevertheless try, obliquely, our evolving constructions or guesses at what the amplitude of the Absolute "must" include. Curiously, figures like Peirce and Kuhn, and of course Cassirer (and, more distantly, Kant), need two distinct foci of reasoning that are forever intertwined: one conjecturally centered in a finitist way on what may be problematically "given" when viewed against the accumulating guesses of the second kind; the second, conjecturally centered in the infinitist way on what, interpretively, continually recovers the dialectically promising "totality" of what, by our lights, conforms best with the regulative idea of the Absolute. You see here the completely intuitive nature of Hegel's contribution and, as it were, the various historied, locally disciplined scientific strategies Peirce, Cassirer, and Kuhn provide in this larger Hegelian spirit. Cognition, in the Hegelian sense, has this dual structure: a phenomenologically promising minimal contribution to knowledge that we are forever obliged to supersede and an endlessly totalizing interpretive review of what is thus given read against the continuing history of all such efforts, which cannot ever be confirmed as knowledge finally secured.

I do indeed believe that this cartoon summary of the present state of philosophy is more or less correct. Pragmatism *is* the leanest form of naturalism committed (often too vaguely) to the post-Hegelian analysis of historicity and encultured life. Yet it never pursued these themes forcefully or adequately enough during or even since its classic days. Were we to search Peirce and Dewey thoroughly, and even if we added James, Mead, Schiller, and Lewis to our sources, we would still find that pragmatism's classic phase had hardly touched the fresh possibilities focused by Kuhn's late daring, and certainly never equaled the robust inquiries of its own most congenial near contemporaries, that is, of Marx and Nietzsche, fired by the same Hegelian impetus that best defines its own inspiration. Pragmatism *has* indeed been given a second life through the well-known minor scuffle between Rorty and Putnam,[8] but it has still to justify that gift.

We are not entirely clear about Peirce's and Dewey's mastery of Hegel. The joke is that Royce taught Peirce Hegel, and Peirce taught Royce logic. Questions have been raised about Dewey's competence in German; but his fluency in reading Karl Rosenkranz's biography of Hegel (1844), which apparently has never been translated into English, has been taken to settle the matter. Dewey wrote a one hundred–page typescript on Hegel's philosophy toward the end of the nineteenth century, chiefly occupied with the *Encyclopaedia* and the transition from the *Phenomenology*, which confirms that he saw a distinct continuity between Hegel and American pragmatism.[9] But the record becomes noticeably sparse thereafter.

To be perfectly candid, pragmatism's recent labors have favored a rather doubtful sort of nostalgia for certain dogmas that never actually congealed or were ever rightly "corrected" (during its classic phase) in the manner now so weakly approved. It has converted the rebel courage of its first champions into the formulaic fixities of Peirce's "realism," Dewey's "antidualism," James's "existential pathos"—and remarkably little else. It has no cutting edge, no frontier undertaking, no challenge to lay before the profession at large. The standard themes are certainly "there," of course, buried in plain view. But they block the continuation of pragmatism's unfinished encounter with the rest of the Eurocentric tradition, which has (in its various careers) surely eclipsed pragmatism's development after the 1950s, a pragmatism that cannot yet be rightly said to have rekindled or extended its own energies. It is still comparatively inert, uncertain, unsure of its original mission, relatively arrested among the disconnected pieces of an unfocused and poorly remembered vision. It will surely dwindle once again—perhaps mortally—if it cannot demonstrate the recovery of its historical role in the first or second decade of the new century.

All of philosophy's major movements are similarly at risk, however. Analytic philosophy has spent its best energies among reductionisms and extensionalisms that have proved entirely delusive (as in early Carnap, the Wittgenstein of the *Tractatus*, Russell's logicism, Quine's behaviorism, Sellars's eliminativism, Chomsky's innatism): it's now scrambling to recover its relevance by way of whatever it finds to be the saving themes of Kant, the post-Kantian idealists, Hegel, Nietzsche, Husserl, Heidegger, and the poststructuralists, whom it had earlier so unceremoniously dismissed. The recuperative impulse in American analytic philosophy (in Brandom, McDowell, Rorty, Putnam) is undoubtedly honest and well intentioned; but it is also noticeably awkward, improbable, disoriented, not a little desperate.

In a somewhat parallel way, the continentals have been too often attracted to extreme (or bizarre) forms of the "extranatural" interpretation of the human (certainly, at the highest level of authority, in Husserl and

Heidegger and, less commandingly though fashionably enough, in figures like Levinas, Apel, Lacan, the French feminists, the structuralists, and poststructuralists). The continentals have overreached themselves and have had to retreat to more modest options—notably, by way of naturalistic revisions and compromises (for instance, in the later work of Merleau-Ponty, Sartre, Gadamer, Derrida) and, among American continentals and their allies, Hubert Dreyfus, John Haugeland, Mark Okrent, Joseph Rouse, Frederick Olafson, William Blattner, David Woodruff Smith, Alva Noë, Dan Zahavi, Jean Petitot, and even Richard Rorty.[10]

None of the grand movements of the Eurocentric world is now in a position of notable strength: each has become inflexibly wedded to doctrines that were once justifiably admired but are now more or less vestigial, outmoded, inadequate, arbitrary, unfinished, repetitive, as among late Husserlians, for instance, gambling on the assumed apodicticity of transcendental phenomenology; or the Heideggerians, gambling on the inexplicit relationship between *Dasein* and "natural" persons or between the ontic and the ontological; or reductive materialists, risking all on the irrelevance of history and the denial of the different metaphysics of the cultural world; or the Kantians and post-Kantians, committed to the belief that universalism can always be empirically approximated by rational consensus; or the analytic (or scientific) naturalists, relying on the assumption that normative distinctions can always be replaced, without loss or disadvantage, by causal distinctions. These are all dead issues: the graveyard of philosophy's elephants.

We must turn back to Kant and Hegel to find the unfinished future, and we must overcome the inertia of World War II and its long aftermath to match the courage of the first half of the twentieth century. We are indeed committed to the evolving forms of a priori questioning but not to apriorisms that claim to deliver substantive necessity and apodicticity. We are led by the unforced convergence of the principal movements of Western philosophy that now feature the question of naturalism's adequacy or inadequacy; as a result, we cannot fail to explore the possibility of a more focused rapprochement between pragmatism and analytic and continental philosophy. There are hardly any options there that are not dialectically obligatory. More than that, pragmatism is itself distinctly unfinished (in a way analytic and continental philosophy is not)—as a result of its own scattered history. Peirce, James, and Dewey had remarkably little in common: they largely avoided one another, apart from the need to resolve the scandal regarding the analysis of truth. Yet they come together now, quite easily, from their diverse beginnings, on the analysis of the flux, evolution, history, societal process, naturalism, and even a minimal form of fallibilism.

The whole of Anglo-American philosophy, however, remains remarkably slack on the nature of history, intentionality, phenomenology, and enculturation.[11] These are absolutely central to the inquiries of continental philosophy. Furthermore, pragmatism and analytic and continental philosophy have favored very different views of the adequacy of naturalism. In this regard, the whole of Eurocentric philosophy has resources noticeably richer than those of any one of the principal movements within the tradition; its parts tend, therefore, to favor a certain natural division of labor, which might now contribute profitably to a genuine rapprochement.

When you see all of this, you see the plausibility of Hegel's dialectical reasoning: characteristically, the oppositions that arise in the historical process arise out of the material interests of the functioning moieties of some inclusive society; their "contradictions" are normally "sublated" by an evolving resolution within that evolving society, which, accordingly, will generate cognate oppositions of their own that must again be *aufgehoben*. If you see this entire process as a form of rational choice and freedom, then you understand at once why whatever solutions the encompassing society is prepared to adopt can hardly fail to be dialectically "necessary." So the telos of the process is itself trivially imminent (and "necessary"). In this entirely unproblematic sense (hospitable to plural, even competing commitments), whatever "is," "ought" ("dialectically") to be as it "is": which is to say, we view our choices in a normatively reasonable light. Where we still see an unacceptable limitation or defect, we admit a substantive tension that may yet have to be overcome.

So the "logic" of the rapprochement I've sketched is no more than one possible thread of philosophy's "progress." It cannot be entirely contrived: it evolves from the actual, effective engagements of the functioning cohorts of a committed society. The logic identifies no formal necessities therefore: the necessities are, rather, "material" or "concrete" commitments already embedded in the possibilities of future resolution dawningly perceived in the contradictions we actually encounter. ("Necessity" is itself an artifact of interpretive appreciation within the terms of historied habits.)

Here, I trace the deep informality of Hegel's conception of the logic of dialectical reasoning in order to confirm that there is no secret telos or necessity in Hegel's own vision—no matter how literal minded his arguments may seem at times.¹² The pragmatists are hardly bound to any formal strictures regarding their own "Hegelian" bent as a consequence of any closer reading of Hegel himself. I've fitted a loose version of the dialectic to the plausibility of the rapprochement I advocate—rather than pretend that we know how to proceed rigorously the other way around. The marvel is that the philosophical project suited to our time seems transparently obvious—in the sense of outflanking the conceptual doldrums of the age. If we adhered, rather, to Kant's transcendental original, our reasoning could never be dialectical in Hegel's sense—and would never need to be. It would also never suit the primacy of the historical flux. But if Hegel's critique of Kant is at all compelling (as I believe it is), then the a priori conditions of "possibility" (of knowledge) must themselves be a posteriori proposals in accord with "dialectical necessity"—and then the Kantian (transcendental*ist*) undertaking will be literally impossible. Hence, to admit historicity is to undermine the essential (the would-be) conceptual truth of the entire Kantian system: furthermore, if we admit that Kant correctly grasped the need for a transcendental turn in our second-order inquiries, then, on the argument before us, there can be no escape from the Hegelian dialectic or something very much like it. But to admit that much is also, effectively, to admit the necessity of the rapprochement I've been endorsing.

The argument, then, comes to this: (1) Western philosophy has been stalemated at the end of the twentieth century; (2) nevertheless, the principal movements of the Eurocentric tradition have now converged on the question of the adequacy or inadequacy of a naturalistic account of the central problems of philosophy; (3) "modern" modern philosophy is itself cast in terms of Kant's transformative analysis of the transcendental nature of the question of the "possibility" of knowledge; (4) but Hegel's critique of Kant's account of transcendental inquiry exposes Kant's arbitrary and indemonstrable use of certain would-be privileged powers of reason; so that (5) the only possible correction of Kant's innovation, consistent with (3), requires historicizing transcendental reasoning itself, or construing Kant's transcendental necessities as "dialectical necessities," which is to say, we must concede that the a priori is never more than an a posteriori posit; furthermore, (6) as it happens, pragmatism is the leanest variant of the Hegelian intuition, wedded to naturalism and the doctrine of the flux and the Darwinian continuum; also, (7) all the principal movements of current Eurocentric philosophy—pragmatism, analytic philosophy, and continental philosophy—draw their resources from, or are affected by their conformity with, the philosophical innovations produced by the work of Kant and Hegel, consistent with (3)–(5); (8) pragmatism also champions a moderate version of naturalism, whereas analytic philosophy has favored in its most influential efforts indemonstrable, extreme, reductive and/or scientific versions of naturalism ("naturalizing"); and continental philosophy, extreme forms of extranaturalism ("antinaturalizing"); in addition, (9) pragmatism adheres, at least implicitly, to some extent even explicitly, to Hegel's master themes of historicity and enculturation, whereas analytic philosophy characteristically avoids both or treats both reductively; hence, (10) in its attempt to reconsider—and resolve—philosophy's present stalemate (1), pragmatism rightly claims a productive advantage in pursuing the prospect of a rapprochement among the main movements of the Eurocentric world, but it is an advantage that supersedes its own hegemony. What's needed, then, still exceeds the gains collected as items (1)–(10).

What I am proposing here might, not unfairly, be termed a dialectical prophecy. It's a prophecy because it sketches a genuinely inventive, but also a possible future that the present currents of philosophy could actually support. It is not a merely autobiographical confession, though I am indeed personally committed to it and find it viable and convincing. It's a dialectical prophecy because it's a fair candidate for persuading currently active philosophers of every stripe that it does indeed harbor the best philosophical policy we are likely to advance among all the competing Eurocentric currents that can now claim an active following, and because in being that it captures what Hegel means by "dialectical" necessity. It's not literally necessary—certainly not fated—in the plain sense that history may still discount it or pass it by. In that sense, dialectical necessity is always retrospective: what was rightly necessary *ante*, in the dialectical way, is always identified, *post*, among the actual turns of history; wherever our commitment proves inadequate to our evolving vision, we simply offer an extended dialectical correction and move on.

This helps to define the sense in which the normative in philosophy, science, and morality is always practical or praxical, the sense in which the practical is always concretely grounded in the actual flux of life and thought, the sense in which what is normative in practice is not quite the same as what is normative (and still "practical") in a utopian spirit a little distance beyond the primacy of the practical. In short, I see no way of explicating the sense in which pragmatism is genuinely and promisingly "Hegelian" without explaining the sense in which to understand that is to understand the rationale of the rapprochement that a review of the whole of Eurocentric philosophy now recommends dialectically, wherever it may be viewed from the competing vantages of pragmatist, analytic, and continental philosophy. In that sense, the philosophical future, as much as any moral/political future, constructs its own appropriate dialectical past.

Notes

Chapter 1

"Pragmatism's Advantage" is considerably altered and revised from an earlier version originally presented at a conference at Utrecht University, The Netherlands, June 26, 2003, and published in *Ars Disputandi* 3 (2003).

1. Both Rorty and Putnam have been distinctly productive, and each has made a definite bid to lead pragmatism in a fresh direction that would have engaged the strongest currents of Eurocentric thought (as each saw matters). See Joseph Margolis, *Reinventing Pragmatism: American Philosophy at the End of the Twentieth Century* (Ithaca, N.Y.: Cornell University Press, 2002).

2. For a detailed account of the fortunes of American analytic philosophy, see Joseph Margolis, *Unraveling of Scientism: American Philosophy at the End of the Twentieth Century* (Ithaca, N.Y.: Cornell University Press, 2003).

3. For an extended discussion of Apel and Habermas, see Chapter 3.

4. See, for instance, Michael Tomasello, *The Cultural Origins of Human Cognition* (Cambridge, Mass.: Harvard University Press, 1999). Tomasello, who is a specialist in evolutionary anthropology, assembles a considerable body of evidence in favor of the uniqueness of the human infant's *primate* intelligence, along general Darwinian lines. But he fails utterly—I find it hard to fathom—to distinguish with care the difference between primate and *enlanguaged human* understanding. I take his failure to lend support to the idea that the "self" evolves, artifactually, through enculturing processes (tethered to the acquisition of a natural language but not confined to language alone) that transform the use and development of our primate intelligence by linguistic and cultural "penetration." Kant, I remind you, for all his insistence on transcendental reason (which clearly implicates the self—the *ich denke*, as Kant puts it) never manages to *explain* the basis for positing an *ich* at all. The discussion in the first *Critique* at § 16 is remarkably weak—and hobbled by Kant's fears regarding the paralogisms of assigning too large a power of conceptual invention to the self, beyond the system of the categories, which really makes no sense without an account of the other.

5. See, for instance, Richard Dawkins, *The Selfish Gene*, 2d ed. (Oxford: Oxford University Press, 1989). Dawkins is a committed Darwinian, but he finds it impossible to reduce the processes of cultural transmission (and "selection") in Darwinian terms.

6. For a sense of the opposite tendency, see Charles Taylor, *Hegel and Modern Society* (Cambridge: Cambridge University Press, 1979), which is itself a summary of Taylor's *Hegel* (Cambridge: Cambridge University Press, 1975). For my own reading of Hegel's contribution vis-à-vis Kant, see "The Point of Hegel's Dissatisfaction with Kant," in *Hegel and the Analytic Tradition*, ed. Angelica Nuzzo (New York: Continuum, forthcoming). I've formulated a more systematic interpretation of Hegel in a manner congenial to pragmatism but confined within the terms of the philosophy of art, in *On Aesthetics: An Unforgiving Introduction* (Belmont, Calif.: Wadsworth, 2009); and in "The Greening of Hegel's Dialectical Logic," in *The Dimensions of Hegel's Dialectic*, ed. Nectarios Limnatis (New York: Continuum, forthcoming). Regarding Hegelian aspects of Dewey's thought, see note 16.

7. Karl Marx, "Contribution to the Critique of Hegel's *Philosophy of Right*," in *Karl Marx: Early Writings*, ed. and trans. T. B. Bottomore (New York: McGraw-Hill, 1964), p. 43 (italics in original). For a further, unsympathetic, almost wooden analysis of Marx's account of human nature, see Jon Elster, *Making Sense of Marx* (Cambridge: Cambridge University Press, 1985), chaps. 2, 6. Elster goes too far in his efforts to ensure that Marx will not be seen to be committed to a collective subject. He fails to come to terms with the important complication that Marx's thought, as well as Hegel's, requires the admission of collective *predicates* that can be attributed to individual human *subjects*—as with language, culture, and class interests, for instance. The right way to recover Hegel, I suggest, is to construe *Geist* as Hegel's compendious summary of what would now correspond to the themes of "externalism" with regard to mind and brain in recent discussions of the philosophy of mind—in particular, what may be instructively called "cultural externalism." For a general overview of the literature, see Robert A. Wilson, *Boundaries of the Mind: The Individual in the Fragile Sciences* (Cambridge: Cambridge University Press, 2004).

8. See Daniel C. Dennett, *Consciousness Explained* (Boston: Little, Brown, 1991).

9. For a well-known version of a standard misunderstanding, see Karl R. Popper, *The Poverty of Historicism*, 2d ed. (London: Routledge and Kegan Paul, 1960).

10. Edmund Husserl, *Ideas: General Introduction to Pure Phenomenology*, trans. W. R. Boyce Gibson (New York: Macmillan, 1931), § 32 (italics in original). See also Edmund Husserl, *Cartesian Meditations: An Introduction to Phenomenology*, trans. Dorion Cairns (The Hague: Martinus Nijhoff, 1960), fifth meditation. I freely concede that Husserl's evolving, more "balanced" theory may be reread in what amounts to a "Hegelian" direction, embedding transcendental phenomenology in a natural world encountered in the flux of experience: that is, in short, in the sense of construing the transcendental a priori as itself an a posteriori proposal fitted to evolving experience (for instance, in accord with *Ideas II*). But I find it hard to believe that Husserl meant to jettison the strong theme advanced in *Ideas I*, and I don't believe the two accounts can be reconciled. The adjustment seems to me to be convincing—with or without Husserl; it also favors a viable rapproche-

ment, per Hegel's conception of phenomenology, with the best prospects of pragmatism. See note 36 for a better sense of the opposed readings of Husserl.

11. For an account of Heidegger's excesses regarding truth and knowledge, see Joseph Margolis, "Heidegger on Truth and Being," in *Heidegger and Plato: Toward Dialogue*, ed. Catalin Partenie and Tom Rockmore (Evanston, Ill.: Northwestern University Press, 2005).

12. See John McDowell, *Mind and World*, 2d ed. (Cambridge, Mass.: Harvard University Press, 1994, 1996).

13. See John Dewey, *Logic: The Theory of Inquiry* (New York: Henry Holt, 1938).

14. See, for instance, Martin Heidegger, "Plato's Doctrine of Truth," in *Pathmarks*, ed. William McNeill, trans. Thomas Sheehan (Cambridge: Cambridge University Press, 1998).

15. See Hubert L. Dreyfus, *Being-in-the-World: A Commentary on Heidegger's Being and Time, Division I* (Cambridge, Mass.: MIT Press, 1991).

16. See John Dewey, *Experience and Nature*, 2d ed. (New York: Dover, 1958). See also John R. Shook and James A. Cook, *John Dewey's Philosophy of Spirit, with Dewey's 1897 Lectures on Hegel* (New York: Fordham University Press, 2009), which presents for the first time in print the typescript text of one of Dewey's lectures on Hegel at the University of Chicago, together with extended analyses and further pertinent information provided by the authors. The text and Shook's and Cook's accounts of it confirm the sense in which Dewey was plainly influenced by Hegel and saw the general lines of a distinct and productive continuity between Hegel and his own version of pragmatism. The account given argues convincingly against the accepted view that Dewey finally broke with Hegel and Hegelian thought in advancing his own pragmatist program. My own gloss is simply that Dewey's mature philosophy (notably in *Experience and Nature*) would be nearly impossible without its Hegelian temperament.

17. See William James, *The Will to Believe* (New York: Longmans, Green, 1907); and Bertrand Russell, "The Definition of 'Truth,'" in *My Philosophical Development* (New York: Simon and Schuster, 1959).

18. For a sense of Peirce's early views along pragmatist lines, see "The Fixation of Belief," in *Collected Papers of Charles Sanders Peirce*, ed. Charles Hartshorne and Paul Weiss, vol. 5 (Cambridge, Mass.: Harvard University Press, 1963); see also Joseph Margolis, "Rethinking Peirce's Fallibilism," *Transactions of the Charles S. Peirce Society* 43 (2007).

19. See W. V. Quine, *Word and Object* (Cambridge, Mass.: MIT Press, 1960), §§ 37–38; D. M. Armstrong, "The Nature of Possibility," *Canadian Journal of Philosophy* 16 (1986); and Nelson Goodman, "Seven Strictures on Similarity," in *Experience & Theory*, ed. Lawrence Foster and J. W. Swanson (Amherst: University of Massachusetts Press, 1970).

20. The theme is developed in the prologue in *Reinventing Pragmatism* and supported in full detail in *The Unraveling of Scientism*. See also W. V. Quine, "Epistemology Naturalized," in *Ontological Relativity and Other Essays* (New York: Columbia University Press, 1969); and Donald Davidson, "The Coherence Theory of Truth and Knowledge" (with "Afterthoughts"), in *Subjective, Intersubjective, Objective* (Oxford: Clarendon, 2001).

21. I take this to be Putnam's best claim among his proposals during the failed phase of his "internal realism," which should not be yielded up in rejecting (with Putnam himself) the Jamesian (or Kantian) subjectivism of *The Many Faces of Realism* (LaSalle: Open Court, 1987). For a pragmatist conception of "scientific realism" of great skill—which I applaud and which seems to me to make exceptionally good use (implicitly) of Peirce's category of Secondness, see Ian Hacking, *Representing and Intervening: Introductory Topics in the Philosophy of Natural Science* (Cambridge: Cambridge University Press, 1983), chap. 1, particularly pp. 22–24.

22. See Edmund Husserl, *The Crisis of European Sciences and Transcendental Phenomenology: An Introduction to Phenomenological Philosophy*, trans. David Carr (Evanston, Ill.: Northwestern University Press, 1970), part 3, focused, for example, at §§ 42, 71. See also Eugen Fink, "Husserl's Philosophy and Contemporary Criticism," in *The Phenomenology of Husserl*, ed. R. O. Elverton (Chicago: Quadrangle Press, 1970).

23. American pragmatists have already noticed a good many affinities. See, for instance, the following texts for some representative specimens that themselves lack a common outlook: Mark Okrent, *Heidegger's Pragmatism: Understanding, Being, and the Critique of Metaphysics* (Ithaca, N.Y.: Cornell University Press, 1982); Mitchell Aboulafia, *The Mediating Self: Mead, Sartre, and Self-Determination* (New Haven, Conn.: Yale University Press, 1986), and *The Cosmopolitan Self: George Herbert Mead and Continental Philosophy* (Urbana: University of Illinois Press, 2001); Sandra B. Rosenthal, *Time, Continuity, and Indeterminacy: A Pragmatist Interpretation of Contemporary Perspectives* (Buffalo: SUNY Press, 2000) and, with Patrick L. Bourgeois, *Mead and Merleau-Ponty: Toward a Common Vision* (Buffalo: SUNY Press, 1991); and Richard Rorty, *Consequences of Pragmatism (Essays 1972–1980)* (Minneapolis: University of Minnesota Press, 1982).

24. See, for a sense of the supporting argument, Newton Garver, *This Complicated Form of Life: Essays on Wittgenstein* (Chicago: Open Court, 1994), chaps. 15–16.

25. See Frederick A. Olafson, *Naturalism and the Human Condition: Against Scientism* (London: Routledge, 2001); see also Joseph Rouse, *Knowledge and Power: Toward a Political History of Science* (Ithaca, N.Y.: Cornell University Press, 1987), and *Engaging Science: How to Understand Its Practices Philosophically* (Ithaca, N.Y.: Cornell University Press, 1996).

26. For an extreme specimen of the sort Olafson opposes, see Henry Plotkin, *Evolution in Mind: An Introduction to Evolutionary Psychology* (Cambridge, Mass.: Harvard University Press, 1998).

27. See Okrent, *Heidegger's Pragmatism*.

28. See Maurice Merleau-Ponty, *Phenomenology of Perception*, trans. Colin Smith (London: Routledge and Kegan Paul, 1962), preface and introduction.

29. Maurice Merleau-Ponty, "Course Notes: Husserl at the Limits of Phenomenology"—that is, Merleau-Ponty's course notes on Husserl's "The Origin of Geometry"—trans. Leonard Lawlor, in *Husserl at the Limits of Phenomenology: Including Texts by Edmund Husserl*, ed. Leonard Lawlor with Bettina Bergo (Evanston, Ill.: Northwestern University Press, 2002), pp. 14–15. (Merleau-Ponty distinguishes between underlined words and italicized words.) See also Leonard Lawlor, "Foreword: *Verflechtung*: The Triple Significance of Merleau-Ponty's Course Notes on Husserl's 'The Origin of Geometry.'"

30. See, for instance, the very careful analysis in Reinhard May, *Heidegger's Hidden Sources: East Asian Theories on His Work*, trans. Graham Parkes (London: Routledge, 1996). I owe the reference to Dr. Andrei Vashestov, a Russian scholar of my acquaintance.

31. Olafson, *Naturalism and the Human Condition*, pp. 18–19.

32. Daniel Dennett, one of the more zealous of the scientistic clan at the present time, insists that bottom-up and top-down analyses are perfectly symmetrical—which favors, of course, bottom-up analyses—but he fails to supply the supporting argument. See D. C. Dennett, *Content and Consciousness* (London: Routledge and Kegan Paul, 1969). Dennett is also candid about his hopes of eliminating persons altogether (no doubt the effect of his having been influenced by several of Sellars's essays). And in *Consciousness Explained*, he throws caution to the winds, risks going off the deep end in an attempt to account for the apparent executive presence of the human subject or self through a bizarre torrent of seemingly undirected neurophysiological firings that somehow produce the semblance of a center of unified intelligence. I take all this to signify an abdication of the essential question: something more than a mere confirmation of dubious continental and pragmatist concerns—I would say, an oblique admission of defeat.

33. See, for a convincing brief, David Boersema, *Pragmatism and Reference* (Cambridge, Mass.: MIT Press, 2009).

34. Olafson, *Naturalism and the Human Condition*, p. 19.

35. Ibid., p. 106.

36. See J. N. Mohanty, *Explorations in Philosophy: Western Philosophy*, ed. Bina Gupta (New Delhi: Oxford University Press, 2002), part 1. Mohanty has published, more recently, a suggestive paper on the inadequacy of "reducing" the naturalistic account of consciousness to the transcendental and reducing the transcendental to the naturalistic. See J. N. Mohanty, "Consciousness: Mundane and Transcendental," in *Philosophy and Science: An Exploratory Approach to Consciousness* (Kolkata [Calcutta]: Ramakrishna Mission Institute of Culture, 2003)—the paper was presented at a seminar held at the Mission Institute in February 2002. (Unfortunately, Mohanty's paper has a number of typographical errors.) Mohanty begins with this seeming paradox: "Consciousness is part of the world, but it is also our only access to the world (including itself)" (p. 41)—a view that is very close to Dewey's. (There is no paradox there.) Mohanty invokes the *epoché* (which, as suggested, instantiates the supposed paradox). But his most important concession runs as follows: "By 'transcendental' . . . is meant not what transcends, or is beyond the world, i.e., Nature, but rather what grounds the possibility of the latter, but for which there would be no objectivity, and [no] object of natural science and therefore no natural science at all" (p. 42). Mohanty explicates "grounds" in terms of the following distinctions: (1) "consciousness alone is self-manifesting [self-conscious]"; (2) "there [can] be [no] consciousness without there being an object of which it is conscious [the *noesis/noema* relationship]"; and, hence, (3) "one may . . . 'bracket' all our beliefs in the world, not make use of them (without having to deny them)—and yet have the essence of consciousness unaffected [the point of the *epoché*]" (pp. 42–43).

Mohanty is one of the most skillful and best-informed phenomenologists of our time, a fact that suggests the importance of the inescapable naturalistic tendencies of his own account, that is, its conceding elements of naturalism opposed to the "naturalizing" reductionism or eliminativism of analytic scientism—whether, say, in Quine's sense or in Churchland's. Mohanty specifically shows the latter's account to be paradoxical. Mohanty's "phenomenological" distinctions are pretty well confined to the human paradigm and (probably) cannot be extended reliably to the animal world (because of the absence of language); but if language is essential, then there cannot be any principled disjunction between the naturalistic and the transcendental *within the bounds of the natural world*. In short, the phenomenological must itself be thoroughly naturalistic in at least that regard. Broadly speaking, at the level of language, it is very difficult to make any claims of modal necessity (except trivially or deductively) that cannot also be rendered plausibly as contingent generalities; also, at the level of language, it is very difficult to distinguish between the would-be rules of language and the would-be rules of thought. The contingencies of language, therefore, threaten the pretensions of Husserl's essential disjunction.

The Norwegian philosopher Espen Hammer has recently presented a paper that, however respectfully, very plausibly opposes Mohanty's (and Dagfinn Føllesdal's very different, Fregean-inspired) readings of Husserl's theory—along historicized lines that require abandoning Husserl's well-known transcendental*ism*. Hammer's unpublished paper "Husserl and the Inner-Outer Distinction" was presented before the Philosophy Department, Temple University, in February 2009. I am indebted to him. Nevertheless, the first volume of Mohanty's two-volume overview of Husserl (which admittedly ends before the appearance of *Ideas II* and the *Crisis* volume) certainly suggests no substantial departure from an apriorist stance. (I wait to see the argument of vol. 2.) See J. N. Mohanty, *The Philosophy of Edward Husserl: A Historical Development* (New Haven, Conn.: Yale University Press, 2008). I would say Hammer's Husserl is distinctly Hegelian.

37. I give a fuller account in my *Historied Thought, Constructed World: A Conceptual Primer for the End of the Millennium* (Berkeley: University of California Press, 1995).

38. It may be helpful to take note of the various ways in which the thesis being advanced would not be allowed in any of the following well-known accounts, which take very different stands on scientism: Noam Chomsky, *New Horizons in the Study of Language and Mind* (Cambridge: Cambridge University Press, 2000); John R. Searle, "Reductionism and the Irreducibility of Consciousness," in *The Rediscovery of the Mind* (Cambridge, Mass.: MIT Press, 1992), chap. 5; Jaegwon Kim, *Supervenience and Mind* (Cambridge: Cambridge University Press, 1993). Wittgenstein insists, in the *Tractatus*, in a number of remarks around 5.62, that the "solipsist" is "correct" in what he means in speaking of the world as "my world," that is, at least, that the solipsistic "I" cannot be found in that world. He opposes the doctrine in the *Investigations*, which suggests some degree of convergence with pragmatism's version of naturalism, though the full import of the argument is open to dispute. See also P. S. M. Hacker, *Insight and Illusion: Wittgenstein on Philosophy and the Metaphysics of Experience* (Oxford: Oxford University Press, 1972).

39. See Margolis, *The Unraveling of Scientism*.

40. See Martin Heidegger, "The Age of the World Picture," in *The Question concerning Technology and Other Essays*, trans. William Lovitt (New York: Harper and Row, 1977).

41. As in the motto "natural but not naturalizable," the executive theme of my *Reinventing Pragmatism*.

42. See Paul M. Churchland, *A Neurocomputational Perspective: The Nature of Mind and the Structure of Science* (Cambridge, Mass.: MIT Press, 1989), chap. 1.

43. Olafson introduces the terms (Heidegger's terms) "presence" and "transcendence" in a careful way: "presence," he says, is to be used "for expressing the status of those entities that are present to someone" (that is, human subjects); and "transcendence" applies "to the entities—human beings—to which other entities are present." See Olafson, *Naturalism and the Human Condition*, p. 86. Heidegger would count these distinctions as "existentialia," a term that conveys a meaning rather close (in certain restricted respects) to that of the Kantian transcendentals and the strongest possible disjunction between *Dasein* and "mere things"; but the term *is* primarily addressed to the existential rather than to the cognitive—and implicates the duality of *Dasein*. (It cannot be made to support the transcendental closure of anything like Kant's categories.)

44. These distinctions are quite enough to defeat such theories, for instance, as those advanced by Paul Churchland and Daniel Dennett, without drawing dubious consequences from the distinctly abstract "phenomenological facts" Olafson advances. The argument applies, for instance, to Churchland's notorious claim that the "folk-theoretical" approach to mental and personal traits is so hopelessly mistaken (as an empirical "theory") that it should be utterly rejected as beyond repair; it applies as well to Dennett's equally notorious claim that "Science" requires that we abandon all reliance on first-person reports and avowals regarding mental states. See Churchland, *A Neurocomputational Perspective*; also Dennett, *Consciousness Explained*, and "Quining Qualia," in *Consciousness in Contemporary Science*, ed. A. Marcel and B. Bisiach (Oxford: Oxford University Press, 1988). (Olafson clearly has Churchland's doctrine in mind.)

45. Joseph Rouse, *How Scientific Practices Matter: Reclaiming Philosophical Naturalism* (Chicago: University of Chicago Press, 2002), pp. 13–14. Rouse brings his argument to bear against the views of figures like "Frege, Husserl, early Wittgenstein, Carnap, and Cassirer (among many others)" (p. 30). For a sense of Dewey's contrary account, see John Dewey, *Theory of Valuation*, in *International Encyclopedia of Unified Science*, vol. 2, no. 4 (Chicago: University of Chicago Press, 1939).

46. It is useful to consider in this connection Wittgenstein's examination of the *continuity* of our questioning notions of "clarity" and "necessity" (and therefore of the norms for applying each) in empirical, philosophical, and mathematical contexts. The pursuit of these issues provides plausible grounds for reading the later Wittgenstein as a more or less congenial figure viewed from the pragmatist perspective. It would be too much to say that Wittgenstein was a pragmatist or a neopragmatist. But he makes a very strong case for disallowing the appeal to mathematical reasoning as separable from and yet normative for empirical and philosophical reasoning—which goes very much against Frege's conviction (and the conviction of Fregeans like Michael Dummett). Consider, for instance, § 46, part 3 (read in the context of the run of remarks at §§ 43–48), in Ludwig Wittgenstein, *Remarks on the Foundations of Mathematics*, ed. G. H. von Wright, R. Rhees, and G. E. M. Anscombe, trans. G. E. M. Anscombe (Oxford: Basil Blackwell, 1964). This

seems to strengthen the prospects of a "naturalism" akin to the pragmatist and continental intuitions pitted (here) against the "naturalizing" preferences of analytic scientism. See also the very helpful discussions offered in Juliet Floyd, "Wittgenstein, Mathematics and Philosophy" and Hilary Putnam, "Rethinking Mathematical Necessity," in *The New Wittgenstein*, ed. Alice Crary and Rupert Read (London: Routledge, 2000).

47. I have tried to demonstrate in *Historied Thought, Constructed World* the coherence and merit of a theory in accord with something akin to the tally given in the text.

48. Contrast the views of Fred I. Dretske, *Knowledge and the Flow of Information* (Cambridge, Mass.: MIT Press, 1981); and Claude Shannon, *The Mathematical Theory of Communication* (Urbana: University of Illinois Press, 1948). On Peirce's theory of signs, see T. L. Short, *Peirce's Theory of Signs* (Cambridge: Cambridge University Press, 2007).

49. This was the nerve of Thomas Kuhn's pioneer inquiry. See Thomas S. Kuhn, *The Structure of Scientific Revolutions*, 2d ed. enl. (Chicago: University of Chicago Press, 1970). But Kuhn was unable (through most of his career) to strengthen his analysis effectively, and he gradually turned against the most arresting innovations of his own work (until the last phase of his life). More revealing still, the *problems*—never mind Kuhn's fledgling efforts at analysis (or Paul Feyerabend's "anarchistic" treatment of the same issues)—have been all but eliminated from mainstream analytic philosophies of science.

It needs to be noted as well that there is a substantial collection of naturalistic accounts of history in the American literature that hardly stray into historicity, that run from an adjusted Aristotelianism (as with Frederick Woodbridge and John Herman Randall) to more diverse, more eclectic models variously attracted to pragmatism from the side of an independent naturalism, that are fairly conventional and that never exceed the surprisingly limited daring of Mead and Royce, or that are clearly repelled by pragmatism, as a consequence of favoring the unity of science program (spanning, say, Max Fisch, Morris Raphael Cohen, Ernest Nagel, and Carl Hempel). The problem in all these accounts lies in their characteristic scanting of the emergent features of the cultural world, beyond any physicalist or biologized model. On the use of Aristotle, for instance, see John Herman Randall, *Nature and Historical Explanation* (New York: Columbia University Press, 1958). Aristotle's literal account of the telic nature of biological processes cannot be applied, except figuratively, to the processes of human history and cannot be reconciled with a Darwinian biology.

50. See, for instance, Paul Feyerabend, *Science in a Free Society* (London: NLB, 1978), part 1, especially § 7. See also John Preston, *Feyerabend: Philosophy, Science and Society* (London: Polity Press, 1997), chap. 6; and Margolis, *The Unraveling of Scientism*, chap. 2.

51. See, for instance, Louis Althusser, "Marxism and Humanism," in *For Marx*, trans. Ben Brewster (London: NLB, 1977).

52. See, for instance, Kim, *Supervenience and Mind*.

53. Quine, "Ontological Relativity," in *Ontological Relativity*, pp. 26–27. The citation from Dewey is from *Experience and Nature*, p. 179.

54. Quine, "Ontological Relativity," p. 27.

55. Sandra Rosenthal and Patrick Bourgeois make a very plausible case for considering the pragmatist reclamation of Merleau-Ponty. See their *Mead and Merleau-Ponty*, chaps.

1–2. See also Hans Joas, *G. H. Mead: A Contemporary Re-examination of His Thought*, trans. Raymond Meyer (Cambridge, Mass.: MIT Press, 1997).

56. Dewey, *Experience and Nature*, pp. 178, 180.

57. Ibid., p. 179.

58. Quine's usage is examined in greater detail in Margolis, *The Unraveling of Scientism*, chap. 4. But, for a sense of Quine's running account, see *Word and Object*, parts 1–2.

59. The idea of symmetry here is essential, for instance, to Dennett's treatment of persons, which mimics Quine's behaviorism, though it is not itself a form of behaviorism. See Dennett, *Content and Consciousness*.

60. Quine, "Ontological Relativity," p. 28.

61. See Morton White, *A Philosophy of Culture: The Scope of Holistic Pragmatism* (Princeton: Princeton University Press, 2002), chaps. 3–4. White summarizes his findings very neatly on p. 53.

Chapter 2

"Reclaiming Naturalism" is considerably altered and revised from an earlier version originally presented at a conference, "The Future of Naturalism," at the Center for Inquiry Transnational, in Amherst, New York, September 20–22, 2007, and published in *The Future of Naturalism*, ed. John R. Shook and Paul Kurtz (Amherst, N.Y.: Humanity Books, 2009).

1. Immanuel Kant, *Critique of the Power of Judgment*, ed. Paul Guyer, trans. Paul Guyer and Eric Matthews (Cambridge: Cambridge University Press, 2000), § 83, pp. 298–299 (italics in original). See also G. W. F. Hegel (and F. W. J. Schelling), "Introduction on the Essence of Philosophical Criticism, Generally, and Its Relationship to the Present State of Philosophy in Particular," from *The Critical Journal of Philosophy* 1 (1802), in *Between Kant and Hegel: Texts in the Development of Post-Kantian Idealism*, ed. and trans. George di Giovanni and H. S. Harris, rev. ed. (Indianapolis, Ind.: Hackett, 2000). The essay is generally taken to be the fledgling, as yet inadequate, but essential beginning of Hegel's effort to comprehend human reason as a manifestation of an all-inclusive power of Reason to grasp its own infinite career of self-knowledge. There is an extremely helpful essay by George di Giovanni introducing the collection, "The Facts of Consciousness," which effectively confirms the difficulty of characterizing Hegel's view as fully "naturalistic" in any familiar sense.

2. See *Hegel's Science of Logic*, trans. A. V. Miller (Atlantic Highlands, N.J.: Humanities Press International, 1990), part 1, pp. 55, 63. See the perceptive account in George di Giovanni, "A Reply to Cynthia Willett," in *Essays in Hegel's Logic*, ed. George di Giovanni (Albany: SUNY Press, 1990).

3. See Marjorie Grene, "People and Other Animals," in *The Understanding of Nature: Essays in the Philosophy of Biology* (Dordrecht: D. Reidel, 1974), p. 458.

4. Francisco J. Ayala, "The Three Grand Challenges of Human Biology," in *The Cambridge Companion to The Philosophy of Biology*, ed. David L. Hull and Michael Ruse (Cambridge: Cambridge University Press, 2007), p. 248. See also Richard Dawkins, *The*

Selfish Gene, 2d ed. (Oxford: Oxford University Press, 1989); and Edward O. Wilson, *Sociobiology: The New Synthesis* (Cambridge, Mass.: Harvard University Press, 1975).

It's worth emphasizing that the concept of the "phenotype" risks becoming increasingly vague and equivocal when invoked in accord with treating cultural phenomena as Darwinian "adaptations"—*without* any close linkage to the genetic. (Of course, Darwin himself was deprived of the opportunity to invoke empirical genetics.) For a sense of the inevitable slippage, which obscures the difference between biology and culture (and, therefore, biological and cultural evolution), see Steven Pinker, *The Language Instinct: How the Mind Creates Language* (New York: HarperCollins, 1995). Pinker wrote and published his book just at the time Noam Chomsky was beginning to concede that his doctrine of "universal grammar" was clearly mistaken: Chomsky never abandoned the innatist conviction, though he admitted he had no satisfactory clues about how to replace his former executive thesis. See Noam Chomsky, *New Horizons in the Study of Language and Mind* (Cambridge: Cambridge University Press, 2000). Consider the following specimen remarks from Pinker:

> Because of the language instinct, there is something much more fascinating about linguistic innovation [than mere innovation: borrowing, say, from other languages and introducing variable forms of what is thus incorporated]: each link in the chain of language transmission is a human brain. That brain is equipped with a universal grammar and is always on the lookout for examples in ambient speech of various kinds of rules. (p. 244)

> Evolutionary theory, supported by computer simulations, has shown that when an environment is stable, there is a selective pressure for learned abilities to become increasingly innate. That is because if an ability is innate, it can be deployed earlier in the lifespan of the creature, and there is less of a chance that an unlucky creature will miss out on the experiences that would have been necessary to teach it. (p. 242)

This is surely Lamarckian in spirit, offered without any promising link to genetic theory, whether conventional or revised in some new way. The upshot is that the idea of a distinct form of cultural evolution (catching up the logical difference between biological and cultural properties) begins to fail. (In effect, Dawkins opposes Pinker's lax conception of "adaptation.")

5. Aristotle, *Physics*, trans. R. P. Hardie and R. K. Gaye, 2.2, 193a28–33, in *The Complete Works of Aristotle: The Revised Oxford Translation*, ed. Jonathan Barnes, vol. 1 (Princeton University Press, 1984).

6. For an example of pragmatism's interest in congenial continental figures, see Sandra B. Rosenthal and Patrick L. Bourgeois, *Mead and Merleau-Ponty: Toward a Common Vision* (Albany: SUNY Press, 1991). In the analytic tradition, Alvin Plantinga is well known for his strong efforts to demonstrate the inadequacy of a naturalistic epistemology (and cognate claims) in the direction of the necessity of a supernatural grounding (by way of "natural theology"). See, for instance, Alvin Plantinga, *God and Other Minds* (Ithaca, N.Y.: Cornell University Press, 1967), and *The Nature of Necessity* (Oxford: Clarendon, 1974).

7. As already noted, I take the wording in good part from Marjorie Grene, who shares it with Helmuth Plessner, but the sense is my own.

8. See John McDowell, *Mind and World*, 2d ed. (Cambridge, Mass.: Harvard University Press, 1996). McDowell has just published two new collections of papers, *Having the World in View: Essays on Kant, Hegel and Sellars*, and *The Engaged Intellect: Philosophical Essays* (Cambridge, Mass.: Harvard University Press, 2009). Unfortunately, these appeared too late to be consulted.

9. Edmund Husserl, "Author's Preface to the English Edition," in *Ideas: General Introduction to Pure Phenomenology*, trans. W. R. Boyce Gibson (New York: Collier Books, 1962).

10. I explore this further in "The Point of Hegel's Dissatisfaction with Kant," forthcoming.

11. John McDowell, "Two Sorts of Naturalism," in *Mind, Value and Reality* (Cambridge, Mass.: Harvard University Press, 1998), pp. 192–197. McDowell is referring to the *Nicomachean Ethics*, 1.4, 1095b–6 (which he cites).

12. McDowell, "Two Sorts of Naturalism," pp. 192–194 (italics added).

13. McDowell, *Mind and World*, lecture 4, p. 84.

14. Ibid., p. 85.

15. The only other site among McDowell's papers that I am familiar with that seems to lean, ever so tentatively, in the direction I'm suggesting, appears in John McDowell, "In Defense of Modesty," in *Meaning, Knowledge and Reality* (Cambridge, Mass.: Harvard University Press, 1998), which briefly links Herder's and Hegel's general views on Enlightenment thought in a running critique of Michael Dummett's theory of meaning.

16. See Wilfrid Sellars, "Philosophy and the Scientific Image of Man," in *Science, Perception and Reality* (London: Routledge and Kegan Paul, 1963). For a sustained sense of recent efforts by many hands to liberate analytic philosophy's version of naturalism from the impoverishing constraints of scientism, see Mario de Caro and David MacArthur, eds., *Naturalism in Question* (Cambridge: Cambridge University Press, 2004). The unifying themes seem to affirm that science, rather than man, is the measure of all things. The disjunction seems infelicitous: first, because science is itself the "work of man"; and, second, because, on the argument I've been pursuing, man—the human self—is a cultural artifact, so that what naturalism must include cannot fail to be qualified by what being a self signifies. I'm afraid there's rather little of fresh promise offered—and almost nothing ventured on the theory of the human self or subject or regarding overlooked resources drawn from continental European philosophy, or for that matter, from Darwinian inquiries.

17. McDowell, *Mind and World*, p. 71n.

18. See ibid., p. 5n4: "In much of the rest of these lectures, I shall be concerned to cast doubt on Sellars's idea that placing something in the logical space of reasons is, as such, to be contrasted with giving an empirical description of it." I agree with McDowell here. But it presupposes a deeper account that McDowell nowhere supplies.

19. I should add that I take the papers that form part 4 of McDowell's *Mind, Value and Reality* to confirm just how distant the doctrine of *Bildung* is from his account of

naturalism, apart from his use of it (in his special sense) in explicating Aristotle's ethical naturalism.

20. I've examined Kim's argument more closely in a paper, "Constructing a Person: A Clue to the New Unity of the Arts and Sciences"; see note 50. The decisive clue against Kim's strong form of supervenience, physical realization, and causal reductionism is clear at once from his own definition of the supervenience of the mental:

> Mental properties *supervene* on physical properties, in that necessarily, for any mental property M, if anything has M at time t, there exists a physical base (of subvenient) property P such that it has P at t, and necessarily anything that has P at a time has M at that time.

The definition appears in Jaegwon Kim, *Mind in a Physical World: An Essay on the Mind-Body Problem and Mental Causation* (Cambridge, Mass.: MIT Press, 2000), p. 9 (italics in original). It's meant to suggest a strong form of the unity doctrine. But if you consider that a chess move may be performed in any number of contingent ways (which depend on chess conventions and ad hoc practices), you realize that Kim's definition is invalid: we cannot even tell whether a particular "bodily movement" *counts* as a chess move except top down (that is, by a subfunctional analysis of the molar action that is admitted to be a chess move: in short, an interpretation of the action involved). Hence, the nomological uniformities adduced by Kim are never necessary (in that guise). There's the insuperable complication of the cultural world *if* reductionism fails.

21. For a sense of the puzzling features of McDowell's account of *Bildung*, see Nicholas H. Smith, ed., *Reading McDowell: On Mind and World* (London: Routledge, 2002).

22. John McDowell, "Having the World in View: Sellars, and Intentionality," The Woodbridge Lectures 1997: *Journal of Philosophy* 95 (1998), p. 490.

23. See Margolis, "The Point of Hegel's Dissatisfaction with Kant," forthcoming.

24. That goes well beyond any plausible form of naturalism. Have a careful look, for instance, at the extraordinary account Aristotle offers of the cognitive powers of reason in *On the Soul*, trans. J. A. Smith, in *The Complete Works of Aristotle*, ed. Jonathan Barnes, vol. 1, § 4, 429a13–28, 429b9; also, the account in René Descartes, "The Principles of Philosophy," in *The Philosophical Works of Descartes*, trans. E. S. Haldane and G. R. T. Ross (New York: Dover, 1955), vol. 1, pp. 239–240, 243–244, regarding Principles 51–52, 60 (part 1).

25. See G. W. F. Hegel, *Lectures on the History of Philosophy*, vol. 3, trans. E. S. Haldane and Frances Samson (Lincoln: University of Nebraska Press, 1995), § 3.

26. See, for instance, Ernst Cassirer, *The Philosophy of Symbolic Forms*, vol. 3, trans. Ralph Manheim (New Haven, Conn.: Yale University Press, 1957), part 3. The nerve of Cassirer's "idea of limit" appears as a clear summary at pp. 475–476.

27. This counts heavily against McDowell's "delay" in reclaiming Hegel and "reenchanting" nature—if we mean to recover a viable form of realism, or the norms of moral and political reason that rely, *within naturalistic bounds*, on the resources of "second nature." Consider the following passage from McDowell:

> Aristotle's ethics contains a model of a naturalism that would not stand in the way of a satisfactory conception of experience (and of action, I can now add). The position

is a naturalism of second nature, and I suggested [earlier] that we can equally see it as a naturalized platonism. The idea is that the dictates of reason are there anyway, whether or not one's eyes are opened to them; that is what happens in a proper upbringing. We need not try to understand the thought that the dictates of reason are objects of an enlightened awareness, except from within the way of thinking such an upbringing initiates one into: a way of thinking that constitutes a standpoint from which those dictates are already in view. (*Mind and World*, p. 91)

In my opinion, this threatens to lose the link between Aristotle and Hegel. See also McDowell's congruent reading of Wittgenstein, pp. 92–93.

28. C. I. Lewis, *Mind and the World Order* (New York: Dover, 1929), p. x (italics in original).

29. Ibid., p. 32. See Murray G. Murphey, *C. I. Lewis: The Last Great Pragmatist* (Albany: SUNY Press, 2005), p. 32 (italics in original); and C. I. Lewis, "A Pragmatic Conception of the *A Priori*," *Journal of Philosophy* 20 (1923).

30. Murphey, *Lewis*, p. 139; see Lewis, *Mind and the World Order* (New York: Dover, 1929) pp. 23–27.

31. C. I. Lewis, "The Pragmatic Element in Knowledge," in *Collected Papers of Clarence Irving Lewis*, ed. John Goheen and John Mothershead (Stanford, Calif.: Stanford University, 1970), p. 257; cited by Murphey, *Lewis*, p. 135.

32. See Joseph Margolis, *Pragmatism without Foundations: Reconciling Realism and Relativism*, 2d ed. (London: Continuum, 2007), part 1.

33. See Hilary Putnam, *Ethics without Ontology* (Cambridge, Mass.: Harvard University Press, 2004), pp. 60–63, for a brief but pointed account of "conceptual truths"; and "Rethinking Mathematical Necessity," in *Words and Life*, ed. James Conant (Cambridge, Mass.: Harvard University Press, 1994).

34. Charles Hartshorne and Paul Weiss, eds., *Collected Papers of Charles Sanders Peirce*, vol. 5 (Cambridge, Mass.: Harvard University Press, 1962), pp. 37–39 (italics in original).

35. Edmund Husserl, *Psychological and Transcendental Phenomenology and the Confrontation with Heidegger (1927–1931)*, ed. and trans. Thomas Sheehan and Richard E. Palmer (Dordrecht: Kluwer, 1997), cited by Dan Zahavi (translation modified by Zahavi), in *Husserl's Phenomenology* (Stanford, Calif.: Stanford University Press, 2003), pp. 110–111.

36. Zahavi, *Husserl's Phenomenology*, pp. 72–73. Zahavi paraphrases approvingly a remark of Putnam's: "[I]t is not that the mind makes up the world, but it doesn't just mirror it either," from *Meaning and the Moral Sciences* (London: Routledge and Kegan Paul, 1978), p. 1.

37. Reported in Zahavi, *Husserl's Phenomenology*, p. 73.

38. *Papers of Charles Sanders Peirce*, 5.37 (italics in original). To pit pragmatism against Husserl is not yet to pit pragmatism against phenomenology *tout court*, since Hegel is a phenomenologist and Peirce, a Hegelian phenomenologist. The caveat bears usefully on the strong argument offered in Scott F. Aikin, "Pragmatism, Naturalism, and Phenomenology," *Human Studies* 29 (2006). See also Sami Pihlström, "The Naturalism Debate and the Development of European Philosophy," *Philosophy Today* 46 (2002), cited by Aikin.

39. For a particularly interesting specimen of how the argument might develop, see

Daniel O. Dahlstrom, "Between Being and Essence: Reflection's Logical Disguises," in *Essays on Hegel's Logic*, ed. George di Giovanni (Albany: SUNY Press, 1990).

40. See Joseph Margolis, *Reinventing Pragmatism: American Philosophy at the End of the Twentieth Century* (Ithaca, N.Y.: Cornell University Press, 2002); and *The Unraveling of Scientism: American Philosophy at the End of the Twentieth Century* (Ithaca, N.Y.: Cornell University Press, 2003).

41. Compare Martin Heidegger, *History of the Concept of Time: Prolegomena*, trans. Theodor Kisiel (Bloomington: Indiana University Press, 1985).

42. "With What Must the Science Begin?" in *Hegel's Science of Logic*, trans. A. V. Miller (Atlantic Highlands, N.J.: Humanities Press International, 1990); and vol. 1, book 1, pp. 67–78.

43. I find this compellingly confirmed (unintentionally) in Dan Zahavi, *Husserl and Transcendental Intersubjectivity*, trans. Elizabeth A. Behnke (Athens: Ohio University Press, 2001), see particularly chap. 6.

44. Dan Zahavi, *Subjectivity and Selfhood: Investigating the First-Person Perspective* (Cambridge, Mass.: MIT Press, 2005), chap. 2.

45. Zahavi provides a very useful textual summary of Husserl's evolving treatment of these notions. But the need to vindicate the transcendental "recovery" of the real world does not appear as a serious problem. See Zahavi, *Husserl's Phenomenology*, chap. 2; *Husserl and Transcendental Intersubjectivity*, chap. 1.

46. See Putnam, *Ethics without Ontology*.

47. Sartre follows Husserl here. See J.-P. Sartre, *The Transcendence of the Ego*, trans. F. Williams and R. Kirkpatrick (New York: Noonday Press, 1957). On the distinction between the "egological" and "non-egological," see Aaron Gurwitsch, "A Non-egological Conception of Consciousness," *Philosophy and Phenomenological Research* 1 (1941). For a specimen of the opposed analytic view, see Sidney Shoemaker, "Self-Reference and Self-Awareness," *Journal of Philosophy* 65 (1968).

48. See, for pertinent conjectures, Susan Hurley, *Consciousness in Action* (Cambridge, Mass.: Harvard University Press, 1998); Alva Noë, *Action in Perception* (Cambridge, Mass.: MIT Press, 2006); and Robert W. Wilson, *Boundaries of the Mind: The Individual in the Fragile Sciences* (Cambridge: Cambridge University Press, 2004).

49. Husserl, *Ideas*, pp. 5–11 (italics in original).

50. I offer a version of this thesis in "Constructing a Person: A Clue to the New Unity of the Arts and Sciences," presented at the conference "La Filosofía como Ciudad de las Ciencias y las Artes," October 2008, Valencia, Spain.

51. This tally is, roughly, abstracted from my *Historied Thought, Constructed World*.

52. See Emmanuel Levinas, *Totality and Infinity: An Essay on Exteriority*, trans. Alphonso Lingis (The Hague: Nijhoff, 1979).

53. On Heidegger's account of "facticity" and "exists," see Martin Heidegger, *Ontology—The Hermeneutics of Facticity*, trans. John Van Buren (Bloomington: Indiana University Press, 1988).

54. Martin Heidegger, *Being and Time*, trans. Joan Stambaugh (Albany: SUNY Press, 1996), p. 116; pp. 123–124 in the German pagination.

55. See, for instance, Jerome Bruner, *Beyond the Information Given: Studies in the Psychology of Knowing*, ed. Jeremy M. Anglin (New York: W. W. Norton, 1973), part 3, for a number of pioneer studies in prelinguistic learning and thinking; Michael Tomasello, *The Cultural Origins of Human Cognition* (Cambridge, Mass.: Harvard University Press, 1999); and L. S. Vygotsky, *Mind in Society*, trans. A. R. Luria, ed. M. Cole, V. John-Steiner, S. Scribner, and E. Souberman (Cambridge, Mass.: Harvard University Press, 1978).

56. See the discussion of "conceptual truths" in Putnam, *Ethics without Ontology*.

Chapter 3

"Vicissitudes of Transcendental Reason" is considerably altered and revised from an earlier version that appeared in *Habermas and Pragmatism*, ed. Mitchel Aboulafia and Myra Bookman (London: Routledge, 2002), pp. 31–46.

1. Hilary Putnam, "Values, Facts and Cognition," in *Reason, Truth and History* (Cambridge: Cambridge University Press, 1981), p. 126 (italics in original).

2. Putnam, "Two Philosophical Perspectives," in *Reason, Truth and History*, p. 49.

3. Ibid., pp. 49–50 (italics in original).

4. See G. W. F. Hegel, *Phenomenology of Spirit*, trans. A. V. Miller (Oxford: Oxford University Press, 1977), preface.

5. Putnam, "Two Philosophical Perspectives," p. 50.

6. See, for instance, Hilary Putnam, *The Collapse of the Fact/Value Dichotomy* (Cambridge, Mass.: Harvard University Press, 2002), chaps. 6–7.

7. Ibid., p. 123.

8. Hilary Putnam, *The Many Faces of Realism* (LaSalle, Ill.: Open Court, 1987), p. 28.

9. See Richard Rorty, "Hilary Putnam and the Relativist Menace," in *Philosophical Papers*, vol. 3 (Cambridge: Cambridge University Press, 1998).

10. See Nicholas Cusanus, *Of Learned Ignorance*, trans. Fr. Germain Heron (London: Routledge and Kegan Paul, 1954), p. 11. I have explored the relativistic import of Nicholas's argument in "Motivating Relativism" [Motivazione del relativismo], in *Discipline Filosofiche* 17 (2007).

11. Putnam, *Many Faces of Realism*, p. 29.

12. Putnam, *Reason, Truth and History*, p. 55.

13. Putnam, "Two Philosophical Perspectives," pp. 55–56.

14. See John Dewey, *Logic: The Theory of Inquiry* (New York: Henry Holt, 1938), chaps. 1, 6.

15. Hilary Putnam, *Ethics without Ontology* (Cambridge: Harvard University Press, 2004), pp. 48–49.

16. Ibid., pp. 61–62 (italics in original).

17. Ibid., p. 62.

18. See Joseph Margolis, "Rethinking Peirce's Fallibilism," *Transactions of the Charles S. Peirce Society* 43 (2007).

19. Chomsky has now abandoned his a priori universal grammars. See Noam Chomsky, *New Horizons in the Study of Language and Mind* (Cambridge: Cambridge University

Press, 2000). I see a very strong analogy between Kant's transcendental treatment of Euclid's geometry and Chomsky's treatment of universal grammar.

20. See Hilary Putnam, "Wittgenstein on Religious Belief," particularly the discussion of David Lewis's *Counterfactuals* (Princeton: Princeton University Press, 1973), and "Bernard Williams and the Absolute Conception of the World," in *Renewing Philosophy* (Cambridge, Mass.: Harvard University Press, 1972).

21. Putnam, "Two Philosophical Perspectives," p. 49.

22. Putnam, "Two Conceptions of Rationality," in *Reason, Truth and History*, p. 110. Adorno's remark appears in his *Minima Moralia*: it is, in effect, the central theme of Adorno's book. Gerald L. Bruns uses it as an epigraph to the opening chapter of *On the Anarchy of Poetry and Philosophy* (New York: Fordham University Press, 2006). I simply found it there. It's a sentence that's worth a book. It struck me as the gist of a refutation of a would-be cognate "conceptual truth," often attributed to Hegel, though I think Hegel is much better served by Adorno's actual remark. In any case, if Adorno is right, then I would say Putnam must be mistaken in championing the doctrine of the *Grenzbegriff*.

23. See Joseph Margolis, *Unraveling of Scientism: American Philosophy at the End of the Twentieth Century* (Ithaca, N.Y.: Cornell University Press, 2003), chap. 2.

24. See Richard Rorty, "A Pragmatist View of Contemporary Analytic Philosophy" and "Analytic and Conversational Philosophy," both in *Philosophical Papers*, vol. 4 (Cambridge: Cambridge University Press, 2007).

25. Hilary Putnam, "Facts and Value," in *Reason, Truth and History*, p. 134.

26. William James, *The Principles of Psychology*, 2 vols. (New York: Dover, 1950), 2:296–298, mentioned in James M. Edie, *Edmund Husserl's Phenomenology: A Critical Commentary* (Bloomington: Indiana University Press, 1987), p. 90. Edie's book is unusually instructive (and clear) in assembling the pertinent texts; see particularly chap. 6. On the various topics touched on, see also the following: Aron Gurwitsch, *The Field of Consciousness* (Pittsburgh: Duquesne University Press, 1964); and Maurice Merleau-Ponty, *The Primacy of Perception and Other Essays on Phenomenological Psychology, the Philosophy of Art, History and Politics*, ed. James M. Edie (Evanston, Ill.: Northwestern University Press, 1964). On Lewis, see C. I. Lewis, *Mind and the World Order* (New York: Scribner's, 1929). See also Sandra B. Rosenthal, *Time, Continuity, and Indeterminacy: A Pragmatic Engagement in the Contemporary Perspectives* (Albany: SUNY Press, 2000), particularly chap. 5. Rosenthal provides a natural linkage between Heidegger and Lewis that strengthens the sense of the affinities between pragmatism and phenomenology but also rightly favors (in my opinion) pragmatism's advantages.

I take the occasion (having cited James) to admit that I have never thought much of James's philosophical powers. I believe he had a gift for unusually penetrating intuitions, which many have pondered fruitfully. But he himself seems not to have been able to pursue his best insights with sufficient precision and force to invite a close comparison with the views of other philosophers. Nevertheless, I am struck by Husserl's attraction to James, and even more, by Wittgenstein's intense interest in James. I should mention a recent book by Russell B. Goodman, *Wittgenstein and William James* (Cambridge: Cambridge University Press, 2002), chaps. 1, 6, which shows convincingly that James influenced Wittgenstein philosophically as well as in his personal reflections. But I confess that Goodman's account does not demonstrate (to my mind) that there are any overlooked materials in James's best-known work that are of the first importance philosophically. (Wittgenstein is another matter altogether.)

27. For an early, heterodox use of the Kantian conception that bears comparison with Lewis's notion, see the account of William Whewell's alternative to John Stuart Mill's conception, in John R. Wettersten, *The Roots of Critical Rationalism* (Amsterdam: Rodopi, 1992), chaps. 1–2.

28. Sami Pihlström, *Naturalizing the Transcendental: A Pragmatic View* (Amherst, NY.: Humanity Books, 2003), p. 32 (italics in original); compare p. 31; see also pp. 9, 41n8. See Christopher Hookway, *Truth, Rationality, and Pragmatism: Themes from Peirce* (Oxford: Clarendon, 2000); and for a larger overview of the skeptical and naturalistic issues involving transcendental arguments, Robert Stern, *Transcendental Arguments and Scepticism: Answering the Question of Justification* (Oxford: Clarendon, 2000), chap. 3.

29. See Hilary Putnam, "Sense, Nonsense, and the Senses: An Inquiry into the Powers of the Human Mind," The Dewey Lectures 1994, *Journal of Philosophy* 41 (1994).

30. I find the term used very naturally and aptly in the wake of recovering the essential philosophical questions put at risk, paradigmatically, by Rorty—but also, more instructively, and more subtly, in Isabelle Thomas-Fogiel's *Référence et autoréférence: Étude sur le thème de la mort de la philosophie dans la pensée contemporaine* (Paris: Vrin, 2005), drawing on the entire drift of modern Eurocentric philosophy. Thomas-Fogiel examines a large number of specimen views, drawn chiefly from French and German sources, that support the aptness of her new designation. I am in her debt.

31. Donald Davidson, "On the Very Idea of a Conceptual Scheme," in *Inquiries into Truth and Interpretation* (Oxford: Clarendon, 1984), p. 184. For my own appraisal of Davidson's argument, see *The Unraveling of Scientism*, chap. 2. Compare Donald Davidson, "A Coherence Theory of Truth and Knowledge," in *Truth and Interpretation: Perspectives on the Philosophy of Donald Davidson*, ed. Ernest Lepore (Oxford: Basil Blackwell, 1986), and Richard Rorty, "Pragmatism, Davidson and Truth," in Lepore, *Truth and Interpretation*.

32. See Karl-Otto Apel, *Charles S. Peirce: From Pragmatism to Pragmaticism*, trans. John Michael Krois (Amherst: University of Massachusetts Press, 1981).

33. See, for instance, Susan Haack, *Manifesto of a Passionate Moderate: Unfashionable Essays* (Chicago: University of Chicago Press, 1999).

34. Charles Hartshorne and Paul Weiss, eds., *Collected Papers of Charles Sanders Peirce*, 6 vols. (Cambridge, Mass.: Harvard University Press, 1931–1935), §§ 6.12, 6.343 (italics in original).

35. See Margolis, "Rethinking Peirce's Fallibilism."

36. *Papers of Charles Sanders Peirce*, § 1.366.

37. Ibid., § 6.25.

38. The leanest answer on the realist issue that I offer appears in my "Rethinking Peirce's Fallibilism."

39. *Papers of Charles Sanders Peirce*, §§ 5.121, 5.126.

40. Ibid., § 5.130 (italics in original); see also §§ 5.128–129.

41. Ibid., §§ 5.133–134. See Karl-Otto Apel, "The *A Priori* of the Communication Community and the Foundations of Ethics: The Problem of a Rational Foundation of Ethics in the Scientific Age," in *Towards a Transformation of Philosophy*, trans. Glyn Adey and David Frisby (London: Routledge and Kegan Paul, 1980), p. 287n23.

42. *Papers of Charles Sanders Peirce*, § 5.357.

43. Ibid., §§ 5.133, 5.142, 5.145–150.

44. Ibid., §§ 5.134–136; see also §§ 5.13–126, 5.142, 5.145.

45. See John Dewey, *Art as Experience* (New York: Minton, Balch, 1934), and *Human Nature and Conduct: An Introduction to Social Psychology* (New York: Random House, 1922, 1930).

46. *Papers of Charles Sanders Peirce*, § 5.130.

47. Karl-Otto Apel, "From Kant to Peirce: The Semiotical Transformation of Transcendental Logic," in *Towards a Transformation of Philosophy*, pp. 79–80. See also *Papers of Charles Sanders Peirce*, § 5.382n; and my "Peirce's Fallibilism," *Transactions of the Charles S. Peirce Society* 34 (1998).

48. Apel, "*A Priori* of the Communication Community," p. 280.

49. See *Papers of Charles Sanders Peirce*, §§ 6.36, 5.382n.

50. Apel, "*A Priori* of the Communication Community," p. 262.

51. *Papers of Charles Sanders Peirce*, §§ 5.135–136 (italics in original), which implicitly questions the coherence of Apel's line of reasoning.

52. See Karl-Otto Apel, "Noam Chomsky's Theory of Language and Contemporary Philosophy: A Case Study in the Philosophy of Science," in *Towards a Transformation of Philosophy*, pp. 203–206, 222–224nn101–104. Apel effectively confirms that Habermas still held (at least up to the translation of *Transformation*) to the theories of his (Habermas's) early influential paper "What Is Universal Pragmatics?" in *Communication and the Evolution of Society*, trans. Thomas McCarthy (Boston: Beacon Press, 1979).

53. See Jürgen Habermas, "A Genealogical Analysis of the Cognitive Content of Morality," in *The Inclusion of the Other: Studies in Political Theory*, ed. Ciaran Cronin and Pablo DeGreiff, trans. Ciaran Cronin et al. (Cambridge, Mass.: MIT Press, 1998); "Discourse Ethics: Notes on a Program of Philosophical Justification," in *Moral Consciousness and Communicative Action*, trans. Christian Lenhardt and Shierry Weber Nicholsen (Cambridge, Mass.: MIT Press, 1990); *The Theory of Communicative Action*, 2 vols., trans. Thomas McCarthy (Boston: Beacon Press 1984).

54. Habermas, "Genealogical Analysis," p. 4 (italics in original). Here, Habermas defers to Apel's account of "performative self-contradictions" but avoids an explicit transcendentalism. For Apel's objections (in advance), see Apel, "*A Priori* of the Communication Community," p. 262.

55. For an extremely helpful overview, from the side of current phenomenology, see Dan Zahavi, *Husserl and Transcendental Intersubjectivity: A Response to the Linguistic-Pragmatic Critique*, trans. Elizabeth A. Behnke (Athens: Ohio University Press, 2001), particularly chaps. 6–7.

56. I explore the reasonableness of such an approach for our time in my *Moral Philosophy after 9/11* (University Park: Pennsylvania State University Press, 2003).

57. Lewis, "Pragmatic Conception of the *A Priori*," p. 176.
58. Ibid., p. 177.
59. Ibid., p. 176. (The sense of two sentences is conflated here.)
60. All of this has to do with what is often called the "naturalization" of the transcendental. See, for example, the papers in Paul Beghossian and Christopher Peacocke, eds., *New Essays on the A Priori* (Oxford: Clarendon, 2000), particularly Michael Friedman, "Transcendental Philosophy and A Priori Knowledge: A Neo-Kantian Perspective"; Quassim Cassam, "Rationalism, Empiricism, and the A Priori"; and Stephen Tablo, "Apriority and Existence." See also Pihlström, *Naturalizing the Transcendental*, whose project is, precisely, naturalizing the transcendental. Pihlström reviews an extensive literature linked in different ways to P. F. Strawson's well-known effort to naturalize the Kantian transcendental. A new account of Lewis has appeared recently: Sandra B. Rosenthal, *C. I. Lewis in Focus: The Pulse of Pragmatism* (Bloomington: Indiana University Press, 2007), which emphasizes the holism but not sufficiently (in my opinion) an appraisal of the novel force of Lewis's "intermediary" view. I think there is no way of proceeding further without admitting that both the "empirical" and the "analytic" are constructivist posits. To admit this, however, is to reinterpret the force of Quine's "Two Dogmas of Empiricism" along lines more radical than Quine's—very probably more radical than Lewis ventures as well. There's no settled division to count on; on the contrary, pertinent arguments address the question of how best to specify the would-be difference, if it has any use at all.

61. See Habermas, "What Is Universal Pragmatics?" pp. 21–25; "Genealogical Analysis," pp. 6–7.

62. See, particularly, Jürgen Habermas, "A Reply," in *Communicative Action: Essays on Jürgen Habermas' "The Theory of Communicative Action,"* ed. Axel Honneth and Hans Joas, trans. Jeremy Gains and Doris L. Jones (Cambridge, Mass.: MIT Press, 1991). The most accessible versions of the apriorist objections to Habermas appear in Karl-Otto Apel, "Normatively Grounding 'Critical Theory' through Recourse to the Lifeworld? A Transcendental-Pragmatic Attempt to Think with Habermas against Habermas," in *Philosophical Interventions in the Unfinished Project of Enlightenment*, ed. Alex Honneth et al., trans. William Rehg (Cambridge, Mass.: MIT Press, 1992); and Herbert Schnadelbach, "The Transformation of Critical Theory," in Honneth and Joas, *Communicative Action*.

63. See, for instance, G. W. F. Hegel, *Natural Law*, trans. T. M. Knox (Philadelphia: University of Pennsylvania Press, 1975), pp. 75–78.

64. I had an occasion to raise the question with Habermas during a talk he gave before the Greater Philadelphia Philosophy Consortium more than fifteen years ago—when he actually used the expression "all possible worlds" (signifying what he took to be indefeasibly necessary). He did not, he explained, mean the expression in its technical sense. But I think it is fair to say that he has been struggling all these years to formulate a proper sense of "pragmatic" necessity or to offer an acceptable replacement for his purpose.

I must add a further word here about a related line of speculation that has attracted a number of informed adherents (interpreting Peirce). The most recent summary of (and commitment to) the transcendent*alist* import of Peirce's notion of "transcendent*al* hope" (let me write this as "Hope") appears in Elizabeth F. Cooke, *Peirce's Pragmatic Theory of*

Inquiry: Fallibilism and Indeterminacy (London: Continuum, 2006), chap. 7. Cooke's intention, which, in effect, she shares with Habermas—and with Pihlström, *Naturalizing the Transcendental*, and Kenneth R. Westphal, "Can Pragmatic Realists Argue Transcendentally?" in *Pragmatic Naturalism and Realism*, ed. John R. Shook (New York: Prometheus Books, 2003)—is to naturalize transcendental arguments. The most interesting fact about her own argument is that she does not consider at all C. I. Lewis's successful effort to "pragmatize" the Kantian a priori. I begin with Lewis's achievement: it establishes in the clearest way the distinction between the naturalistic admission of *transcendental* questions and the rejection of *transcendentalist* answers (which I would say accords with Peirce's own conviction). Here, if I understand him correctly, I agree with Christopher Hookway's straightforward observation: namely, "the fact that we should adopt such assumptions [the assumptions of Peirce's transcendental Hope, say] as regulative ideas, as hopes, provides no basis for believing them to be true," in *Truth, Rationality, and Pragmatism: Themes from Peirce* (Oxford: Clarendon, 2000), p. 6 (cited by Cooke). Cooke herself could not be more candid: "Hookway's point that hope must engage the will if it is to affect inquiry will be key for the present account [that is, her own]. . . . Yet while we agree with this view, we will part ways with Hookway and with Peirce in arguing for a specifically transcendental role for hope as a condition for inquiry. In doing so, we will shed light on the fundamentally hopeful attitude of all human thought, while still working within a Peircean theory of inquiry" (p. 134).

Two caveats should serve our present needs. First, "transcendental" questions (à la Lewis or by similar means) are easily construed naturalistically wherever the a priori is rightly construed as a posteriori; second, arguments like Peirce's to the effect that if we wish to support a strong form of realism committed to a mind-independent world, we will have to fall back to something like transcendental Hope, which effectively commits us to the indissoluble union of realism and some form of idealism, and if we require a stronger form of realism, we shall fail. Put in another way, I see no reason for insisting that from the fact that in believing that P is impossible we are rationally prevented from believing that P is true we have discovered a synthetic a priori truth of any kind. This sort of claim, which belongs to the twilight world of Habermas's pragmatic "necessities," is (I anticipate) analytic where it is compelling and indemonstrable where it is intended in the transcendentalist sense. Whatever more may be wanted I shall let stand as a promissory note.

65. Habermas, "Genealogical Analysis," p. 40.

66. See, for instance, Thomas S. Kuhn, *The Structure of Scientific Revolutions*, enl. ed. (Chicago: University of Chicago Press, 1970), § 10.

67. Apel, "Normatively Grounding 'Critical Theory'?" pp. 128, 142–143. There is an excellent exposé of the ur-difficulty that one finds in Apel and Habermas, in a very different (textually unrelated) discussion of Husserl's phenomenologized method, in Maurice Merleau-Ponty, "The Philosopher and Sociology," in *Signs*, trans. Richard M. McCleary (Evanston, Ill.: Northwestern University Press, 1964). Here, late Frankfurt Critical and Husserlian arguments may be made to converge.

68. See Habermas, "A Reply," pp. 232–233.

69. Ibid., pp. 231–232.

70. This is also the crucial difficulty in John Rawls's appeal to rationality, in *A Theory of Justice* (Cambridge, Mass.: Harvard University Press, 1971), which Rawls subsequently attenuated (disarmingly) by the substitution of a candid ideological postulate. Yet Rawls never really abandons the substantive moral universals he advances in *A Theory of Justice* but fails to vindicate. He says as much in his *Political Liberalism* (New York: Columbia University Press, 1993). A very brief but devastating criticism of Rawls's *Theory* may be found in Bernard Williams, "Rawls and Pascal's Wager," in *Moral Luck* (Cambridge: Cambridge University Press, 1981), which suggests to me a similar approach to that of Habermas's theory.

71. Ludwig Wittgenstein, *Philosophical Investigations*, trans. G. E. M. Anscombe (Oxford: Basil Blackwell, 1953), 1:§§ 201–202, 240–242.

72. See Habermas, "Discourse Ethics," pp. 82–98; and Karl-Otto Apel, "The Problem of Philosophical Foundations in Light of a Transcendental Pragmatics in Language" (revised), in *After Philosophy: End or Transformation?* ed. Kenneth Bayles et al. (Cambridge, Mass.: MIT Press, 1987). For Apel's rebuttal of Habermas's view, see Apel, "Normatively Grounding 'Critical Theory'?" pp. 126–128.

73. Habermas, "Genealogical Analysis," pp. 41–42 (italics in original). See also Habermas, "Discourse Ethics," pp. 65–66; and Jürgen Habermas, *Between Facts and Norms: Contributions to a Discourse Theory of Law and Democracy*, trans. William Rehg (Cambridge, Mass.: MIT Press, 1996), p. 556n15.

75. See, for instance, Gayatri Chakravorty Spivak, *A Critique of Postcolonial Reason: Toward a History of the Vanishing Present* (Cambridge, Mass.: Harvard University Press, 1999), p. 9, and the whole of chap. 1.

Epilogue

"Pragmatism and the Prospect of Rapprochement within Eurocentric Philosophy" was first presented at the 10th International Meeting on Pragmatism, São Paulo, Brazil, November 12–15, 2007, and published in *Cognitio* 9, no. 2 (2008), pp. 235–245; reprinted with permission.

1. Thomas S. Kuhn, "The Trouble with the Historical Philosophy of Science," in *The Road since Structure*, ed. James Conant and John Haugeland (Chicago: University of Chicago Press, 2000), p. 115.

2. For the sense of "conceptual truth" invoked here, see Hilary Putnam, *Ethics without Ontology* (Cambridge, Mass.: Harvard University Press, 2004), pp. 60–65.

3. See G. W. F. Hegel, *Faith and Knowledge*, trans. Walter Cerf and H. S. Harris (Albany: SUNY Press, 1977); and *Lectures on the History of Philosophy*, vol. 3, trans. E. S. Haldane and Frances Simson (Lincoln: University of Nebraska Press, 1995), the discussion on Kant in the context of § 3.

4. See Joseph Margolis, *Unraveling of Scientism: American Philosophy at the End of the Twentieth Century* (Ithaca, N.Y.: Cornell University Press, 2003).

5. See Michael Friedman, *A Parting of the Ways: Carnap, Cassirer, and Heidegger* (Chicago: Open Court, 2000).

6. I take this to be the right way to read, say, Thomas Kuhn, Ernst Cassirer, and

Charles Peirce. See Ernst Cassirer, *The Philosophy of Symbolic Forms*, vol. 3, trans. Ralph Manheim (New Haven, Conn.: Yale University Press, 1957), part 3.

7. See G. W. F. Hegel, *The Encyclopaedia Logic (with the Zusätze)*, trans. T. E. Geraets, W. A. Suchting, and H. S. Harris (Indianapolis, Ind.: Hackett, 1991).

8. See Joseph Margolis, *Reinventing Pragmatism: American Philosophy at the End of the Twentieth Century* (Ithaca, N.Y.: Cornell University Press, 2002).

9. The text of what was apparently a series of lectures on Hegel is now being issued for the first time, with commentaries, by John R. Shook and James A. Good, as *John Dewey's Philosophy of Spirit* (New York: Fordham University Press, 2009).

10. See, for instance, Jean Petitot, Francisco J. Varela, Bernard Pachoud, and Jean-Michel Roy, eds., *Naturalizing Phenomenology: Issues in Contemporary Phenomenology and Cognitive Science* (Stanford, Calif.: Stanford University Press, 1999).

11. For a promising counterexample, see Sandra B. Rosenthal and Patrick Bourgeois, *Mead and Merleau-Ponty: Toward a Common Vision* (Albany: SUNY Press, 1992); see also Hans Joas, *G. H. Mead: A Contemporary Re-examination of His Thought* (Cambridge, Mass.: MIT Press, 1997).

12. See John W. Burbidge, *Hegel's Logic: Fragments of a Commentary* (Atlantic Highlands, N.J.: Humanities Press, 1981); and Michael Forster, "Hegel's Dialectical Method," in *The Cambridge Companion to Hegel*, ed. Frederick C. Beiser (Cambridge: Cambridge University Press, 1993).

Index

Adorno, Theodor, 106
agency, 35
Althusser, Louis, 39
analysts and continentals, 2, 3,4, 6, 10, 15–16, 30–32
analytic scientism, 3, 4, 15, 18, 26–27, 30
Apel, Karl-Otto, 4, 6, 111, 114, 115–16
    appraisal of, 119–130
    apriorism (transcendentalism), 111, 117–19
    and Habermas, 4–6, 111–12, 115–16, 119–120, 121–24, 127–29
    on Peirce, 116–19, 121, 123
    pragmatized (semiotized) account of Kant, 117, 119, 121
a priori
    as a posteriori posit, 15–16
    Lewis on, 72, 125
    two senses of, 41–42
apriorism. *See* Kant
Aristotle
    as ancient naturalist, 50, 53–54
    Darwin applied to, 56
    definition of "nature," 53–54
    ethical upbringing ("Bildung"), 62, 63
    First Cause, 54
    McDowell on, 61–66 passim
    nous, 53, 89

Armstrong, David, 14
Ayala, Francisco, 52–53

Bildung
    and Aristotle's *Ethics*, 11
    and Darwinian evolution, 11
    "internal"/"external," 11, 56, 62–63, 68–69
    McDowell on, 11, 62–63 (*see also* McDowell)

"Cartesians" (pre-Kantians), 4, 8, 15
Cassirer, Ernst, 14, 69, 71, 92
Churchland, Paul, 31
cognitive privilege, 12, 19, 57
"conceptual truths" (Putnam), 73–74, 102
constructive realism. *See* constructivism
constructivism (constructivist), 3, 16–17, 19, 24, 32
cultural world
    and nature/culture distinction, 64 (*see also* intentionality)
    not definable biologically, 52–53, 60
    "penetration" (transformation) of nature, 53
    sui generis, emergent, irreducible, 56, 59–60

Index

Darwin, Charles (Darwinian, neo-Darwinian, Darwinizing), 6–7, 10, 12, 16, 40–41, 55–56, 69–70
   and artifactuality of the self, 17, 52–53, 55, 69
   discoveries of, applied to Hegel, 51
   and external *Bildung*, 11, 123, 136
   historicizing, 16, 30
   and transformation of *Homo sapiens*, 55–56
Davidson, Donald
   "common co-ordinate system," 116
   criticism of Kuhn and Feyerabend, 112, 113–14
   and Putnam, 112–14
   on relativism and incommensurabilism, 112–14
   on truth, 38
Dawkins, Richard, 53, 146n5
Dennett, Daniel C., 8, 31, 149n32
determinacy/determinability, 26
Dewey, John, 11, 13, 14, 37, 147n16
   Experience and Nature, 13
   and Heidegger, 20–21, 26
   "indeterminate [and/or 'problematic'] situation," 2, 20, 22, 25–26, 38
   and Quine, 41–46
"doctrine of the flux," 131
Dummett, Michael, 32

emergentism, 65
epistemology, constructivist, 71–72
ethical values and norms, legitimation of, 63–64, 67
Eurocentric philosophy, 2, 4, 33, 36, 40, 47–48, 80, 135–36, 190
   future of, 47–48
   and naturalism, 49, 74
   principal quarrels of, 33
   unity of, 60
evolution, biological and cultural, 59–60, 153–54n4

evolution of language and culture, 6
extranaturalism, 16, 19
   Kant's, 69
   medieval, 54

fallibilism. *See* Peirce
Feyerabend, Paul, 97–98, 112
Frankfurt Critical program, 20

Geist. *See* Hegel
Goodman, Nelson, 14
Grenzbegriff(e) (Putnam), 93–108 passim
   beliefs on, tallied, 94–95
   dilemma regarding, 99–100
   regulative function of, 107–108

Habermas, Jürgen
   and Apel, 4–6, 111–13, 114, 115–16, 119–120, 121–24, 127–29
   appraisal of, 130
   on norms (discourse and morality), 120–21
   on the pragmatic and transcendental, 126–30
   on reason (rationality), 5, 116
   See also universalism
Hare, R. M., 128
Hegel, G. W. F. (Hegelian)
   "Absolute Knowing," 61
   Bildung, 62–63 (*see also* McDowell)
   contra "Cartesianism," 8
   Darwinizing, 51, 56, 66
   Geist, 7, 8, 10, 16, 25, 36, 51, 52
   and human subject (self), 7
   and Husserl, 80–82, 84
   and Kant, 7, 135–39
   on Kant, 7, 15, 58, 71
   McDowell on, 3–4, 59, 61–66 passim
   and naturalism, 58
   phenomenology, 80–81
   on *Vernunft* and *Verstand*, 5, 69, 153n1 (*see also Vernunft*)
Hegelianized Kantianism, 14, 69

Heidegger, Martin (Heideggerean),
    9–10, 12
  aletheia, 9
  appraisal of extranaturalism (*Dasein*),
    89–91
  Dasein and its phenomenology, 9, 26,
    29, 51, 54, 89–90
  and Dewey, 20–21, 26
  and Husserl, 9–10, 12, 21–22, 31–32,
    89–90
  In-der-Welt-sein, 20, 25–26 (*see also*
    Olafson)
  Kehre, 10–12
  as naturalist *manqué*, 90
  phenomenology, 89–91
  and the Void (*śūnyatā*), 23, 27
Homo sapiens, 5–6, 10, 33, 51, 55–56
Hookway, Christopher, 110
human being, analysis of, 27–28, 29–30,
  39–40, 50
Hume, David, 6, 74, 86
Husserl, Edmund (Husserlian)
  appraisal of, 80–87 passim
  epoché, 8–9, 10, 19, 25, 56, 86
  exceeding naturalism, 55, 76–77, 81,
    82, 84–86
  and Hegel, 80–82, 84
  and Heidegger, 9–10, 12, 21–22
  Ideas, 8–9
  and James, 108–10
  "natural attitude" (naturalism), 9, 19,
    24
  and Transcendental Ego, 8, 86
  transcendental phenomenology, 8–9,
    58, 79, 84–86, 146–47n10
  transcendental subjectivity, 75–76,
    85–87
  Zahavi on, 76, 82–84

Idealism (post-Kantian), 17–19, 71
"independent world" vs. noumena, 17–18
information, 34–35, 36
intentional(ity), 60, 88

invariance and flux, 131

James, William, 13–14, 37, 108–10, 111,
    160–61n26
  and Husserl, 108–109
  and Peirce, 13, 14
  use of "Grenzbegriff," 108–109

Kant, Immanuel (Kantian)
  apriorism (transcendentalism), 6, 12,
    14, 15, 17, 18, 25, 50, 51, 57, 69, 73
  on culture, 50–51
  Darwin applied to, 56, 69–70
  faculty of reason, 5
  first *Critique*, 5
  and Hegel, 7, 61, 71, 135–36
  Hegel on, 7, 15, 71, 135–36
  and the human self, 6, 50
  "*ich denke*," 6, 74, 145n4
  McDowell on, 61, 62, 64
  not a naturalist, 58
  transcendentalism, 15, 18, 69, 71–72
  on *Vernunft*, 57, 69
Kim, Jaegwon, 27, 65, 67–68, 156n20
Kuhn, Thomas S., 63, 98–99, 112, 132–34,
  152n49

language
  evolution of, 12, 59
  transformative role of, 59, 60, 69
Lewis, C. I., 43, 72, 82, 124–26. *See*
  pragmatic a priori
"lingual," 60

Marx, Karl, 7–8, 146n7
McDowell, John
  on Aristotle, Kant, Hume, and Hegel,
    11, 59, 60, 61–66
  assessment of, 61–69 passim
  on *Bildung* ("second nature"), 11, 27,
    56, 61–64, 66, 68–69
  on the nature/culture distinction, 64,
    65–66, 155n8

McDowell, John (*continued*)
  on Sellars, 63–69
  treatment of naturalism, 59, 60, 62, 65, 156–57*n*27
Mead, George Herbert, 44, 86
Mendeleev, Dimitri, 97
Merleau-Ponty, Maurice
  "Course Notes" on "Origin of Geometry" (Husserl), 21–23, 43–44
  and Husserl, 12, 21–23, 25
Michelson, Albert, 97
"modern" modern philosophy, 2, 133
Mohanty, J. N., 29, 149–150*n*36
Murphey, Murray, 72

Naturalism (naturalistic) 12, 19, 29, 30–31, 35, 57–59, 152*n*49
  and analytic philosophy, 36
  aporiai and antinomies of, 49–50
  continuum of, and extranaturalism, 21, 54, 55
  definition of, 58
  discontinuity of "modern" analysis of, 59
  master strategies of, 65, 67–68
  medieval, 54
  Pihlström on, 110–11
  and problem of the conceptual adequacy of, 54, 58
  and problem of the definition of culture, 52
  and problem of the difference between nature and culture, 51
  and problem of the human self, 51, 52, 68
  reply to Husserl, 57–58 (*see also* Husserl)
  See also Olafson
"naturalizing" (Quine, Davidson, Rorty), 13, 19, 89, 110
noumena(lism), 17–18, 19, 70
  Kant's letter to Herz, 70–71
  and "mind-independent objects," 96

objective reality, 17
Okrent, Mark, 29–30
Olafson, Frederick, 20, 24–26, 27–29, 30–31, 151*n*43
  "having a world," 20, 27
  on naturalism in Husserl and Heidegger, 24–25, 28–29, 30–31

Peirce, Charles Sanders, 13–14, 37
  abduction, 46–47, 109, 114
  convergence with Cassirer, 14
  on ethics, 117 (*see also* Apel)
  fallibilism, 14, 98, 104
  on Hegel, 75, 77–78
  as Idealist, 13, 17–18
  and James, 13, 14
  and Kant, 14, 114
  on necessity, 73
  on normative ethics and practical reason, 117–18
  not a transcendentalist, 14, 110, 116
  "objective idealism" (Schellingian), 116
  as phenomenologist, 77–78
  Putnam on, 98
  transcendental Hope, 104, 106, 111–12, 114, 115, 116, 118, 163–64*n*64
  transcendental reason, 115–16
phenomenology
  Hegel's, 80–81
  Husserl's, 76, 77, 79, 81 (*see also* Husserl)
  lax sense of, 74–75
  and naturalism, 78–79, 80
  Peirce on, 75–76, 77–78
  and pragmatism, 21, 23–24, 28, 29, 30–31
  preference for Hegel over Husserl, 80–81, 92
  varieties of, 21–24, 25
physical nature and human culture, 51
Pihlström, Sami, 110–11
Plantinga, Alvin, 52, 54
Popper, Karl, 114

poststructuralism (Francophone), 20
pragmatic a priori (Lewis), 109, 124–26
pragmatism (pragmatists)
   classic, 13, 15–16, 34, 70
   and constructive realism, 32, 33
   defined, 34, 36
   drawn to Darwin, 10, 12, 56–57, 137
   and the flux, 134
   for and against analysts and continentals, 1, 2, 3–4, 6, 15, 16, 18–19, 26–27, 34, 36–38, 39–40, 41, 60–61, 78, 87, 136, 140 (*see also* analysts and continentals)
   as Hegelian, 142–44
   and Husserlian phenomenology, 21, 23, 30–31
   and information, 35
   and Kant and Hegel, 13, 16, 18–19, 34–35, 46–47, 70, 135–39, 140, 141
   mottoes, 16, 78
   and naturalism, 16, 18–19, 34–35, 46–47
   and naturalistic account of subjectivity, 87–89
   overview of, 36–38
   unfinished, 140–41
pragmatism's advantage, 1–2, 3, 20, 31, 136
pragmatism's revival, 2
primate communication, intelligence, language, 10, 145*n*4
Putnam, Hilary, 2, 3, 73–74, 83.
   "Brain in a Vat" hypothesis, 97
   "conceptual relativity," 102–103
   "conceptual truths," 73–74, 102, 103–104, 105
   and Davidson, 112–14
   "internalist perspective" (internal realism), 96, 99, 100, 142*n*21
   misreading of Peirce's fallibilism, 98
   pluralism (plurality), 100, 103
   rejection of metaphysical realism ("God's-Eye" view), 94–96
   as relativist, 94, 97, 99
   on truth and reality, 96–98, 101
   See also Grenzbegriff; relativism
Putnam's quarrel with Rorty, 93–99 passim, 101–102
   Grenzbegriffe and relativism, 93–95, 100, 142–44
   need for *Grenzbegriff* (limit-concept), 93–95
   relativism as self-contradictory, 94–95

Quine, W. V., 11, 14, 36, 37, 41–46, 47

rapprochement (Eurocentric), 4, 15, 25, 38–39, 47, 141
Rawls, John, 6, 123, 165*n*70
realism
   constraints on, 33–34
   constructive (constructivist), 17, 32
   and idealism, 17–18
reason
   in Apel and Habermas, 115, 116
   as cognitive faculty, 105–106, 114
   in Peirce, 115
reductionism, 65, 66
relativism (relativist)
   anti-Protagorean thesis on (*Theaetetus*), 99
   Cusa's viable version of, 96, 100
   Davidson on, 112–14
   possible coherence of, 93–94, 98–99
   Putnam and Rorty on, 93–96, 99, 105
   "true in L" not equivalent to "true-in-L," 99
Rorty, Richard, 2, 37, 38
   "linguistic turn," 38
   as postmodernist, 95, 108, 135
   Presidential address (1980), 93 (*see also* Putnam; relativism)
   as relativist, 95, 99
Rouse, Joseph, 20, 31–32

Schelling, Friedrich (Schillingian), 110, 115

"second nature" (McDowell), 11, 60, 63, 66. *See also Bildung*
Sellars, Wilfrid, 66–67, 68–69
selves (persons)
    as agents and subjects, 16
    defined, 30, 52
    emergent, hybrid, artifactual, second-natured, 12, 17, 30, 33, 52, 56, 59, 60, 67
    Hume and Kant on, 6, 74
    "natural artifact," 52, 55, 60, 74
summary argument (and prophecy), 142–44
supernaturalism, 16
supervenientism (Kim), 27

Taylor, Charles, 11, 27
transcendental Hope (Peirce), 114, 163–64*n*64
transcendental inquiry, 16
transcendental necessity, 124–25
transcendental subjectivity (Husserl), 75–76. *See also* Husserl
transcendentalism (apriorism), 17, 73, 124.
    Apel and Habermas on, 127–29
    Lewis on, 124–26
    See also Kant

universalism, moral and discursive (Apel and Habermas), 118–22 passim, 128, 129, 130
utterance, 35, 88

Vernunft
    Hegel on, 51, 58, 69
    Kant on, 57, 69

White, Morton, 46
Wittgenstein, Ludwig, 20, 150*n*38, 151–52*n*46

Zahavi, Dan, 76, 82–84